D0153117

ENTREPÔT CAPITALISM

All of these Securities have been sold. This announcement appears as a matter of record only.

New Issues / April, 1981

$400,000,000

British Columbia Hydro and Power Authority

$150,000,000
14½% Notes, Series FF, Due 1991

$250,000,000
15% Bonds, Series FG, Due 2011

Unconditionally guaranteed as to principal, premium, if any, and interest by

Province of British Columbia
(Canada)

Kidder, Pe
Incorporated

Nesbitt Th

Shearson I

Warburg P
A. G. Becker

Pitfield, M;

EuroPartni

New Court

Nomura Si

New Japar

⌄⌄ ELECTRICITE DE FRANCE

U.S. $1,200,000,000
TEN YEAR EUROCREDIT FACILITY

Lead Managed by

AMSTERDAM ROTTERDAM BANK N V   ARAB BANKING CORPORATION (ABC)
THE BANK OF NOVA SCOTIA GROUP   THE BANK OF TOKYO LTD
BANQUE NATIONALE DE PARIS   BARCLAYS BANK S.A. PARIS
CREDIT AGRICOLE   CREDIT LYONNAIS
NATIONAL BANK OF CANADA   SOCIETE GENERALE

Managed by

BANQUE DE LA SOCIETE FINANCIERE EUROPEENNE   NATIONAL WESTMINSTER BANK
SFE GROUP   GROUP

Jenrette

pany Inc.

lerty Inc.

I, Towbin

ities Inc.

olds Inc.

irica Inc.

, Benson

ities Co.

ca), Inc.

inal, Inc.

ENTREPÔT
CAPITALISM

Foreign Investment and the American Dream in the Twentieth Century

CHARLES R. GEISST

PRAEGER

New York
Westport, Connecticut
London

Library of Congress Cataloging-in-Publication Data

Geisst, Charles R.
   Entrepôt capitalism : foreign investment and the American dream in
the twentieth century / Charles R. Geisst.
      p.   cm.
   Includes bibliographical references and index.
   ISBN 0-275-93894-8 (alk. paper)
   1. Capital market—United States—History—20th century.
2. Investments, Foreign—United States—History—20th century.
3. Capitalism—United States—History—20th century.   4. United
States—Economic conditions—1918–1945.   5. United States—Economic
conditions—1945–   I. Title.
HG4910.G44   1992
332.6'73'0973—dc20   91-34168

British Library Cataloguing in Publication Data is available.

Copyright © 1992 by Charles R. Geisst

All rights reserved. No portion of this book may be
reproduced, by any process or technique, without the
express written consent of the publisher.

Library of Congress Catalog Card Number: 91-34168
ISBN: 0-275-93894-8

First published in 1992

Praeger Publishers, One Madison Avenue, New York, NY 10010
An imprint of Greenwood Publishing Group, Inc.

Printed in the United States of America

The paper used in this book complies with the
Permanent Paper Standard issued by the National
Information Standards Organization (Z39.48–1984).

10 9 8 7 6 5 4 3 2 1

For Margaret

Contents

Introduction

The American Dream has proved to be a strong magnet for adherents and has become the favorite adjective used when describing the American economic experience on an individual level. The idea has weathered many political alliances, economic upheavals, and inequitable applications. Over the years it has taken on remarkably little baggage. It still suggests freedom from want, access to higher education, accumulation of wealth, and probably most important, owning one's own home. All of these elements combine to become the one shared experience that several generations of immigrants and their successors recognize as quintessential to being American.

The present volume is intended as the international companion to the primarily domestic survey of the same topic found in *Visionary Capitalism: Financial Markets and the American Dream in the Twentieth Century* published by Praeger in 1990. Like its predecessor, this book traces the history of the American Dream from the period immediately following World War I, the period in which the United States became a major force in international affairs. In the 1920s, the country emerged from its relative isolation to record the greatest period of prosperity in its short history. Demand for housing, consumer goods, and education all helped further define the American Dream at this time and demonstrated to foreign investors the attractiveness of U.S. investments. As will be seen later, foreign investors responded by increasing their investments, both portfolio and direct, in record amounts, leading to the 1929 crash. Although the resulting economic boom was the greatest recorded until that time, it was not necessarily anticipated. Writing in 1916, the economist Irving Fisher predicted that once the war had ended, pent-up demand would help raise European interest rates and, with them, U.S. rates as well.[1] As true of all such predictions, the opposite occurred in the United States, and the greatest bull market in history until that time helped raise stock and bond prices and drove down short-term interest rates. What could not have been envisioned was the increasingly important role the capital markets would play in raising money during the 1920s. Stocks and corporate bonds became the new investment favorites of the public rather than government war bonds, and the incredible demand for both allowed interest rates and the cost of equity financing to move lower over the course of the decade rather than to rise. As will be seen, the market for new corporate bond issues became so strong that foreign companies and governments were able to borrow freely, enabling the United States to become an exporter of long-term capital to the rest of the world.

Accompanying the newly acquired international political power was an international financial power that had the potential for abuse. Dealings in the period after the war were actually an improvement over some financial shenanigans that had occurred before and during it. When Woodrow Wilson dissuaded a consortium of international banks from making a $300 million high-interest loan to China, it marked the end of the "dollar diplomacy" that had been practiced for several decades. Dollar diplomacy was nothing more than the U.S. version of "sterling diplomacy" practiced by the British in gaining an empire during the latter half of the nineteenth century. It meant that foreign governments that could not repay loans made by bankers risked military action against them by the bankers' home countries, which could often end in foreign domination of their countries either through the means of production or directly through government overthrow. But World War I effectively ended U.S. aspirations for commercial expansion through those means. After the war, the general economic boom beginning in 1922 saw U.S. influence extend itself through investments and lending without the implicit threat of military backing of private interests. U.S. interests would certainly continue to be extended through investments abroad, and in a political sense, would come to be seen as a more sensible way to hold the world order together, especially during the 1920s. That was certainly an improvement on the sort of financial and political meddling the United States had engaged in with Mexico just prior to U.S. entry into World War I— meddling that led many Mexicans and Americans to state, not light-heartedly, that the real capital of Mexico was New York City, not Mexico City. After the war foreign investment began to replace direct intervention. The Dawes loan to Germany after the invasion of the Ruhr in 1923 helped forestall another war when Germany fell behind in its war reparations. As one commentator of the period noted, "Private foreign investments have been considerably more useful as an aid and protection to navies than navies have been as an aid and protection to foreign investments."[2]

This attitude would not prevail for long, however. Despite numerous loans

from the Western allies to bolster its foreign exchange reserves and the
mark, Germany embarked on the path to war in the 1930s. The fact that
German companies and the German government had invested in the United
States, borrowed on the New York bond market (the "Yankee" market, for
foreign borrowers), and paid their interest and principal payments on time
ultimately meant little as the world again prepared for war after the invasion
of Poland. The Germans would provide the only exception to the rule concerning foreign investment in the United States. Of all the major investors
in the United States, the Germans were the only group to prove that the
power of foreign investment sometimes paled in comparison to the power
of navies.

The reason that economic meddling in the United States by foreign investors did not become a major issue prior to the 1920s was that the origin and
distribution of those foreign investments, both portfolio and direct, were
from friendly cousins rather than potential hostiles. Since the early part of
the nineteenth century, both types of investment had largely been held by
British, Canadian, Dutch, and northern European investors. Being closely
akin to the vast majority of its investors, the United States did not view
foreign investment as inimical to public good. Added to that was an economic
reality: the United States was dependent to a great degree upon foreign
capital. Prior to World War I, the United States had been the greatest debtor
nation in the world. Nevertheless, its reaction to increasing foreign investment was mostly favorable. From both a business point of view as well as a
governmental position, Americans welcomed the infusion of foreign capital;
in fact, they recognized their dependence upon it. If complaints were heard,
they usually were from the investors' home countries, suggesting that their
U.S. investments were not always in their best interest.

Being a magnet for foreign capital, the U.S. was rather lax about reporting
exactly who owned what. As will be noted throughout this survey, how the
statistics are compiled has improved enormously since World War II, having
come under intense scrutiny in the 1970s, especially when disproportionate
amounts of Arab and Japanese investments were suspected. But historically,
the bulk of investment from a single country has been from Great Britain.
The other side of the coin is that Canada and Britain have been the major
recipients of U.S. direct investment abroad. Although our topic in this book
is foreign investment in the United States, it should not be assumed that
British and Canadian investments in the United States represent one-way
investments.

The reasons for the heavy concentration of British investment in the
United States has been a topic of long and intense discussion. For most of
the nineteenth and twentieth centuries, British money has accounted for
between 30 and 40 percent of total foreign investment in this country, both
direct and portfolio. Until the late 1980s, when portfolio investments were
supplanted periodically by investments by the Japanese, it was assumed

natural that British money would find its way to Wall Street, to manufacturing and banking, or to the insurance sectors as a means of diversifying from sterling. This assumption persisted despite the fact that U.S. investments often yielded less than comparable British investments for U.K.-based companies, especially when the hidden costs of doing business in the United States were factored into the equation. Despite the fact that many U.K. companies at certain times have been less successful in North America than have U.S. or Canadian firms, their relative inability to attain maximum profit did not necessarily dissuade them.[3] While it may be difficult to quantify, the cultural link between North America and Great Britain appears to have proved a boon when returns alone suggest otherwise.

The precise quality of the United States that makes its investments so alluring to foreigners has often been identified as its combination of political and economic stability. Not having to fear confiscation or political intrusion, foreign investors have placed funds in the United States hoping to take advantage of U.S. productive capacity, ingenuity, and other qualities usually cited as characterizing American business. While all of this may be true, it overlooks the element essential for all investment. As will be seen in the following pages, money came to the United States in the nineteenth century simply because investors were seeking a rate of return greater than that available in European markets. The potential for profit plus U.S. receptiveness to foreign investment provided that more tangible attraction.

In the years leading up to World War I, the United States remained comfortably insulated against the political winds blowing across Europe. While Europeans were debating the ideas of Marx and Proudhon, and the International movement was gaining strength among the working class, many of whom had little to lose by pressing for redistribution of wealth, Americans were on a slightly different path. Though the labor movement in the United States developed during the same period, and the novels of Frank Norris and Upton Sinclair displayed the same social concerns as did those of Emile Zola, American ideas concerning wealth and the means of production remained radically different from those of Europeans. Wealth was something to be attained—an ideal worth striving for, not to be redistributed but to be accumulated. While much of Europe was busy reading Zola and Marx, Americans favored the novels of Horatio Alger, stressing self-reliance and hard work. Surplus value was not considered theft by the American capitalist class; instead, it was an end in its own right. Any ideas that did not hold private property, accumulation of wealth, and spending in high regard were indeed considered alien.

During this period, the modern U.S. economy emerged; about two-thirds of the gross national product would be driven by consumer spending. The economy was in high gear, and it was considered foolish to meddle with a good thing. The Republican administrations of the 1920s understood the attitude well. As Will Rogers wrote in 1925, "The next time a politician gets spouting off about what this country needs, either hit him with a tubercular tomato or lay right back in your seat and go to sleep. Because this country has got too big to need a damn thing." This was perhaps the core of the American Dream in a mundane but abstract sense. The practical side saw it deeply imbedded in U.S. financial institutions.

Even strident foes of capitalism during the Depression recognized the fundamental strengths of the U.S. economy. In an interview in the *New York Times* (March 18, 1933), Leon Trotsky, living in exile in Turkey, said that he believed the U.S. financial system would eventually right itself from the Depression: "The American hegemony's future inevitable growth will signify nothing but this—the penetration of all our planet's contradictions and diseases into American capital foundations." In traditional Marxist language, Trotsky recognized the historical basis for what would later be known as the "American century." No force would be able to stop the ineluctable drive of American capitalism—at least not at that time. Trotsky's was a more simple view of the same idea expanded upon by Lenin in *Imperialism*. Writing prior to the 1917 Revolution, Lenin summarized imperialism as the highest stage of capitalism—the process by which capitalism expanded internationally. Integral to that process is what he called financial capital, spread and propagated by a financial oligarchy—namely, the banks of the industrialized countries. Financial capital was money concentrated in the largest commercial banks, not coincidentally founded or run by the Morgans or Rockefellers in the United States and loaned to industrial companies for expansion. In more contemporary terms, Lenin was referring to commercial loans made by banks. In the early part of the century, those sort of loans were somewhat more crucial to industrial development than they are presently, since banks furnished companies with medium- and long-term capital as well as short-term working capital loans.

Although the bond and stock markets were highly developed prior to the war, the 1920s would be when they would play an even more crucial role in financing U.S. industry, at the expense of commercial banks. It was for that reason that the banks were so quick in attempting to acquire securities houses or develop investment banking subsidiaries after World War I. Recognizing the changing trend in finance, they were determined not to be left behind. And this time period was conducive to growth, looked at from either an American or a Leninist point of view. The *New York Times* itself, in its news summary on the same day the Trotsky interview was published, saw the quote in a slightly larger context: "Trotsky is not often found seeing eye to eye with Stalin but on one subject they do agree . . . both think that the decline and fall of the United States is still a considerable distance away."

In the 1920s, perhaps the most strident domestic critic of U.S. socioeconomic development was Thorstein Veblen, whose *Theory of the Leisure Class* first appeared in 1899. Although this book was written in the style of classical political economy, its descriptions and analyses had a strangely contemporary ring. Describing what he termed conspicuous consumption, Veblen delineated the manner by which people accumulate goods for vicarious consumption—the consumption of goods beyond the level necessary to survive. In more advanced societies, this consumption becomes conspicuous, and as such becomes the surrogate for people's predatory nature. The accumulation of goods becomes part of a person's nature and the individual seeks to accumulate as much as possible in much the same manner that more primitive ancestors showed off martial costumes or acquired women by carrying them off. When the book was first published around the turn of the century, Veblen's popularity soared, and he gained the distinction of being one of the best known economists of his time. After World War I, his tongue-in-cheek descriptions became particularly apt for the fast-moving generation of the 1920s.

On the surface, it appears that Veblen was describing the American Dream in abstract terms. However, his cynicism shared a quality with Lenin and Trotsky that provides a small testimony to the American Dream. In all cases, they were critical but yet equally impressed by the strength and breadth of U.S. markets and institutions. Perhaps there is ample proof of that in Veblen's behavior shortly before his death. He too succumbed to the pie-in-the-sky dream in the last year of his life by foolishly investing a portion of his life savings in a speculative stock prior to the 1929 market crash, losing about half his savings in the process. The bull market of the 1920s had finally caught one of conspicuous consumption's most outright critics and snared him for a loss.

On the international side of the coin, one could assume J. A. Hobson's position outlined in his own study *Imperialism*, originally published in 1902 but still widely read in the 1920s, that foreign investment was actually a form of imperialism. It represented the darker side of successful economies—the sort that found its best U.S. manifestation in dollar diplomacy. Having developed their manufacturing to a high degree, the British had sought new markets for those goods. Wealthy societies, if they intended to remain wealthy, would seek foreign outlets for their domestic production and their capital as well. Overseas investment was just another form of survival in a manufacturing world. The export of capital was nothing more than economic imperialism: profits in search of new worlds to conquer. This was also the general argument used by Lenin. However, if that argument is accepted at face value, the corollary would naturally be that any country that had been the recipient of a large amount of foreign capital would also be "invaded" by imperialistic forces of sorts. The history of the United States, especially in the post–Civil War period to 1914, provides a distinct antithesis to that position. Having been highly dependent upon foreign investment in the nineteenth century, many U.S. industries, especially the railroads, would not have been able to develop without funds from northern Europe. But this was not considered imperialistic, and it did not bring with it undue foreign influence; instead, it was viewed simply as good business. There were many cases when foreign investors thought, sometimes with good reason, that Americans were in fact treating them as less than first-class investors by providing poor investment information or attempting to sell them investments that could not be sold to Americans. Whether indeed it was American practice to dump questionable investments in the laps of eager British investors is impossible to prove, but it was suspected nevertheless.[4]

THE ENTREPÔT, PAST AND PRESENT

Achieving the American Dream has always depended to an extent on foreign capital, but the type and structure of that capital has changed its complexion over the last hundred years. In the nineteenth century, most foreign investment was in the bonds and stocks of the railways and mining companies—expansionist industries for which the country was well known at the time. The nature of that investment began to change after World War I, when the United States became a net exporter of long-term capital at the same time it was becoming a net importer of short-term capital. The trend began to develop during the 1920s and would last for approximately thirty-five years. The U.S. financial markets would be used by foreigners to raise long-term capital, mostly bonds. There were no restraints on the movement of funds, and money was free to leave the country and re-enter, although there were implications for the gold stock as a result.

It was through this use of U.S. financial markets that the United States became an entrepôt, or trade intermediary. The markets would be used by foreigners, on occasion, to raise funds to be taken outside the country. The simple idea was that dollars raised would be dollars eventually spent in or with the United States, especially for trade purposes. But there was little evidence to suggest that the money raised in the country was being used to buy U.S. manufactured goods and agricultural products. While many Republicans in the 1920s felt that access to the markets would help the balance of payments and the U.S. economy in general, the fact was that foreigners were using the U.S. capital markets simply to acquire the only freely accessible capital in the world. In both postwar periods, capital controls in most countries prohibited foreigners from raising funds. But this was not the case for the U.S. capital markets. The one U.S. experiment in blocking access to the markets—the Interest Equalization Tax (1963–74)—ended with limited success eleven years after it was enacted.

After World War I, when New York began to compete with London as a net exporter of capital and the center of international finance, the U.S. employed the entrepôt concept as successfully as the British had in the immediate past. In order to lure business away from London, U.S. capital markets stood ready to supply long-term capital to the rest of the world. When the New York bond market blossomed after the recession of 1920–

21, that part of the entrepôt concept became a reality. Foreign companies and governments came to rely upon the New York capital market as a place to raise funds—as far as Americans were concerned, they hoped it was to buy American-made goods. Little direct evidence would ever support that hope.

The capital export part of the entrepôt concept succeeded quite quickly. The other part of the equation, attracting dollars back to the United States, would take more time to bear fruit. London's success in the nineteenth and early twentieth centuries was due to the premier role sterling played in international finance—a role that the dollar was rapidly assuming but had not yet reached. At the outbreak of war in 1914, David Lloyd George summed up Britain's preeminent role in international finance in practical terms: "We are transacting far more than the whole of our own business [in London]; we are transacting half the business of the world by means of paper transactions . . . paper which was issued from London has become part of the currency of commerce throughout the world."[5] Many U.S. business transactions, especially international ones, were still financed from London rather than from New York. But with Britain's decline in the international marketplace and the constrictions placed on the sterling in the 1930s, the dollar began to rise as the premier trading currency. In the 1920s, a concerted effort was made to keep U.S. interest rates below those in Britain, aimed partly at developing an entrepôt market where foreigners could raise dollars.

That strategy worked quite well until the early 1960s, when the eurobond market emerged, based primarily in London. For the first time, the international financial marketplace had a entrepôt market in the strict sense of the word: a market where foreigners could raise funds in a currency not necessarily their own, to be used for international investment purposes. At the time, sterling was still under exchange controls, so the intent was clear from the outset: foreigners would be able to access London in order to raise funds in currencies other than sterling (primarily U.S. dollars), using London as the market but not the ultimate source of funds.

At the same time, U.S. companies and banks began to extend their operations internationally, and their overseas investments with their financial outflows made the United States a major supplier of capital. As will be seen, this trend hit its apex in the 1960s, when U.S. direct investments abroad outnumbered foreign direct investments in the United States by a ratio of about 5 to 1. The political and social consequences were felt almost immediately, as the tide of international public opinion began to turn against U.S. multinational companies accused of everything from rapacious transfer pricing to meddling with developing countries' monetary affairs, to outright economic imperialism. The outcry then was louder than that Japan experienced twenty years later, perhaps because, unlike the Japanese, the U.S. economic ideology was interwoven with a pragmatic political ideology deeply resented in many quarters.

From the nineteenth century to the end of World War II, accurate tracking of foreign investment in the United States was taken somewhat light-heartedly by both the Department of Commerce and the Treasury. Unlike many other aspects of U.S. history, even two world wars did not engender a fear of foreigners that might have resulted in accurate surveys of foreign investment. That is not to say that the wars did not create an awareness of the problem. During both conflicts, the property of enemy countries was seized for the duration, and the financial strains of the conflicts, especially for the British, brought many foreign investments to light although most were already recognized. Nevertheless, some investments were perceived as a threat to national security, causing the Department of Commerce to closely monitor direct foreign investment in a more consistent manner.

Two pieces of legislation passed in the mid–1970s, prompted by the enor-mous holdings of dollars by the Organization of Petroleum Exporting Coun-tries (OPEC) and the acquisition of U.S. hard assets by the Japanese, prompted the U.S. government to assess foreign holdings on a regular basis and report those findings. It will be the contention here that these holdings, although substantial given the short time in which they were accumulated, did not have a negative effect upon U.S. business, but rather, helped erode some of the insularity that has traditionally characterized the American way of doing things.

In *Visionary Capitalism*, I noted a trend in the origin of student loan programs in the United States. All of the elaborate mechanisms for the programs, including the founding of the Student Loan Marketing Associa-tion, or Sallie Mae, could be traced back to a single event that had a profound effect upon the American psyche—the launching of the Soviet Sputnik in 1957. The reaction from Congress was to institute the loan program under the penumbra of national defense legislation. The original program became known as the National Defense Student Loan Program. Thus a basic part of the American Dream was interwoven with government assistance under the "threat" to the national security.

But that was not the first time this sort of equation was used in this peculiar form of American political calculus. The federal agencies founded during the last year of the Hoover administration and during the first two Roosevelt administrations were also based on such principles. Although many of those agencies later became identified with certain sectors of the economy, their original intent was to "combat" fiscal problems brought on by the Depres-sion. The development of the contemporary mortgage assistance agency—the Government National Mortgage Association, or Ginnie Mae—continued this trend. As part of Lyndon Johnson's Great Society programs, the Ginnie Mae apparatus was used to declare "war on poverty" by seeking to produce over twenty-eight million new units of residential housing. As with the student loan program and the Depression-era agencies before it, the intent was to accompany socioeconomic goals with a rallying cry. The American solution to social problems thus required Congress or the president to declare "war" on them. This approach re-emerges in the 1970s and 1980s, when Congress began examining the increased direct foreign investment in the United States in terms of whether national security was imperiled.

The issue of foreign acquisition of U.S. assets within the last twenty years has both a visible and a blind side. The visible coincides with fears that the United States has become a second-rate economic power, falling behind both Germany and Japan in terms of productivity and quality of manufactured goods. The blind side refuses, or fails, to recognize that foreign portfolio investments are growing as rapidly as foreign direct investments. Investment, and then liquidation, of U.S. securities by foreign investors can have a much more volatile effect upon the financial markets and asset values, and can prove more deleterious to the financial system than can direct investment. Even though direct foreign investment has produced fewer jobs and a smaller aggregate paycheck for the American worker than might be imagined, the contribution to the domestic economy is much more pronounced than that created by (normally) short-term investment in U.S. securities.

The benefits of direct foreign investment many times have been overlooked in favor of political or xenophobic considerations, especially in the 1980s. As foreign companies bought existing U.S. industries or opened start-up companies, many introduced production skills and management styles markedly different from those traditionally practiced in the United States. As will be seen later, this contrast in styles ultimately benefited the consumer by producing higher quality goods. But the price paid for these changes was a loss of market share for many long-standing U.S. industries such as automobiles and consumer electronics. And loss of market share to either imports or domestic goods designed elsewhere had a distinctly nationalistic overtone: did the influx of foreign capital and foreign-made goods signal the end of the American century?

The patriotic view of U.S. dominance of industrial production and innovation established following World War I tends to overlook simple economic geography. Making ample use of both domestic and foreign capital, U.S. industry was able to dominate much of international trade while enjoying relative physical isolation. Success in both world wars, plus heavy exports of long-term capital after World War I, ensured success for much of the twentieth century. However, the relatively long period of peace since 1945 also ensured that the United States would have competition from Europe and Japan once their economies emerged from the effects of the war. By the 1970s, that competition was beginning to appear in earnest, and when it actually arrived on our shores in the form of visible investments, the result was predictable: pundits would claim that the American success story was in its twilight and that the American Dream had become somehow irrevocably altered. The fact was that the United States now had international competition.

In examining the history of foreign investment during the twentieth century, one fact becomes clear. Foreign investment has always been present in the U.S. marketplace, in varying degrees. Limitations have existed only on certain industries deemed vital for defense.[6] Direct investment has been noticed only when the nationality of the investor has not been northern European. When there is competition from foreigners, the American Dream has been considered under attack. Over the years, one of the major problems surrounding this topic has been that of measuring foreign investment. For years, no one could adequately claim to know exactly how many U.S. real property or financial assets were held by foreign interests. As a result, invisibility was the best way a foreign-owned firm could avoid the occasional probing public eye. Perhaps no other single economic topic of such vast potential importance has had such a spotty statistical history.

STATISTICAL PROBLEMS

Although the amounts of foreign investment in the United States appear to be relatively consistent, there have been changes in the manner in which those investments have been counted. As will be seen in Chapters 1 and 4, official surveys of direct foreign investment in the United States were inaccurate at best until methods began to be changed in the 1980s. The consistent pattern was in the way investments were valued; usually these amounts were reported as the book value (historical cost) of a direct investment. In the 1920s and 1930s, however, the method of accumulating those values was somewhat suspect. Usually, surveys were sent by the Department of Commerce to companies known to have foreign ownership, and their responses became the basis for the statistics reported.

Aside from determining the valuations, there was also the matter of defining a direct investment. In the 1980 benchmark survey of foreign investments taken by the Department of Commerce, a *direct foreign investment* was defined as an investment that gave a foreigner controlling interest in a U.S. company—that is, an investment in which a foreigner owned 10 percent or more of an American company's stock (or its equivalent in the case of private companies). Prior to 1980, *controlling interest* was defined as owning 25 percent or more of the stock. While the numbers reported in this study appear quite consistent over time, the figures reported after 1980 are more inclusive than those preceding that time. The figures for the early years often were not defined at all. Controlling interest was reported only if the company was totally in foreign hands or believed to be substantially held by foreign interests. Therefore, it is quite possible that foreign interests before the 1970s were much more prevalent than indicated in the official statistics.[7]

The value of foreign portfolio investments in the United States was more accurate, since securities were and are valued on a current market basis.

But again, until about 1960, the totals depended upon the response rate of the banks and brokers occasionally providing the raw data for foreign portfolio activity. In the case of stocks and U.S. Treasury bonds especially, their increasing values during certain periods (the 1920s, 1950s, and 1980s especially) have to be understood on a market basis. Reported figures show the current value of securities held by foreigners. In periods of substantial market movements, the values reported may increase substantially without one additional dollar of new investment being made. Nevertheless, the figures for portfolio investment are probably more accurate than the direct investment figures because of the current-value basis consistently used over the years, despite the fact that the numbers at one time may not have been particularly accurate.

Because of measurement problems, plus the statistical storm that arose in the 1980s when foreign investments purportedly equaled or exceeded what U.S. companies had invested abroad, the Commerce Department announced in 1990 that it was attempting to place measurement of U.S. direct investments abroad on a current basis. This change occurred after numerous complaints concerning the value of U.S. foreign direct investments. Traditionally, the values had been registered on a historic basis. At the same time, it was acknowledged that U.S. investments abroad were more long-standing than many foreign direct investments in the United States and therefore may have been valued at unrealistically low levels. The whole issue came to the surface when foreign direct investment in the United States exceeded U.S. direct investment abroad for the first time in 1988, using traditional accounting methods. As will be seen, the usual historical proportion had been about 5 or 6 to 1, with U.S. investments abroad exceeding foreign direct investments in the United States. Politically, the question was simple: was America being bought up by foreigners or were the statisticians simply using poor data?

The questionable data and ad hoc methods employed are nevertheless indicative of the atmosphere surrounding the entrepôt market. For years the historical basis for valuing U.S. assets and liabilities overseas, as well as direct investments in this country, was recognized as faulty but tolerated as long as it was clear that political repercussions would be minimal. But once the tide began to change, new accounting methods for recent as well as historical valuations were adopted. The matter of the national security arose again. Questions that were first raised after the OPEC price rises of the 1970s were again asked in the late 1980s. Some of the most vocal expressions came in 1990, after Matsushita Corporation of Japan purchased a majority share in New York City's Rockefeller Center for $6.4 billion. While the worries over foreign ownership did not require Congress or the president to declare "war" on the problem, clearly the American Dream was again under attack in the people's imagination.

Throughout this study, *foreign investment* is taken to mean private investment—that is, the flow of private capital across national boundaries. Official government flows of capital have not been included because many times these occur for reasons quite distinct from the reasons companies make foreign investments. For instance, governments may grant loans or credits, or make other investments in a foreign country, in order to provide economic support or relief. The economic circumstances that prompt these measures can be the direct opposite of those that promote private investment in a country. The American Dream in the twentieth century finds its best manifestation in private foreign investment flows, into either directly held U.S. assets or portfolio investments. The United States has been a great importer of human capital throughout its history. Importing investment monies has also played a critical but less visible role, and its importance cannot be understated.

NOTES

1. Irving Fisher, "The Rate of Interest After the War," American Academy of Political and Social Science, *The Annals* 68 (November 1916), p. 250.

2. Eugene Staley, *War and the Private Investor* (Chicago: University of Chicago Press, 1934), p. 100.

3. On this topic see, for instance, John H. Dunning, *Studies in International Investment* (London: George Allen & Unwin, 1970), especially Chapter 6.

4. See Mira Wilkens, *The History of Foreign Investment in the United States to 1914* (Cambridge, MA: Harvard University Press, 1988), especially Chapter 16.

5. Quoted in "London and New York as Financial Centers," American Academy of Political and Social Science, *The Annals* 68 (November 1916), p. 265.

6. See the Organization for Economic Cooperation and Development, *Controls and Impediments Affecting Inward Direct Investment in OECD Member Countries* (Paris: OECD Publications, 1987), for a summary of those U.S. industries protected from direct foreign control by federal or state regulations.

7. See also Edward M. Graham and Paul Krugman, *Foreign Direct Investment in the United States* (Washington, DC: Institute for International Economics, 1989), pp. 135–44.

ENTREPÔT
CAPITALISM

1

Boom and Crash

Emerging victorious from World War I, the United States embarked on a period of unparalleled optimism. The years immediately following the post-war recession of 1921–22 witnessed unprecedented growth in consumer spending, home building, demand for education, and speculation in the stock market. American participation in the war had brought a newfound sense of confidence and power. The 1920s became a period of spending in which people from all walks of life enjoyed the benefits of the unique position the country had attained. In international financial terms, the period also had tangible consequences: the United States was no longer a debtor nation. After decades of imbalances, its accounts with the rest of the world were finally positive.

As with all periods of growth, the optimism was not without its more restrained side. The severe recession and a farm crisis in 1920–21 tested the framework of the Federal Reserve and the new Farm Credit Administration created only two years before. But that particular crisis and the subsequent strains it placed on the banking system were triggered by mechanisms that belonged more to the nineteenth century than to the twentieth. For instance, there was a very wide range of interest rates prevailing in the country at the time. Mortgages on single-family homes as well as on farms varied greatly depending upon geographical area and the peculiarities of local banking systems. For instance, generally it was more expensive to borrow from a bank in the West than one on the Eastern Seaboard. The country did not yet enjoy the standardized interest rates and structures that would eventually lead to more even-handedness and cohesion in the financial sector. But that did not deter the economy from prospering. The financial markets enjoyed unprecedented growth, Wall Street boomed, and all sectors of the economy benefited—although the banking system was not quite up to the challenge in structural terms. Investors of all sorts, ranging from the wealthy to the humble, speculated in shares while at the same time many banks were failing. Within ten years, the developing crisis would end in the stock market crash of 1929 and the Great Depression. A similar pattern would be repeated several times in the course of twentieth-century U.S. financial history. Fortunately for the markets, only the first time ended in a depression. The disastrous economic events of 1929–1933 produced a panoply of laws and regulations intended to ensure that the financial system would never again reach the brink of disaster.

After World War I, the booming markets and the optimistic tone of the Republican administrations under which they had occurred displayed a continuing sense of power and well-being. During this period, foreign investors also began to return to U.S. investments after being temporarily absent during the war years. However, the attractiveness of American investments was not new. The same foreign investors that had helped finance railway and mining investments in the nineteenth century and in the earlier part of the twentieth century returned. During the war they had liquidated many U.S. securities to raise money for the war. Between 1915 and 1916, foreign investors liquidated over $800 million par value of U.S. railroad securities, valued at about $600 million in market terms. In the two years between 1914 and 1916, an estimated $1.5 to $1.75 billion was sold back to American investors.[1] This selling had a sobering effect on the new issues market in the United States but helped the stock market gain an even greater reputation internationally for its ability to provide funds fairly efficiently. The British, for example, sold large amounts of U.S. securities. Those in the hands of the British government were liquidated for cash or used for collateral for loans made with the banks or bonds floated in the market. In addition, the British government kept large stocks of gold in the United States during the war, helping keep U.S. interest rates low. That kept the rates of interest they incurred on their dollar loans low as well.

When private foreign investors returned after the war, their preferences changed and investments were now directed more toward manufacturing companies and less toward railroads. But their return was both for the same and for different reasons at the same time. The shape of the U.S. economy and its markets had begun to change and, when coupled with international financial developments, it proved a great lure for capital in search of a safe home and a decent return. Concurrently, conditions in the international marketplace during the 1920s were substantially different from those before and during World War I. While capital, mainly from northern Europe, was invested in the United States in increasingly larger amounts each year to 1929, developments in the nature of U.S. capital markets plus changes in the foreign exchange market were largely responsible. The political element—that is, of money seeking a safe haven—obviously played a role but financial considerations were initially more important than were political ones. The last thing on investors' minds in 1920–21 was another war. Returns dictated where their money was invested.

Although the foreign exchange system was somewhat different in the 1920s than during the war, and the financial markets were essentially unregulated, it was neither real property nor stocks that attracted foreign investors. The majority of foreign investment in the United States was portfolio investments in the form of bonds, both corporate and governmental. This was not a new trend: most investments in the nineteenth century and most of the twentieth followed the same pattern. While many immigrants sought political and economic refuge, drawn by the possibilities of home ownership and economic betterment, the immigrant status of most foreign capital depended upon yield and the easy movement of capital.

In the nineteenth century, foreign investors clearly preferred bonds. The secretary of the treasury estimated that in 1853, almost 60 percent of the bonds of Boston, Massachusetts, and Jersey City, New Jersey, were held by foreigners. New York City bonds registered slightly more than 25 percent foreign ownership. When foreigners did make equity purchases, banks were a favorite. Some New York City banks (the Bank of New York was one example) had about 10 percent of their equity in foreign hands. Some New York insurance companies followed the same pattern. But the favorite investment of foreigners in the nineteenth century—railroads—was primarily a matter of bond investment rather than equities.[2]

During the Civil War, foreign investors made a massive divestiture of U.S. securities. But shortly after the cessation of hostilities, their investments again rose quickly, and by 1870 estimated foreign investment totaled about $1.5 billion. More than half of that amount was in the form of U.S. Treasury bonds and about equal amounts of the remainder were in municipal securities, railway bonds, and equities. What was never particularly clear was the origin of the monies. In the twentieth century, when reporting measures were improved, the major investment groups would more easily be identified, but in the nineteenth century the assumption was that most of the funds were northern European, especially British, with lesser amounts coming from Canada, Cuba, and Latin America.[3]

As the major attraction for foreign investors, bonds may at first appear to have been a curious choice. Unlikely to afford the investor the same opportunities for gain as common stocks, bonds were known, especially in the nineteenth and early twentieth centuries, mainly for their fixed-income qualities rather than for capital gains based upon interest rate movements. But this is precisely the sort of investment foreign investors seemed to prefer, especially given the nature of foreign exchange trading and differences in interest rates. As the 1920s began, the financial environment appeared even more conducive to fixed income investment, and investment monies began to pour into the country from various, but mostly familiar, sources. As the ensuing years would show, the type, length, and nature of foreign investment in the United States would depend to no small degree on the ability of the investor to move capital on short notice—conditions in the foreign exchange markets and tax considerations by the Internal Revenue Service notwithstanding.

THE MOVEMENT OF CAPITAL UNTIL 1929

While much has been written about the extent and type of foreign investment in the United States in both the nineteenth and early twentieth centuries, most of the early figures cited are actually no more than estimates, and many times very crude estimates at that. Writing in 1927, the Department of Commerce admitted, "No census of foreign investments in the United States has ever been taken and estimates of their total vary widely."[4] Most of these estimates or figures appearing in other studies were surveys taken by the government usually among banks, securities dealers, or insurance companies on a one-time basis and did not pretend to be comprehensive over time. And sometimes the results were slightly embarrassing, to say the least.

One such example can be found in that 1927 Commerce Department study. Citing prewar estimates of long-term foreign capital invested in the United States, the study estimated the amount at somewhere between $4.5 *million* to $5 *billion* in 1914. When tallying the amount from northern Europe alone, the report gave the amount at $6 trillion, although when indicating the breakdown by country the total was a more reasonable $6 billion.[5] Despite some poor reporting, one fact did emerge from even these crude estimates that would take on greater significance after the war: over half of that $6 billion originated from Great Britain, with the bulk of the balance from Germany, France, and the Netherlands.

Aside from the periodic reports commissioned by Congress or government agencies, the actual amounts of foreign investment in the United States were reported along with the amount of gold that entered or left the country on an annual basis. Gold movements were of special importance because most industrial countries still adhered, or hoped to return, to the gold standard, as had been the case prior to the war, and the strength or weakness of the dollar on the foreign exchange markets depended upon the country's gold stock. Unlike the foreign exchange standard that would emerge after World War II, the period leading up to the stock market crash and depression of the early 1930s relied on gold as the central numeraire for measuring the relative value of currencies.

The gold exchange standard, as it was more properly known, and the relative stability of the dollar prior to 1914 were partly responsible for the popularity of U.S. portfolio investments during the 1920s. After the war and the recession of 1920–21 had passed, the dollar took on a new luster in the wake of the devastation. Of the three major currencies, only the dollar remained stable during the early to mid–1920s. The pound and the French franc varied from their prewar exchange parities. Political instability continued to reign as well. The Austro-Hungarian empire no longer existed, and many major European economies were wracked with uncertainty. The German mark was virtually destroyed and the sterling would soon be under additional international pressures. Under these circumstances, the dollar naturally took on international significance.

Central to the period 1922–29 was continued adherence to the gold standard by the major central banks. Currency values were fairly stable in terms of their value in gold and also against each other. In theory, this reduced the risk an investor might incur if he sold one currency in favor of investments in another. Unlike investors in the latter part of the twentieth century, an international investor in the late 1920s faced some foreign exchange volatility, but not a significant amount.

The investment climate in the early 1920s was influenced by two factors, one practical and the other theoretical. Before any stability could be reached in the foreign exchange markets, the matter of German war reparations and the value of the mark would have to be settled. As the German currency depreciated after the war, it had a negative effect on the French franc and neighboring currencies. For there to be growth and stability in Western Europe, the mark would have to be stabilized. And once the mark had reentered the foreign exchange market, market participants would react to the new environment and its potential for future change by adopting a fashionable theory of foreign exchange movements, hoping to anticipate future exchange movements. Both of these developments would ultimately help the dollar and dollar-denominated investments.

The stabilization of the German mark was accomplished in late 1924 with the floating of the Dawes loan. For several years prior to then, bankers on both sides of the Atlantic had fostered the idea of having Germany borrow money to bolster its central bank reserves and stabilize the mark. After a long bout with hyperinflation during the early years of the Weimar Republic, inflation had finally been contained by the new chancellor, Gustav Stresemann, and the stage was set for Germany's reemergence onto the international financial scene. Though political and credit issues surrounded the loan proposal for several years, it was finally floated in the autumn of 1924, in both the United States and Europe. Politically, the loan was an expedient because Germany's failure to keep up its reparations payments had led to occupation of the Ruhr by some former Allied powers. Bankers from J. P. Morgan & Company were particularly active in the negotiations, and the loan emerged as an international bond issue rather than as a traditional bank loan. The U.S. tranche was valued at $110 million, with an equal amount floated in the European capital markets.[6] The borrowing did help stabilize the mark, and it assumed a fixed dollar value on the foreign exchange markets that lasted until the end of the decade.

Trading foreign currencies under what appeared to be relatively stable conditions, at least among the major currencies, still contained elements of uncertainty, however. Foreign exchange rates in the immediate postwar period were fluctuating and the price swings in some currencies, especially those in Europe, were deemed inimical to postwar recovery and reconstruction. A return to the gold exchange standard was thought to be the most advantageous action since it would stabilize the market. The pound sterling in particular was most often discussed in this context since it was the major reserve currency at the time and would remain so until World War II. By advocating a return to gold, the major central banks showed a desire for the relative price stability that had prevailed prior to the war.

The idea of returning to a gold standard for sterling was not without its detractors, however. While central bank authorities on both sides of the Atlantic favored the move, other influential economists and bankers were opposed. Montagu Norman, governor of the Bank of England, and Benjamin Strong, governor of the Federal Reserve Bank of New York, were both proponents and eventually won the day, although John Maynard Keynes, among others, was opposed. Sterling was stabilized in the early spring of 1925 with the assistance of both the Federal Reserve and a syndicate of banks headed by J. P. Morgan & Company.

Each of the central bank governors had national objectives in fostering a return to the gold standard. Both sides saw the need for a stable international market, while the British additionally saw the return to gold as a resumption of London's preeminent role in international finance. Conversely, Strong saw an advantage for New York to assume a more prominent role in international finance than had previously been the case. Under cooperative arrangements, New York would for a time maintain its interest rates below London's, hoping to become a center in which foreigners would utilize U.S. capital markets by borrowing in the bond market or selling new stock in the equities market.[7] That particular objective was met in the years immediately following, but the interest-rate factor also came into play in the foreign exchange markets. During the period immediately following the return to the gold standard, the U.S. discount rate was maintained at one percentage point lower than the Bank of England's equivalent rate. But at the same time, inflation in the United States crept ahead that of Britain, so a peculiar situation arose whereby the country with the higher interest rates had the lower inflation rate. The foreign exchange markets responded to that anomaly by adopting a theory for trading currencies that took into account inflation rate differentials.

During the 1920s, an earlier theory of foreign exchange pricing gained favor among traders and became a cause célèbre. This was the idea of purchasing power parity—a theory advanced by the economist Gustav Cassel of Stockholm in several articles and books published during and after the war.[8] The approach dovetailed with the new foreign exchange environment forged by the Federal Reserve and the Bank of England. Cassel had addressed the age-old problem of determining the forces that affect foreign exchange rates. Why did the market attach a premium to some currencies while treating others more poorly? In brief, his theory—which has lasted until the present—stated,

> Our willingness to pay a certain price for foreign money must be due to the fact that this money possesses purchasing power as against commodities and services in that foreign country. . . . When the two currencies have undergone inflation, the normal rate of exchange will be equal to the old rate multiplied by the quotient of the degree of inflation in the one country and in the other. . . . The rate that has been calculated must be regarded as the new parity between the currencies.[9]

According to this idea, one could predict a foreign exchange role if one could accurately calculate future inflation rates by interpreting current economic statistics. However, the implications of the theory are manifold and quite complicated. If the general theory reflected the reality in the foreign exchange markets, along with some other theories periodically used, the actual mechanism that affected the rates was a contentious issue. For instance, did the convergence toward a new parity work its way through the system through prices that were affected by the exchange rate mechanism, or did the exchange mechanism affect prices in turn? The traders' view was the more immediate one: the mechanism affected prices, not vice versa. Therefore, if a trader could have made an intelligent guess concerning inflation trends and applied those calculations to the market, he should have been able to position himself correctly in the markets to favor one currency over another.

This sort of posturing was true of the spot market and also applied to the other section of the foreign exchange market—the forward market, where currencies trade for future short-term delivery at prices that are established in the present. Prices for forward delivery were a matter of conjecture, with traders, economists, and speculators all attempting to predict those prices so they could position themselves in the present for a potential profit in the future. Obviously, the forward price of a currency was dependent upon the current (spot) price, and the forwards would be quoted at a premium or discount to the current price. Forward prices were also surrounded by some considerable theories, but they did have one major stalking horse that dominated the market in the 1920s and beyond. This was known as the theory of interest rate differentials, and one of its best-known exponents was John Maynard Keynes.

Keynes maintained that the difference between the spot and forward price for one currency versus another was the difference between the interest rates of the two countries involved.[10] If the pound was quoted at \$4.80 spot, and the difference between British and U.S. interest rates was 2 percent, then the forward pound rate would be adjusted by that same percentage. Supply and demand would naturally enter the picture, and forward prices would diverge slightly from these arithmetic differences, but if the divergence became too great then arbitrage would ensue, closing the gap.

The interest-rate differential method was and remains the practice in the foreign exchange markets for pricing forwards. But the factors that went into pricing spots remained of greatest interest and stimulated greatest controversy. The difference between purchasing power parity and other theories, especially those that base the price of a foreign exchange on a metallic standard, is that purchasing power theory signals a constant change in the parities between two currencies. Different economic statistics, interpreted differently by traders, would logically necessitate quickly changing rates, which would in turn produce changing prices if the theory held. But the mid–1920s did not witness rapidly changing parities. On the contrary, sterling held at \$4.80 between early 1926 and mid–1931. The same was true of the reichsmark and the French franc after 1926. Because of the return to gold, the purchasing power parity theory did not hold and the markets remained steady until abolition of the gold standard during the Depression. Adherents to the theory suffered heavy losses in the markets during the early 1920s, proving that, at least in general, markets adhere more to supply and demand than they do to theories.

The foreign exchange losses were not confined to bankers and professional traders; these dealings had been made by other strata of society as well. After World War I, the first great financial swindle of the twentieth century was exposed in Boston, Massachusetts. Thousands of small savers, notably Italian immigrants, were swindled out of their savings by Charles Ponzi, who sold an investment fund based upon gains supposedly derived from the foreign exchange markets.[11] The Ponzi scheme claimed to take advantage of discrepancies in the market by effectively selling short other currencies against the dollar and covering them later at lower prices. While the fraud occurred a long distance, both geographically and socially, from the centers of trading in New York City and London, it illustrated the fascination for both foreign exchange sales and putative exponential gains that dominated the period. In all cases, it was the relative stability of the dollar in the foreign exchange markets that drew investors, making Benjamin Strong's desire to see the markets host to foreign securities issuers a reality.

The 1920s were a period of increased foreign activity in U.S. markets, but direct investments remained on the modest side, hovering around \$1.5 billion. The idea of the United States as a safe home for foreign money had not yet become embedded in investor psychology. On the contrary, earlier confiscation of some \$525 million in investments from the Central Empire

(Austria-Hungary) was still fresh in investors' minds, and by 1926, $150 million was still unclaimed by, or not returned to, the original owners. From the 1920s to World War II, this action and similar ones prohibited the United States from becoming a truly safe haven in the universal sense.

With a relatively low rate of inflation and interest rates below those of Britain, the United States benefited from foreign capital after the return to the gold standard, but not necessarily by attracting foreign buyers to its hard or real property assets. In 1927, it was estimated that $28 million was invested directly by foreigners, much of it in the rayon industry. While that number rose to $35 million in 1928, it fell back to its 1927 level in 1929.[12] Those numbers are suspect owing to poor survey methods; nevertheless, they are quite small in relation to the amount of U.S. bonds bought by foreigners and the amount of dollar-denominated bonds borrowed by foreigners in the same period. The safe haven idea was not at work here; low interest rates were mainly responsible for this flow of funds.

The U.S. capital markets benefited from this funds inflow in two respects. First, foreign issuers of securities, mainly bond borrowers, used the New York bond market to secure long-term capital because of the relatively low cost of money. Second, investors continued to purchase U.S. bonds because of their currency stability. As long as the foreign exchange markets remained relatively stable, investors would find bonds attractive, since they did not have to worry about the prospect of a currency depreciation that would diminish their returns. Volume in the bond markets reflected this heightened activity. And changes in U.S. investment banking practices also helped immeasurably.

Although the 1920s are best remembered for the increase in the price of common stocks that eventually led to the market crash of 1929, the decade is also well known for the development of the bond market, especially for corporate and foreign issues. During the period that actually began in 1916, the corporate bond market began to expand, although the war and consequent U.S. Treasury borrowings forestalled further development until the 1920s. Nevertheless, the bond market was sophisticated enough to raise funds for the U.S. Treasury, domestic corporations, and foreign borrowers. It is estimated that between 1914 and 1916 alone, the market raised $1.7 billion in foreign loans, mostly for Canadian and European borrowers.[13] After the war, the United States became a major exporter of long-term capital and the bond markets developed to a higher degree.

Commercial and investment banking practices developing at the same time helped ensure the success of the long-term markets. In 1916, First National Bank of New York acquired Halsey Stuart & Company, a New York investment bank and broker, with the specific intent of entering the corporate securities market by underwriting and distributing corporate bonds. Following the war, other commercial banks entered the market by underwriting bonds of both domestic and foreign borrowers. Domestically, this increase in long-term borrowing signaled a new era of optimism for U.S. industry, which had previously relied more on direct borrowing from commercial banks, usually for the short or medium term. With the war behind them, American companies were now laying out capital investment plans funded with more long-term debt than ever before. The era of the 1920s was not only an investor's boom; industry also shared in the optimism.

After 1925, commercial banks made some headway in underwriting and distributing corporate stocks as well as bonds, with the McFadden Act of 1927 allowing them to do so legally. They had been dabbling in those markets for several years prior, however much of that activity was in bonds. In many cases, their interest in bonds was more than that of an investment banker. In 1924–25, the total volume of foreign bonds floated in the United States was $1 billion. This market became technically separate from the domestic market and was known as the Yankee bond market, a name that is still in use. Of the amount issued, some $500 million was purchased by Federal Reserve member banks for their own portfolios.[14]

The motive for this investing was twofold. First, the banks could collect the underwriting fees for these issues, enhancing their profitability. Second, if the banks kept the bonds as their own investments rather than selling them, the yields would be higher than the ordinary investor would have received for the same bond because the underwriting fees, when subtracted from the face value, would produce a higher return at a lower booked price. The incentive for entering the bond business was so strong that, by the eve of the crash in 1929, commercial banks had come to dominate the business at the expense of the remaining independent investment banks that had not been purchased in the previous twelve years.

Many of the foreign bonds issued during the 1920s proved to be poor risks when the 1929 crash and the Depression finally came. Despite the fact that the new foreign bond issues helped the United States gain prominence as an exporter of long-term capital, regulations for assessing investor risk were virtually nonexistent. It was assumed that the underwriters would be diligent and would not underwrite and sell a bond for a borrower who was less than creditworthy. As it turned out, that diligence was lacking in many cases, and numerous defaults occurred. Ironically, these patterns of default were repeated almost sixty years later in the bank syndicated loan market.

The number of foreign bonds floated in New York in the period 1920–29 reflects the high activity hoped for by Benjamin Strong, with the return to the gold standard. In 1920, the amount was $585 million, rising to $928 million in 1924. Between 1925 and 1928, the amount in foreign bonds floated rose from $1 billion to around $1.3 billion before falling back in 1929 to $670 million.[15] The nationality of the borrowers is critical since many issues defaulted in the early 1930s as international economic conditions deteriorated. Using 1927 as an example, Germany accounted for the largest amount in new issues ($220 million), followed by Canada and Newfoundland ($268 million), other European borrowers ($350 million), and Latin America ($360 million).

Not everyone saw foreign borrowing as conducive for a growing U.S. economy. The German loans in particular met with some opposition from U.S. industry because they were, in effect, helping to finance a major industrialized competitor. The Department of Commerce, under Herbert Hoover in the 1920s, came to recognize that "new German loans are frankly intended to develop foreign trade in competition against American firms."[16] The department tried, mostly in vain, to tie agreements with foreign borrowers to a specific use of funds, but the attempt met with opposition on Wall Street. The underwriting commissions were too important to investment bankers to tolerate any government meddling. This caused one Commerce Department official to comment in 1927 that the houses had an "utter disregard for all interests outside their own."[17] However, little could be done in this period of a laissez-faire market to stem this outflow of dollars into the hands of foreigners. Even if there was a general concern, it was nevertheless understood that investment bankers would always check with the State Department before agreeing to underwrite a foreign bond or loan. The government's major concern was that nations in arrears to the United States might enter the private loan market without first paying back their government debt. If a foreign company issued stock on the U.S. market, however, the Commerce Department would offer little opposition.

The same relaxed atmosphere did not extend to the realm of imports however, an area where successive Republican administrations practiced a more protective policy to shield American industry. In 1922, Congress passed the Fordney-McCumber Act, raising tariffs to their highest level in history. The president was given the power to adjust the tariffs in order to equalize differences in production costs between foreign and American products. Equally, he was empowered to impose embargoes on countries discriminating against the United States in trade. True to form, the administrations did very little to lower tariffs, in most cases keeping the levels high to emphasize American enterprise, production, and patriotism. This created the somewhat untenable position of exporting capital through the bond markets while at the same time closing the import market to foreign goods.

The popularity of the U.S. bond markets in the 1920s can be attributed to two factors that were less visible to investment and commercial bankers than they were to the borrowers of dollars. For foreign exchange purposes, the decade can conveniently be split into two chronological periods. The first was the time ending in 1925, in which the major currencies were floating and the dollar was quite strong against the franc and the pound. The second was the time from 1926 to 1930, when the currencies were stable and the dollar's value against sterling was suspect, owing to terms set for the return to the gold standard. Both periods witnessed strong growth in foreign issues for quite different reasons.

In the earlier period, an international borrower needing funds would be drawn to dollars because of uncertainty regarding most other currencies. After 1926, when stability returned to the currency markets, the dollar would have appeared somewhat overvalued, especially against sterling. As mentioned earlier, U.S. interest rates were lower than the British although U.S. inflation was higher. In these circumstances, the dollar should eventually have undergone a realignment against the pound. If that had been the case, those borrowing dollars would have been able to retire their debt with less of their native currency than had previously been the case when the dollars were borrowed, effectively making the borrowing cheaper. Thus, the relative strength of the currency between 1926 and 1930 was a magnet for borrowers willing to take a somewhat speculative stance against the dollar.

The ease with which these various borrowers could access the market was another factor in favor of the dollar and the bond markets. In the absence of any particular regulatory authority, only the states that had blue-sky laws could require more disclosure of a borrower's financial position than underwriters might have been willing to offer. The easiest way around these disclosure requirements was simply to avoid the states that applied them. When many Latin American borrowers, along with some from Eastern Europe, failed to meet interest payments in the early 1930s, it subsequently was discovered that many were literally bankrupt at the time they had borrowed. Revelations of that sort helped fuel the regulatory fires that would culminate in the Securities Act and the Glass-Steagall Act of 1933.

A good deal of this stock market activity was attributed to foreign investors, despite their modest interest in equity investments for the longer term. This can be attributed to international arbitrage among securities that had more than one stock market listing. Listing stocks on foreign stock exchanges was a fairly commonplace practice, especially for larger, well-known companies. These dual listings presented speculators with profit opportunities through both the foreign exchange market and the stock markets operating on different international times. Owing to relatively slow international communications, mainly via telex, and the incipient volatility of the U.S. stock markets during the period, investors were able to buy the same security in one market while selling it in another, profiting from what would appear to be a small difference in price. This practice was known as interexchange arbitrage, and could be practiced anywhere a share was recognized for trading. It was possible for a relatively small number of shares to be turned over so frequently that the total turnover for a year could appear quite substantial. It is estimated that prior to the crash in 1929, this activity generated trading volume worth approximately $750 million per year.[18] The U.S. part of these commissions was fairly sizable, and contributed to the balance of payments in both 1928 and 1929, as well as in the years immediately preceding.

Although direct foreign investment remained less than $100 million in any particular year during the 1920s, the penchant of foreigners for trading U.S. securities was robust until the crash in October 1929. An estimated $1.5 billion in domestic securities was sold to foreigners in 1928 and again in 1929. Certainly not all of this amount can be attributed to bond investments. U.S. brokers regularly advanced margin money to foreign accounts, usually at slightly higher rates than for domestic investors. Canadian investors were especially noted for speculating in U.S. stocks, and were among the most adept at practicing interexchange arbitrage. On balance, Canadians were long-term borrowers and short-term lenders to the American banking system, but on the stock market side they were among the best-known speculators.

The picture that emerges of international investments and investment behavior in the United States in the 1920s is not materially different from that on the domestic side. Despite some poor and spotty record keeping, distinct patterns emerge from the period. The most obvious was the preference for Americans to invest outside the country while foreigners tended to speculate in U.S. markets. In 1927 and again in 1930, the value of total U.S. investments abroad exceeded that of foreign investment in the country. Before the 1929 crash, $18 billion had been invested abroad versus $6.6 billion domestically. In 1930, the figures were $21.5 and $8.5, respectively. Of the 1927 figures, U.S. direct foreign investments totaled $6.6 billion while total foreign direct investments were undetermined. In 1930, the U.S. amount increased to $8 billion while direct foreign investments in the United States were estimated at $1.4 billion.[19]

Part of the explanation for this imbalance is undoubtedly the wealth effect created by victory in World War I. Not having to rebuild a ravaged economy, the United States was in a better position to invest in foreign countries than many other nations. The newfound prosperity, enjoyed by individuals and their institutional intermediaries alike, created opportunities in investments such as the bond business developed by commercial banks, and those opportunities drew many customers through aggressive selling and advertising.

Somewhat less evident is the fact that all the stock market speculation, especially in margin accounts, and the rise in interest rates prior to the crash, drew a number of foreign investors to the United States, through channels not quite as obvious as those already described. After the war, many countries used the dollar for official international and domestic transactions in place of their own currencies. For example, the dollar was the currency of preference in many Caribbean and Latin American countries, Cuba and Argentina probably the best examples. These dollar holdings naturally would have to be returned to the domestic banking system if their holders wanted to

earn interest. Although technically expatriate, the dollar balances were deposited in U.S. banks, thereby making the United States an importer of
short-term capital. As interest rates rose just prior to the market collapse of
October 1929, these deposits found their way into the market for short-term
lending, especially for margin money. The result was that foreigners were
indirectly helping to fuel stock market speculation by making margin money
available.[20]

In traditional banking terms, the country was borrowing short and lending
long—a classic mismatch whether it be on a balance sheet or in balance-of-
payments terms. However, in trade terms the situation looked somewhat
more sanguine. The U.S. trade balance with the country's oldest and largest
trading partners remained favorable, and U.S. capital markets continued to
supply debt and equity to both domestic and foreign companies and governments. But the international financial system, more fragile than many
had imagined, began to send out warning signals that would culminate in
the stock market crash and subsequent depression.

EXTERNAL INFLUENCES ON THE MARKETS

In several Commerce Department documents produced during the 1920s,
reference is made to American prosperity and how those from outside the
country desired to participate in it. However true that may have been, part
of the foreign investment attracted during that time had also to do with
common language and political traditions. During the 1920s, as in decades
past, the major trading partners of the United States were Britain and Canada. In balance-of-payments terms, this relationship was one in which Americans greatly benefited.

From 1921 to 1929, the United States imported more goods and services
from the British and Canadians than from any other nation. In some cases,
the imports exceeded those from other continents, such as South America
or continental Europe. The value of British and Canadian imports accounted
for between 20 and 25 percent of all general imports for the decade. On the
other side of the ledger, the picture was even brighter: exports to those two
countries accounted for about 30 to 35 percent of all U.S. overseas sales. Of
the two, Britain was the better export market, a trend that would last until
the end of World War II.

These figures help explain why Canadian borrowers, especially the federal
government and the provincial governments, borrowed so heavily in the
Yankee bond market. The borrowings were used to help finance purchases
of goods from the United States. In the businesslike Republican 1920s, this
was exactly the sort of international capital transfer that was desired, since
the trade figures supported these borrowings. But this was more than simply
a case of foreigners wanting to participate in U.S. prosperity or to buy U.S.

manufactured and agricultural goods. There was also a lack of competitiveness in the international marketplace.

The United States was one of the few places in the world where capital could be raised and exported without incurring governmental restrictions. The other major source was the British capital market. The stock markets of remaining European economies were small in comparison and, as were their bond markets, they were still recovering from the war. But the London markets were constrained by capital controls in the 1920s, as they would be for decades to follow. Capital was not free to enter the United Kingdom, as it was in the United States. That one fact alone helped give rise to New York's increasing importance in international finance.

British capital controls actually began during the war and continued in one form or other until 1924. When sterling returned to the gold standard in 1925, formal controls were lifted and "informal" controls took their place. But these less formal restrictions still affected overseas borrowers or raisers of equity capital. The Bank of England applied indirect pressure on foreign borrowers of sterling, effectively limiting their access to the London market. This was done so that foreign borrowers would not compete with the British, keeping pressure off interest rates. After 1925, even these controls were lifted but by that time foreign borrowing had shifted to New York because of the lower U.S. interest rates negotiated by Montagu Norman and Benjamin Strong.

Though foreigners had limited access to the London market, British firms were free to raise funds domestically for the acquisition of foreign investments. Equally, British institutional investors were given free rein to purchase foreign securities in overseas markets. From an official perspective, these informal controls were designed to protect British monetary policy from external influences, but they had another effect that diminished Britain's invisible account on the balance of payments. Foreign securities that normally would have been issued in London in the absence of controls now found their way to centers such as New York, where they were purchased by British or Commonwealth investors and taken back to London for trading. The London Stock Exchange had always had a reputation for trading foreign as well as domestic stocks. In a somewhat convoluted manner, London continued to attract trading capital, while New York earned the underwriting commissions for bringing the new issues to market.[21]

With regard to foreign direct investments in the United States, certain types of manufacturing and agriculture attracted interest. In addition to the manufacturing of rayon, there was some foreign investment in citrus farming, especially in Florida. But manufacturing remained the dominant foreign interest. From railroads and natural resources in the nineteenth century, foreign preferences had switched to manufacturing in the 1920s. Also suspected, but not proved by adequate data, were mortgage investments held by foreigners, especially British and Canadians. The same two groups also accounted for most new, substantial investments in U.S. companies in 1929: Of the 78 investments made by foreigners in U.S. companies between 1921 and 1929, 22 were made by Canadians and 15 by British investors.[22]

Despite the fact that American prosperity was usually cited as the reason for foreign interest in U.S. investments, the issue was somewhat more complicated. The country's role as an entrepôt was enhanced by a favorable foreign exchange environment, low interest rates, aggressive commercial and investment bankers, lack of regulations affecting borrowers and lenders, and no serious competition from the London market. But it was apparent that foreign capital was not financing the American Dream as it would become defined after the Great Depression. The main thrust of foreign investment leading up to the 1929 crash was, in keeping with the times, more speculative than long-term. Until 1920, it had also been opportunistic but had tended to be more long-term than short-term in nature.

THE CRASH AND ITS AFTERMATH

The character of the international financial system forged by the fixed exchange rate system ensured that a worldwide decline in prices and values would follow the stock market crash of 1929, leading to the Great Depression. The market crash was the principal cause of the Depression, which was effectively exported to the rest of the world through the exchange rate mechanism. For instance, the gold exchange standard involved fixed exchange rates, and as long as those rates were maintained, prices and incomes in different countries tended to move together.[23] International portfolio diversification would mean little, since all of the major economies would fall victim to the same set of economic misfortunes. The only economies that did not suffer were those that were not on the fixed monetary or gold exchange standards.

One example of the speculative nature of foreign-held securities is the average price of U.S. shares held by foreigners versus all those listed on the New York Stock Exchange. In 1929, the average price of a common share was $55.25 while the average price of a foreign-held common share was $87.00. Similar comparisons can be found in preferred stock: the average price of a listed preferred share was $77.50 while the price of a foreign-held share was $94.00. After the crash, when values of all shares fell dramatically, the losses incurred by foreigners were proportionately greater than those suffered by domestic investors.[24]

All the investors who had loaned money to the call market in New York, both domestic and foreign, saw the banking institutions that had made the loans come under severe pressures and, in some cases, eventually fail under the weight of irretrievable loans and lost funds. But the allure of lending short-term to the call money market was quite strong because of the enormous speculative nature of the stock market involving all segments of society, from the dabbling of Herbert Hoover's famous "bellboys" all the way to traditional institutional investors. With margins granted by brokers ranging from 10 to 20 percent of the value of the stocks involved, the potential for high earnings was too strong for many institutions to resist. Thus, the boom market of the 1920s involved foreign investors as well as Americans from both ends of the spectrum—share investors themselves as well as their banking counterparts, the lenders.

One of the first victims of the drop in share prices was the new foreign issues on the Yankee bond market. The link between the falling equity market and the diminution of new issues is not immediately obvious, but the connection involves the structure of the investment banking industry at the time, before the regulations imposed by the Glass-Steagall Act of 1933.[25] Although foreign exchange rates would ordinarily be expected to be a major cause in a drop in new foreign issues, the exchange value of the dollar remained relatively stable during 1929. Instead, it was the nature of bond borrowers themselves that caused the curtailment. Before adequate investor protections were introduced, the only vetting a foreign bond would receive was the implicit blessing of its underwriter. The financial condition of the borrower, whether a domestic corporation or a foreign entity, would be made known only through the best efforts of its underwriters. Consequently, many new issues brought to market were bonds of poor quality, especially among the foreign borrowers.

Many of the issues brought to market during the 1920s subsequently defaulted, among them bonds of several Latin American and Eastern European borrowers. Some foreign issues actually fared well in the post–1929 environment and were so popular among investors that they traded at premiums to their issue price in the lower interest rate environment that developed. As soon as the stock market turned sour, however, the number of new issues dwindled. In 1928, new issues of Yankee bonds had totaled some $1.25 billion; by the end of 1929, the number was about half, $670 million.[26] Investor reaction was responsible for this drop. The bond market became as vulnerable as the stock market as soon as investors realized that some bonds were as risky, if not more risky, than common stocks. But this reaction did not end in 1929. Subsequent defaults of many foreign bonds aroused indignation among investors, who thought they had purchased relatively safe investments. The underwriters that brought the issues to market ultimately were blamed for not being diligent enough in determining their clients' creditworthiness. As a result, foreign bonds were classified as corporate bonds in the Securities Exchange Act of 1934, and would henceforth be required to register with the newly created Securities and Exchange Commission before they could be sold to the public.

While the bond and stock markets provided the most attractive magnets for foreign capital in the 1920s, the number of direct foreign investments was not insubstantial, as later statistics would eventually show. But if the

1920s had to be viewed in terms of foreign investment, the results would be no different than for domestic investment: interest in the markets was fueled by a speculative fever that hit its height in 1928, before eventually slowing and creating the crash in the autumn of 1929. The combination of capital exports through the bond markets, capital imports through the money market, and the protective trade environment created by the Fordney-McCumber Act set the stage for perhaps the greatest U.S. export of the decade—depression. Whether the market crash and the slowdown that followed is viewed in exchange terms or simply in trade balances, it is clear that the world's leading capital provider had set the stage by providing long-term funds on one hand while putting a damper on imports on the other. As a result, the early part of the next decade would witness a continuance of the trend until the Depression ended and foreign investment interest reappeared.

NOTES

1. Gordon B. Anderson, "The Effect of the War on New Security Issues in the United States," American Academy of Political and Social Sciences, *The Annals*, November 1916, p. 121.

2. U.S. Senate, "Report of the Secretary of the Treasury in Answer to a Resolution of the Senate Calling for the Amount of American Securities Held in Europe & Other Foreign Countries, on the 30th June 1853," Executive Document No. 42, 33rd Congress, 1st Session, 1854, p. 22 ff. It should be noted that the distinction between *bond* and *stock* is not always clear in nineteenth- and early twentieth-century financial usage. In some cases, *stock* means *bond*, following British use, while in other cases *equity* is used to make the distinction. As a result, reading statistics of the period can often be difficult.

3. U.S. House of Representatives, "Report to the Special Commissioner of the Revenue upon the Industry, Trade, Commerce &c. of the United States for the Year 1869," Executive Document No. 27, 41st Congress, 2nd Session, 1869, pp. xxvi–xxxi.

4. U.S. Department of Commerce, "The Balance of International Payments of the United States in 1927," Bulletin Number 552, May 1928, p. 22.

5. Ibid. The amount of British investment in the United States during the war, originally estimated by Sir George Paish in *The Statist* of February 14, 1914, became the basis of many of the official U.S. "guesstimates" done in the 1920s. He estimated that in 1913, of the total of £160 million of new capital raised in Britain for overseas ventures, £18.70 million was destined for the United States, second only to Canada in the amount of British capital investments. At the same time, of the total of £3.70 billion invested by the British overseas, about £754 million was invested in the United States, making it the largest single recipient of British overseas investment.

6. The Dawes loan, or bond, was set at a 7 percent coupon for twenty-five years and was issued at a discount to yield 7.75 percent. It was quite profitable for the banks that underwrote it. The full amount of underwriting fees amounted to five full points. The issue price was 92, but the cost to the underwriters was only 87 (both

percentages of par, or 100). As it turned out, the loan was never actually paid back in full. After Herbert Hoover's moratorium on debt in 1932, an international conference at Lausanne arranged for Germany to pay off the loan in one amount, disregarding the original terms of the loan. Although there would be an outstanding balance after this time that would lead to further friction, Germany's main creditors maintained a flexible attitude so that the integrity of the German financial structure would be maintained. For a full discussion of the terms and circumstances of the Dawes loan, see Stephen V. O. Clarke, *Central Bank Cooperation, 1924–31* (New York: Federal Reserve Bank of New York, 1967). A political and diplomatic interpretation of the loan can be found in Eugene Staley, *War and the Private Investor* (Chicago: University of Chicago Press, 1935).

7. Clarke, *Central Bank Cooperation*, pp. 72–73.

8. The theory of purchasing power parity was not actually new to Cassel and could be traced back to the Salamanca School and David Ricardo. See Paul Einzig, *The History of Foreign Exchange*, 2nd ed. (London: Macmillan, 1970), p. 264.

9. Gustav Cassel, *Money and Foreign Exchanges after 1914*, cited in Einzig, *History*, p. 265.

10. Most notably in his *Tract on Monetary Reform*, 1923.

11. The Ponzi fraud involved investing in a plan that purportedly took advantage of foreign exchange movements by investing in international reply coupons which could be bought from post offices around the world by paying for them in the local currency. In theory, a person holding coupons in one country could redeem them in another. If the currency rate was in his favor, a gain could be made. In short, the coupons were theoretically fungible. Ponzi sold the idea mostly to Italian immigrants in and around Boston. He satisfied the early investors by paying them off with funds taken from other investors, creating what became known as the Ponzi scheme, later to become generically known as a pyramid scheme. After being exposed by newspaper articles in the *Wall Street Journal* among others, the Ponzi fraud became known as the largest swindle in American history to date.

12. U.S. Department of Commerce, "The Balance of Payments in 1927, p. 41.

13. Gordon B. Anderson, "The Effect of the War on New Security Issues in the United States," p. 125.

14. Federal Reserve System, *Bulletin*, November 1925, p. 782.

15. U.S. Department of Commerce, "The Balance of Payments in 1927" and U.S. Department of Commerce, "The Balance of International Payments of the United States in 1929," Bulletin No. 698, 1930.

16. Quoted in Joseph Brandes, *Herbert Hoover and Economic Diplomacy* (Pittsburgh: University of Pittsburgh Press, 1962), p. 193.

17. Ibid., p. 194.

18. U.S. Department of Commerce, "The Balance of Payments in 1929," p. 53.

19. U.S. Department of Commerce, *Historical Statistics of the United States: Colonial Times to 1970*, Vol. 2 (Washington, DC: U.S. Bureau of the Census, 1975), p. 869.

20. As will be seen in later chapters, the creation of the eurodollar market in the 1960s obviated the need for foreigners to deposit funds in domestic banks. Equally, once the repatriation of eurodollars by domestic banks was effectively blocked by the Federal Reserve for domestic lending purposes, the impact of these offshore deposits on the domestic banking system could be minimized.

21. See Alec Cairncross, *Control of Long-Term International Capital Movements* (Washington, DC: The Brookings Institution, 1973), Chapter 4. The British stamp tax, a government tax on securities turnover, was also a factor dissuading some borrowers and investors from using the London market and would remain as such for the next sixty years.

22. U.S. Department of Commerce, *Foreign Investments in the United States* (Washington, DC: U.S. Government Printing Office, 1937), p. 41.

23. See Milton Friedman and Anna Schwartz, *A Monetary History of the United States, 1867–1960.* (Princeton: Princeton University Press, 1963), p. 359.

24. U.S. Department of Commerce, *Foreign Investments*, p. 100.

25. For a more detailed explanation of the condition of the corporate bond market for both domestic and foreign issues prior to the October 1929 crash, see Charles R. Geisst, *Visionary Capitalism: Financial Markets and the American Dream in the Twentieth Century* (New York: Praeger, 1990), Chap. 1. The poor quality of many foreign and domestic issues also helped characterize the period 1920–40 as one of high bond defaults in general, especially compared to issues subsequently brought to market between 1940 and 1965.

26. U.S. Department of Commerce, "The Balance of Payments in 1929," p. 22.

2

Depression and War

New as a creditor nation in the 1920s, the United States assumed a role it was unaccustomed to filling—providing other industrialized and developing nations with long-term capital. But as the number of foreign bond issues in New York began to fall off in 1929, economic activity rapidly slowed down, the stock market averages continued to plunge, and the country and the world sank into a depression. The new U.S. role of entrepôt came to an abrupt halt as capital, for whatever purpose, became scarce and long-term investment took a back seat to immediate short-term needs. However, foreign investment in the United States remained remarkably stable during the Depression despite economic conditions, and shortly thereafter the country would adopt a more sober view of market speculation, consumption, and of its own role in international finance.

One of the major shortcomings of the Republican administrations of the earlier boom years was their attitude of putting immediate business first, even if that meant overlooking the obvious long-term implications of their policies. An example of this one-sided optimism was the Commerce Department's classification of foreign bonds floated in New York as "foreign investments." The obvious advantage was the number of underwriting commissions that Wall Street reaped from these issues and the boost those numbers gave to the balance of payments. But those numbers belied the fact that capital was being exported in large quantities, in many cases to major manufacturing and agricultural competitors. The myopic emphasis on short-term tangible profits had been one of the major characteristics of the Coolidge administration in particular, and it suited Wall Street well. Attitudes began to change with the Hoover administration, especially after the crash, and those changes certainly continued in the subsequent Roosevelt administrations.

The similarity between the tenor of the Fordney-McCumber Act and the purchasing power parity theory of foreign exchange rates remains one of the striking financial features of the 1920s. The equalization provision of the tariff was remarkably similar to the notion that prices align themselves owing to the leveling of exchange rates between two countries. If there were discrepancies between the price of U.S. product and an import, the presidency had the power to raise (the usual action) or lower the tariff rate. In 1930, the tariff situation was exacerbated by enactment of the Hawley-Smott Act—a textbook cause of the Depression. Actually, the new tariff act was nothing more than a modification of the Fordney-McCumber measure, with the equalization and flexible provisions of the original tariff kept intact. The major modification was the method by which the provisions were administered. Unlike the Fordney-McCumber Act, the Hawley-Smoot bill gave the Tariff Commission the power to initiate investigations into purported inequities in tariffs and trade, and to recommend necessary changes to the president. (The original tariff had vested that power solely in the president.) As it turned out, Herbert Hoover signed the measure into law because he appreciated the administrative change, shifting more power to the tariff commission. The new Act exacerbated an already precarious international trade situation. Many foreign governments retaliated with similar measures, and the Depression was given additional impetus by a curtailment in international trade.

At the same time, the number of international loans floated in the New York market continued the decline that had begun in 1929, after almost a decade of unabated growth. By 1931, new issues had fallen to a fraction of the 1928 record. The drop in international economic activity was more serious, however, than a simple drop in new bond issues might suggest. In May 1931, the Kredietanstalt, Austria's largest commercial bank, began suffering liquidity problems and the Austrian government had to search for international loans to help restore the institution. In June 1931, President Hoover suggested a moratorium on all international payments due to the United States during the following year, provided other creditor nations took similar action. Two months later, a consensus was reached although some debtor nations were still being pressed by short-term creditors to pay off loans due immediately.

Given the state of both the U.S. and European economies, it would be natural to assume that foreign investment in the United States would have fallen, as did foreign bond issues. This was not the case, however. Portfolio investments were assumed to drop, although there was still scant evidence to support such conclusions owing to poor record keeping by various agencies. Despite the increasing number of bank failures in the country, the general deflation of prices, and the drop in securities values, direct foreign investments remained remarkably stable. They were so stable because of the value of the dollar on foreign exchange markets—remarkable since the press was blaming commercial and investment bankers for the massive bank failures and destruction of savings.[1] The major factor that propped up the dollar was gold: the United States held in reserve about 35 to 40 percent of the world's supply of gold.

In 1931, Great Britain had to abandon the gold standard. The Labour government was unable to withstand the pressures brought upon the pound, *inter alia*, when Germany froze British bank assets during the German banking crisis of 1931. The value of the pound had dropped during the first six months of that year, stabilized, and then dropped drastically by almost 15 percent just before the gold standard was abolished. The dollar began attracting flight capital as never before, despite the Depression. It began to fluctuate against the pound owing to speculation by foreigners, but on balance, the ability to get gold rapidly restored confidence in the dollar despite otherwise gloomy economic news.[2] Since the United States remained committed to the gold standard, the value of the dollar stayed relatively strong. But the deterioration of the pound also brought on demands to devalue the dollar, and relative dollar stability was achieved only as other major currencies fluctuated widely. That situation in turn added pressure to realign the currencies, and the dollar was naturally affected. One result of the currency crisis came in 1931, when the Federal Reserve raised the discount rate to prevent erosion of the dollar, and made funds readily available to commercial banks.

The crisis of the early 1930s, when combined with the somewhat loose Republican policies that characterized the 1920s, aided the dollar and strengthened the U.S. reputation as a haven for foreign money. As mentioned earlier, the same characteristics essentially stabilized direct foreign investment, since there were no obvious incentives for liquidating U.S. holdings. Hot money was again attracted to the United States despite interest rates that were still below those in Europe and a moribund stock market.

Another more far-reaching effect of Britain's abandonment of the gold standard was the international depreciation of currencies, continuing until 1934. After the crisis of 1931, currency blocs, or areas, were created whereby many countries linked their currencies to either sterling or the dollar. Those that followed sterling allowed their currencies to depreciate with it. This group included many of the Commonwealth countries and former colonial possessions. At the same time, the dollar was allowed to depreciate, and the currencies of those countries that tied themselves to it naturally followed suit. The dollar depreciation was accompanied by exchange restrictions designed to prevent further capital exports. At the same time that President Roosevelt declared a national banking holiday in March 1933, another executive order was passed effectively taking the country off the gold standard.

The order prohibited export of gold and also prohibited banks from dealing in foreign exchange except for normal business requirements. As a result capital movements were less free than they had been prior to 1931. The depreciation policies of the United States and Britain both had one common objective: by allowing their currencies to depreciate, it was assumed that exports would become cheaper and imports more expensive. This proved to be a difficult objective, however, especially in the United States, owing to the Hawley-Smoot Act.

The temporary moratorium on international payments due to the United States, and the general lack of activity in new issues in the capital markets, changed the nature of American foreign trade. Unlike the more open 1920s, when the bond markets were used to supply capital for buyers of U.S. goods, among other purposes, the 1930s saw the United States become a net exporter while its foreign investments actually declined. This new position was created by the Depression and the fear it caused in the markets. Despite restrictions on capital movements and foreign exchange speculation, the dollar was now in demand as a haven for hot money, and any benefit of exporting more goods than the country was importing was offset by the inflow of foreign capital seeking a safe home. The idea of U.S. markets as an entrepôt for foreign capital had changed substantially from the prior decade. Now, the principal investment attraction of the United States was political. While far from ideal, foreign capital was voting for U.S. policies that appeared to protect capital, if not allowing it to move as freely as possible.

THE DECLINE OF THE ENTREPÔT

As early as 1932, there was official recognition that the financial markets could not aid U.S. trade as they had since World War I. For the next fifteen years, this would be a task of government. But this was not a Republican response; the first salvo in this new war came from the Roosevelt administration, when it created the Export-Import Bank of the United States in 1934. The Eximbank, as it became popularly known, was destined to join the Reconstruction Finance Corporation and the Federal Home Loan Bank Board—institutions created during the Hoover administration—as mainstays of the New Deal. The functions of all three institutions, along with the many other agencies created in the 1930s, subsequently would be expanded under the Roosevelt administrations immediately before, during, and after World War II.[3]

The Eximbank was modeled after existing import-export agencies used by many major nations to foster their foreign trade, although to stimulate exports rather than imports. The basic idea was to (1) provide loans or credits to U.S. exporters so that they could sell products abroad, or (2) to make loans and credits available to foreign buyers of U.S. goods: two different methods to achieve the same purpose. The Eximbank ordinarily made these loans for specific purposes only; general-purpose loans were not made for either importers or exporters.[4]

Agencies of this type were already in operation in Britain, Sweden, Germany, France, and Japan. The United States had not needed such an organization in the past because the bond markets had served in the same capacity. But since conditions had changed so dramatically, the markets could no longer be relied upon. The Eximbank received its charter from Congress, which was also responsible for setting its capital limits. The bank was expanded several times during the Roosevelt and Truman administrations before the Republicans again assumed the White House in 1954. The Eximbank operated on what would become classic agency lines, in that it functioned separately from the government, funding its operations through the bond markets and then lending the money to its clients. The U.S. experience with an import-export agency varied over the next fifty years, ranging from successful to mediocre. The volume and ability of the capital markets to fund both domestic and foreign companies and governments meant the Eximbank would never attain the stature of its foreign counterparts. But during the 1930s, it was designed to stimulate foreign trade.

As noted earlier, foreign direct and portfolio investments continued despite the Depression and the banking crises of 1932 and 1933. Although interest rates in the industrialized countries were raised in response to Britain's abandonment of the gold standard, U.S. rates were lower by at least two or more percentage points. In some cases, the higher rates elsewhere might have attracted hot money, putting selling pressure on the dollar, but since convertibility to gold and political safety were key considerations, foreigners opted for dollars and dollar-denominated investments. America's streets were literally paved with gold, with the exception of the period 1933–1936, when the Tripartite Agreement was passed. About the same time, the confusion about how much foreigners owned in the United States began to abate as the Department of Commerce started assembling credible statistics on foreign investment. Although the circumstances of the early 1930s were difficult, the foreign-investment picture was nevertheless clearer than it had been before.

As mentioned in Chapter 1, prior to 1929, estimates of foreign investment in U.S. securities had been based largely upon anecdotal evidence. Most conclusions were that the major investors were British, Dutch, Swiss, French, and German with substantial pockets of money from Latin America. While better record keeping did not dispute these assumptions, it helped provide a clearer picture of where foreign investment monies originated and provided some insights into what sorts of investments were preferred, both during and after the Depression.

After the currency crisis of 1931, the gold standard underwent a radical transformation. Linkages among the currencies of the industrialized countries were strengthened, as the massive rush to depreciation showed that the gold standard had effectively been abandoned. Currencies now began to float against each other, although Washington, London, and Paris made several attempts to establish a new monetary order. They finally did so with the Tripartite Agreement of 1936. The five years in the interim, however, were not devoid of foreign investment. On the contrary, foreign investment in the United States was certainly alive and well, if not robust.

Direct investments remained stable during the period 1934–36 and even gained marginal ground. The book value of long-term direct investments increased from $1.5 billion in 1934 to $1.65 billion two years later.[5] Manufacturing proved the major allure to foreign investors, accounting for 35 to 40 percent of the total. The second most popular form of direct investment was financial institutions—mostly banks, insurance companies, and trust companies. This investment distribution was somewhat different from that preceding World War I, when a majority of foreign investment was in the railroad industry. During the 1920s, many railroad bonds had been redeemed or refunded, and many shareholdings were liquidated in favor of manufacturing, although there remained some foreign interest in U.S. transportation in general. Foreign interest in U.S. financial institutions was constant, however, and was a major source of funds.

British direct investments remained the largest foreign sector in the United States in 1934, and manufacturing was one of the favorites, especially textiles. Of a total of $678 million in British foreign investments, 25 percent was in textile production. The insurance industry, normally made up of U.S. subsidiaries of British companies, was the most popular in the service sector, registering $231 million.[6] Canadian investment was second and Dutch investment third. The Canadian penchant was for transportation (mainly railways), while the Dutch favored the petroleum industry. The total for all foreign direct investment was some $1.5 billion.[7]

As mentioned earlier, the amount of direct investment increased gradually over the next two years. The same was not true of portfolio investments, however. Between 1934 and 1936, the amount of common stock held by foreigners doubled, while the amounts in corporate bonds and preferred stocks registered only marginal increases. Bonds and preferred shares did not increase in popularity owing to low interest rates. The allure of common stocks explains the post-Depression rebound in the market indices. The Dow Jones Industrial Average, at a low of 85.5 in 1934, touched a high of 110 in 1934 before proceeding to 148 in 1935 and 184 in 1936. On the other hand, yields on corporate bonds fell from about 4.5 percent to 3.5 percent. While that sort of drop in yield indicated a chance of capital gains in the bond market, those gains could not match the ones registered by common stocks during the same period. The amounts of portfolio investment would increase until the recession of 1937, when they would again fall.

Interest in common stocks was both a continuation of the speculative fever that had gripped investors in the 1920s and a natural tendency to bargain-hunt for cheap securities with the intention of recouping some of the losses experienced in the 1929 crash. Stocks became so popular that the total amount held by foreigners in 1934 was almost as much as the total for direct investments. But except for the increases in common stock held, the esti- mated $4.38 billion in foreign investment in 1934 was acquired before the Depression and, in some cases, before the World War I.[8] While foreign direct investment did not increase during the Depression, neither did it decrease, as might have been expected.

Common stocks began to increase in popularity among both domestic and foreign investors during the general interest rate decline that had begun in late 1933. Both stock and bond market rallies were aided immeasurably by a strong dollar, which had begun a marked improvement against the pound and the French franc in early 1933 after extraordinary banking and currency measures were introduced by the new president, Franklin Roosevelt. The confidence displayed in the new Democratic president proved to be the turning point in the Depression and the end of the decline in the markets.

For example, foreign portfolio investments increased at a healthy pace. The percentage of foreign-held shares in U.S. corporations rose steadily from 1929 to 1936. In 1929, foreigners held an estimated 2.06 percent of the common stock of American companies, rising to 3.81 percent in 1936. The percentages also rose for preferred stock, from 2.12 percent to 2.81 percent.[9] But the pattern of investment remained the same as it had been prior to the crash: for the most part, holdings were concentrated in the stocks of the largest corporations, almost all listed on the New York Stock Exchange. Foreigners preferred listed shares for the same reason as did domestic inves- tors: unlisted (over-the-counter) stocks had fared much worse than NYSE stocks since the 1929 crash. On average, a listed share lost 32 percent of its market value between 1929 and 1936. But investors were compensated to an extent by an almost 90 percent increase in dividends over the same period. Unlisted stocks performed much more poorly, losing 75 percent of their market value while dividends decreased by 80 percent.[10]

In 1934, foreign preferences for common stocks centered on those listed on the NYSE and represented about 85 percent of all foreign share holdings. At the end of the year, the price of an average share was $18.68, while the average foreign-held share was valued at $22.78. Total foreign holdings of NYSE shares amounted to about 3 percent of the total outstanding, and tended to be confined to larger corporations. Significantly, these were the shares traded in the heaviest volume, again illustrating the foreign preference for short-term trading profits.[11] Even after the Depression had hit bottom and recovery had begun, foreign activity in U.S. markets did not change substantially. Foreign direct investment remained constant, share specula- tion increased as it had in the past, and corporate bonds—and to a lesser extent preferred stock—continued to draw more conservative investors.

The bond markets at this time presented investors with an incentive that would end in 1936: Interest on certain types of corporate bonds, called industrial bonds, effectively was tax-free. Naturally, this type of issue drew all sorts of investors, and foreigners especially tended to favor these corporates over Treasury issues or municipalities. The absence of tax proved especially important, since yields were at a twenty-year low and any yield incentive could help offset potential foreign exchange risk.

During the 1930s, the political and investment climates began to change and the United States became the direct beneficiary. The policies of the Roosevelt administration favored investor protection. The disclosure requirements of the Securities Act of 1933, regulation of the stock markets established by the Securities Exchange Act of 1934, the deposit insurance at commercial banks and thrift institutions instituted in 1933 and 1934, and the Public Utility Holding Company Act of 1935 all helped create a more favorable investment climate, even if every one of the protections did not affect every investor. Equally, the provisions of the Eccles Act, or Banking Act of 1935, helped further structure and refine the Federal Reserve system, expanding the powers of the central bank. The loose policies of the 1920s and the easy-market attitude of both business leaders and Republican administrations were replaced by a regulatory atmosphere that took a dim view of market manipulation and self-aggrandizement. As the tide of public and government sentiment changed, so too did the markets, rising from the depths of the Depression in a more orderly fashion than they had in the latter part of the previous decade. While this would appear to have discouraged foreign investors, many of whom were accustomed to wild markets and get-rich opportunities, the new atmosphere helped rather than hindered foreign investment in the United States.

After the debt moratorium of 1932, bonds were less favored among many foreign investors, although there remained substantial domestic investment in them for reasons already mentioned. The interest paid to British, Dutch, and French residents—the major bond investing groups—declined. The yields on bonds were low, especially when compared with the dividends on common stocks. The AAA long-term bond yield continued to fall after Roosevelt's election, and by 1935–36 it had fallen as low as 3.5 percent—the lowest yield on a quality bond since the war. Despite the fact that the world economy was only beginning to recover from the worst depression of the century, the safety factor often attributed to U.S. investments decidedly took a back seat to the speculative.[12] The hot money had not become any cooler as a result of improving economic conditions; it still moved with great velocity seeking high speculative returns.

In the years immediately prior to 1936, the foreign exchange markets were more volatile than during the 1920s. The dollar-pound relationship especially tested U.S.-British relations and helped destroy, at least temporarily, the amicable and close relationship that had developed between Montagu Norman and Benjamin Strong. Currency problems dominated foreign affairs perhaps more than at any other time during the postwar period. At the heart of the dispute between the two countries was the gold content of the dollar and sterling, respectively, and the impact one currency would have upon the other as both countries sought depreciation in the hope of economic recovery.

In January 1934, Franklin Roosevelt explained his administration's policy concerning gold: "The suspension of gold payments, followed by a progressively rising dollar-price for gold, was therefore designed to contribute to the rise in commodity prices which we felt was essential to restore the purchasing and debt-paying ability of the American people."[13] In an attempt to reflate the economy in early 1934, the dollar was fixed against gold at $35 per ounce. This was after several years of currency volatility whereby both sterling and the French franc had depreciated by as much as 30 percent against the dollar. The rush to purposeful devaluation strained relations among the three allies, and lacked a common support effort for the currencies. Several attempts at three-way agreements had failed in the mid–1930s, and the Roosevelt administration had come to rely on gold as the major tool in its attempts to reflate commodity prices and the economy. However, as would be proved shortly, unilateral declarations concerning currency values were a thing of the past; if the currency market was to be restored to some stability, an agreement between the major industrialized countries was necessary.

The declining currency situation went hand in hand with the deteriorating political climate in Europe. German and Italian expansion could be viewed as military alternatives to failing domestic economic policies. With the dollar overvalued in relation to the franc and sterling, the United States was also experiencing a net inflow of gold. Viewed in a purely political context, this flow was interpreted as a lack of confidence in those countries suffering gold losses and a vote of confidence in the United States. This growing international prestige began the view of the United States as a safe political haven for money, much as its more traditional role was a home for refugees. It also aided the political fortunes of Franklin Roosevelt, who faced another election in 1936. The idea of reflating commodities put him in good stead with farmers, who were experiencing a drought in the Mid-west. The inflow of gold also helped him in the financial community, a group that had been looking askance at many of the New Deal policies, especially the financing attempts of the Reconstruction Finance Corporation (RFC).[14]

As mentioned earlier, the currency situation was stabilized in October 1936, when the United States, Britain, and France reached the Tripartite Agreement. The impetus for the agreement was France's need to devalue the franc. The majority party, the Popular Front of Leon Blum, had pursued domestic policies that increased costs for French industry and brought the franc under pressure. The Tripartite Agreement allowed for devaluation of the franc without a similar response by the Americans and the British. The three governments also agreed to maintain convertibility of their currencies into gold, and to confer with each other if further depreciation of the respective currencies should be needed. In order to maintain stability in the foreign exchange markets, each country would buy or sell currencies or gold through a stabilization fund. The gold standard was effectively a dead issue, as the major trading nations recognized the futility of attempting to dictate currency values unilaterally. The depreciation race of the early 1930s was thus over, although war clouds were beginning to appear as Germany went its own way in response to financial pressures. The major industrialized countries would ally in order to foster economic growth and fight off the threat of the Axis, and the 1930s quickly became a period of inefficacious nationalism leading the world to the brink once again. George L. Harrison, president of the New York Federal Reserve Bank, remarked in 1936 that "the result [of the past six years] has been a tangible network of defensive measures such as the depreciation of currencies, the arbitrary control of foreign exchanges, and the restrictions of trade through embargoes, quotas, clearing agreements, licenses, and tariffs."[15] The Tripartite Agreement ended that particular phase of the post-crash economic cycle, although ironically it would not be given real teeth until World War II had run its course.

WAR, UNCERTAINTY, AND CAPITAL INFLOW

Even before the Tripartite Agreement was reached, the United States began to experience an inflow of capital on such a large scale that it would change the country's position from creditor back to debtor. As the European political climate deteriorated, capital began to flow west at an ever-increasing rate, accompanied by an inflow of gold. Equally, U.S. foreign investments began to diminish in the face of uncertainty. That combination affected the capital markets perhaps more than any external event since World War I. Investor behavior quickly began to change, anticipating war. New direct investments leveled off; the major activity now was the flow of flight capital into both long- and short-term markets. In 1934, the estimated amount of foreign investments was $1.8 billion; by the end of 1939, it had risen to only $1.9 billion. But during the same period, the amount of short-term deposits by foreigners grew from around $680 million to $3.2 billion. Meanwhile, interest in common stocks continued the trend begun earlier in the decade: Foreign common stock holdings increased from $1.4 billion in 1934 to over $2.4 billion in 1939. Corporate bond investment remained flat, and holdings of preferred stocks registered only a marginal increase.[16] The second half of the 1930s was a speculative period for foreign investors, but for reasons quite different from those in the 1920s.

During the immediate pre–World War II years, most foreign investment originated from Britain, Canada, France, the Netherlands, and Switzerland. Investments from Germany and Italy stopped completely when their re-

spective governments blocked currency movements abroad and began seiz-
ing foreign assets of domestic investors. Canadian investments also did not
show signs of increase since Canadians, as did U.S. investors, generally
began to curtail investments abroad because of political uncertainty, regardless of location. Then a phenomenon peculiar to the financial markets
began to take place, with a positive effect on the markets. Discounting the
possibility of war, especially after Italy's invasion of Ethiopia in 1935 and
Hitler's invasion of the Rhineland in 1936, investors began to direct funds
into the markets, supporting stock market indices and bringing down yields
on long- and short-term instruments. By 1940, yields on bonds had fallen
by 0.5 percent from 1936 levels. The Dow Jones Industrial Average had
remained in about the same range since the recession of 1937, and only
dropped substantially after official U.S. entry into the war. While foreign
investment continued in stocks rather than bonds, it appears that bond yields
benefited more than the stock market by marking a noticeable decrease in
returns and financing costs.

As Europe plunged into war, the British and Canadians restricted the
movement of capital and required holders of foreign securities to register
them with the appropriate authorities. After 1939 in both cases, fresh foreign
investment would be severely curtailed until the war ended. Equally, the
political situation put an end to the Tripartite Agreement in 1939, as French
and British resources were reallocated to the war effort. After three years
of stabilization and capital flight, the United States had virtually cornered
the market for gold. The American Stabilization Fund, operating under the
guidelines of the agreement, bought foreign currencies or gold whenever
the value of the dollar increased in the exchange markets. But the United
States never held those currencies for more than twenty-four hours; it converted them to gold daily to avoid risk.[17]

The pessimistic years immediately prior to 1940 were not without a lighter
side. In October 1938, Orson Welles presented his famous *War of the Worlds*
radio broadcast, and there was reason to believe that most Americans perceived a Martian invasion a greater threat than one from Hitler. At the same
time, a Gallup poll showed that most Americans approved of the Munich
Agreement negotiated among Germany, Britain, Italy, and France. Europeans, however, had reason to be less sanguine. They lacked a European
collective security system to contain Hitler, one of the "lessons of Munich"
that would lead to establishment of the United Nations in the next decade.
In a similar way, financial and economic stabilization procedures tried under
the Tripartite Agreement would eventually be incorporated into the Bretton
Woods Agreement beginning in 1944.

During the 1930s, the United States remained isolated from international
affairs, maintaining an official neutral position with respect to events occurring in Europe and the Far East. This neutrality, plus the relative financial
strength exhibited after the worst of the Depression had passed, made the

United States an even more appealing haven for foreign capital. But even as the appeal grew stronger, capital controls and prohibitions against foreign investment by most major industrialized countries made the haven unattainable. Safety and growth of capital would have to wait until the war had finished.

Of the $1.8 billion foreigners had invested directly in the country as of 1937, about 50 percent was in manufacturing. It was estimated that over 1,100 companies were controlled by foreigners.[18] As seen earlier, the major investors remained British and Canadian; between them they accounted for over 70 percent of all foreign investment. German firms were strong in chemical production, while the British and Dutch were strong in textiles. British interest in the service sector remained concentrated in insurance and banking. Canadians were primarily interested in manufacturing and transportation, notably railways. But as sizable as some of the foreign investments were, in most cases they did not represent more than 5 percent of the total capital invested in any one U.S. industry. On aggregate, the amount of foreign investment was substantial and widespread, but foreign firms did not exercise much dominance over U.S. industry or services.

While foreign investment remained stable, if not increasing exponentially except for investments in common stocks, the newly developing institutions that were designed to protect the American Dream saw little foreign capital. Although some foreign investment in bonds of the Farm Credit banks or the Federal National Mortgage Association may have been suspected, there was little record keeping to monitor foreign ownership in U.S. Treasury issues or quasigovernment issues. Examining the pattern that emerged over the twenty-year period from 1920 to 1939, there is little reason to suspect that foreign capital was attracted to noncorporate debt securities when stocks, direct investments, and corporate bonds with substantial tax breaks were (or had been) available. And the next decade would not witness any substantial changes in this pattern, especially after interest-rate pegging of Treasury securities was begun in 1942.

Taxes helped dissuade foreign investors from choosing low-yielding U.S. investments. The Revenue Act of 1936 called for payments of dividends, interest, rents, and royalties to foreigners to be taxed at the source. This is more popularly known as a withholding tax, and in 1937 it amounted to about 9 percent of income. In that year, income paid to foreigners on U.S. investments amounted to $97.5 million, representing about a 5.2 percent rate of return on the average investment.[19] Using that estimate, the tax income generated by the withholding tax would have been around $8.5 million on total direct investments of about $1.8 billion. Appearing somewhat small, the return nevertheless was about 1.5 percent more than the return on a high-quality corporate bond. When compared with common stocks for the same year, the return was quite healthy. For instance, the total return on common stocks was a minus 35 percent—the worst return since 1931 and the second worst return recorded between 1926 and 1987.[20]

Once the United States entered World War II, the international investment climate changed substantially. The U.S. markets took on new baggage that remained throughout the war years and, in some cases, became part of its financial system until after the Korean War. The major factor in the markets was again the United States government, whose borrowing needs dominated the fixed-income markets, in many cases crowding out corporate and foreign borrowers. Bank behavior also changed, affecting the asset-liability mix of commercial banks, and many foreign firms were closely supervised, with the assets of belligerents seized as they had been during World War I. The foreign exchange market again entered a state of flux after the Tripartite Agreement ended. The atmosphere was poor for international investment.

The U.S. markets braced for the war effort, and although the Dow Jones Industrials Average touched a five-year low in 1945, some new companies producing new drugs and electronic equipment appeared, making the investment climate somewhat brighter. Treasury bill yields remained in the 0.2 to 0.3 percent range, long-term Treasury bonds yielded 2.5 percent, and long-term corporate bonds yielded about the same. In fact, long-term Treasuries remained in the same general range until after the Korean War, more than ten years later. This remarkable stability in yield levels was due to the Federal Reserve's official pegging of Treasury bill yields. In 1942, the central bank announced that it stood ready to buy or sell bills at a yield of 0.375 percent. This policy had the net effect of quieting the market, since it helped eliminate the fear of capital loss due to interest rate risk. Obviously, it also helped reduce the Treasury's cost of borrowing for the war effort. But the Federal Reserve was not necessarily being altruistic in this matter, since the message of bill stability was aimed primarily at commercial banks, traditionally the largest holders of Treasury bills.

During the war, commercial banks were encouraged to hold Treasury securities as assets, in many cases displacing more traditional commercial loans. While this helped the Treasury financing immensely, it also crowded out other borrowers. As a result, the mix of loans as a proportion of total bank assets declined and investments rose.[21] While this proved beneficial in the long run, it also kept rates on short-term deposits low—not ordinarily the best inducement for foreign flight capital. But even though yields and quoted interest rates were low prior to the official pegging, the amount of foreign-owned assets was still a subject of some speculation since survey methods employed by the various agencies were suspect.

After Germany invaded Denmark and Norway, the United States undertook a census of all foreign-owned assets. Immediately, Norwegian and Danish assets were frozen so that they could not be used by the Germans for

their war effort. In 1941, the freeze was extended to all other European
assets in the country, those of Italy and Germany included. Only at that
time did the United States gain a clear picture of the extent of foreign-owned
assets. The result was somewhat surprising. The estimate at the end of 1939
was that total assets were in the range of $9.4 billion—$6.2 billion in long-
term investments and $3.2 billion in bank deposits. The new survey, based
on assets of all sorts held as of June 1941, found $12.74 billion in total assets,
a gain of $3.3 billion in the intervening year and a half, a period of increasing
European capital controls and general retrenchment.[22]

What was particularly significant about the wartime survey was its reve-
lation that individuals held over $2.6 billion of those assets while corporations
held about $8 billion. In fact, the actual number of individuals was put at
around 132,000, while over 23,000 foreign corporations held the larger of
the two amounts.[23] Although previous figures were not particularly reliable,
this large number of individuals, plus the relatively large amount they held,
illustrates that the United States was becoming a haven for money endan-
gered elsewhere. Since all of these foreign funds were held in dollars in
U.S. institutions, the increase in capital inflow also helped strengthen the
dollar on foreign exchange markets.

The United States derived great financial benefit from the war. In addition
to the funds that poured into U.S. banks, the Lend-Lease program, initiated
in 1941 to assist those countries fighting the Axis powers, provided demand
for U.S.-made capital equipment and machinery. Franklin Roosevelt's classic
remark that vulnerable foreign countries should make use of the program
in order to "put out the fire in your neighbor's house before your own burns
down" succinctly described the economic warfare the United States was
waging against the three Axis powers without actually committing itself to
the hostilities. At the same time, many foreign countries were shifting bank
balances to the United States in order to protect them against possible enemy
seizure and also to pay for anticipated war costs. These funds found their
way mostly into short-term deposits, Treasury bills, or gold accounts at the
Federal Reserve. While the markets would benefit directly or indirectly, no
significant shift in ownership of U.S. assets occurred with these funds. Safety,
not ownership, was the primary criterion.

The funds flow and the census of foreign-owned assets proved what had
already been known subjectively: the most extensive foreign investments
were made by the British, Swiss, and Canadians. But the census also showed
the precise holdings of U.S. bonds—corporates as well as municipal and
government issues. Always considered the most solid and reliable of U.S.
investments, bonds were the ideal form of foreign investment, at least viewed
from official American eyes. Creditors tended to be the most passive of
investors, and did not represent a controlling interest in a domestic company.
The only negative factor of a foreigner's holding a domestic bond was the
debit on the balance of payments account when interest was paid. And along

with the special studies of the Commerce Department, the survey fortunately cleared up some confusing terminology that had plagued the market since the nineteenth century. For instance, there was an end to the nineteenth-century practice of lumping together stock and bond holders as "investors" and the British practice of calling bonds "stock."

Of the $12.74 billion in foreign-held assets, British investors held some $3.2 billion, Swiss investors held $1.2 billion, French investors accounted for $1.0 billion, and Canadians held $1.7 billion. The balance was held mostly by other Europeans and, to a lesser extent, by Asians and South Americans. The actual distribution of those assets was $4.24 billion in gold, $2.7 billion in securities, and $2.3 billion in direct investments, with the balance divided among real property, estates and trusts, and other assets. Of all securities, stocks were most popular, with $1.84 billion outstanding. Of the debt securities, corporate bonds emerged as the largest category with $219 million. Holdings of U.S. Treasury obligations were about equal, amounting to $213 million.[24]

Despite the war, it appeared that investors still preferred the capital appreciation potential of stocks over the low yields on bonds, a trend that had begun in the mid–1930s. However, another suspected reason for this preference was the potential for anonymity and the ability to avoid withholding tax. At the time, corporate bonds were held mostly in bearer form— that is, they were not registered in the name of the beneficial owner—but they were held for a long-term. (The bond-investing techniques of the 1970s and 1980s, calling for active management of bond portfolios, had not yet come into vogue.) As a result, investors were apt to buy a bond and hold it for a long period—certainly for longer periods than common stocks were held. Despite anonymity, tax implications could still arise, especially if tax laws were subsequently changed. A stock held in nominee form, however, where the owner was disguised by the depository holding the securities on his behalf, had a better chance of avoiding tax entirely, leaving few if any footprints behind.[25]

Foreign interest in government bonds was minimal during this period, as the low number given earlier illustrates. But to attribute the minor interest to low yields alone does not present a complete picture. Between 1935 and 1940, government debt had grown by $14 billion, a 50 percent increase. Included in that amount was an increase in Treasury bonds as well as new agency obligations, created during the New Deal, bearing a government guarantee. In 1940, one-third of all Treasury obligations were held by commercial banks. Of the $48 billion in outstanding obligations, only 0.5 percent was held by foreigners. While indebtedness obviously increased, so too did some Treasury management techniques. Most important, the Treasury's sinking-fund provisions were abandoned in the late 1930s in favor of what has become known as rollover financing, or refunding. Rather than set aside funds each year for an issue's eventual redemption, the Treasury simply used a new borrowing to retire a maturing one. While that technique was less cumbersome than operating sinking funds for ever-increasing amounts of Treasury debt, it broke with a tradition of debt management and appears to have dissuaded foreign investors from increasing their holdings in Treasury securities at a time when relative safety of capital was of paramount importance.

Most countries adopted foreign exchange and capital controls during the war to protect their currencies and domestic economies. Values on the foreign exchange market were, for the most part, pegged and fluctuations were discouraged. Forward markets, as well as the spot markets, were also placed under restriction so that forward speculation would not affect spot values. Most of the controls were deemed an overall part of economic warfare, but unlike the period prior to World War I, most of the belligerent countries were better prepared for the defense of their currencies.[26] These controls naturally diminished the amount of fresh capital committed to foreign investment. While less reliant on foreign capital than in past periods, the United States did become a net exporter during the war, mainly because of the Lend-Lease Act. The entrepôt nature of the U.S. financial markets was effectively moribund.

After U.S. entry into the war, the pegged interest rates had a stabilizing effect upon the yield curve, but price inflation surged because the country's resources were committed to the war effort. This provided a further disincentive to whatever foreign investment might have been available, since it would have produced a negative rate of return. At the same time, foreigners were being forced to liquidate many of their U.S. investments. British investments changed substantially, as they had during the Civil War and World War I, to meet the financing needs of the U.K. Treasury. The U.S. Treasury estimated that in 1937, over half of the U.S. production of borax, rayon, and potash was in foreign hands, namely British and German. In 1941, the British sold back to the Americans a controlling interest in the American Viscose Company, giving them effective control again of the rayon industry. At the same time, the Alien Property Custodian, charged with protecting U.S. assets from enemy control, shifted controlling interest in German-held potash and borax production to U.S. sources. In the same year, the British government negotiated a loan with the RFC for $425 million to help finance the war effort. The British also liquidated many of their equity holdings and in some cases margined off holdings of equities to raise cash. They pledged part of their stock in the Brown and Williamson Tobacco Company with the RFC as collateral for the loan. In almost all cases, private British overseas holdings were involved, since the government had assumed the right to seize overseas assets for the war effort.

The task of the Alien Property Custodian was not easy because foreign-company holdings were registered through nominee or custodian arrangements. German and Japanese holdings were suspect during the war, but the exact ownership of many assets could not be proved. This raised the curious situation whereby U.S. investments helped finance the war efforts of the Axis powers while U.S. allies, such as the British, were forced to liquidate their U.S. assets to pay for loans and advances. While the Treasury acknowledged the problem, it also noted that little could be done to remedy it, given the state of disclosure laws and willing intermediaries.

This curious situation did not harm America's reputation as an entrepôt, although new money was not finding its way into the markets as it had in the 1930s. The store of value that had built up over the years in certain foreign holdings was now proving useful to the balance of payments, under totally different conditions. Although the United States was no longer financing trade with itself by lending long-term, as it had in the 1920s, many of the investments foreigners had made previously were now bearing fruit by helping to pay for U.S. goods and materials necessary for the war effort.

During the war years and immediately after, much of the American Dream was financed by domestic sources. Foreign investment in government agencies was minimal, if not nonexistent; most bond purchases were by domestic sources. The stock market retreated to prewar levels and took until 1944 to again reach 1940 levels. Domestic automobile production was halted in 1942, and production of heavy domestic appliances ceased soon thereafter. The economy was geared for the war effort, and all notions of peace and prosperity, in the public mind since the early 1920s, had disappeared. The American public's favorite investment or savings vehicle was no longer a hot stock or real estate; it was war loans issued by the Treasury and Victory bonds. Estimates vary as to the number of individuals who bought war bonds, but what is clear is that they represented the largest Treasury financing ever. Even though large amounts were subscribed for, the number of individual subscriptions failed to live up to Treasury expectations. Nevertheless, the number of subscriptions by nonbank financial institutions far exceeded expectations.[27]

Perhaps patriotism as such had not diminished but the ability or incentive to save had to some extent. Disincentives for fresh investments clouded the horizon for both foreign and domestic investors. The Roosevelt administration pushed series of tax increases through Congress in an attempt to raise revenues and redistribute the tax burden. One of these increases quickly became known among detractors as the "soak the rich" program because it increased the maximum tax brackets for the wealthy. In reality, the taxes imposed during wartime were fairly progressive. The maximum tax rate for the majority of individuals—those earning between $500 and $3,000 per year—was only about 9 percent; the maximum rate for those earning above $100,000 was about 70 percent. But the American Dream had receded for the majority of the population, for whatever reason.

Almost immediately after peace with Japan was concluded, tax reductions were put into effect in order to stimulate the U.S. economy. The stock market responded with a gain, and the Dow Jones Industrial Average touched 200 for the first time in fifteen years. But the international system would need more stimuli if it was to be instrumental in the massive rebuilding of Western Europe. The Bretton Woods Conference, which had been ongoing since 1944, supplied valuable structural support for this new project. The basic mechanics of the earlier Tripartite Agreement reemerged even before the war was officially over, in a new system designed to cover all countries, both the major trading countries and their blocs, or satellites. In the absence of global war, the next thirty years would produce the greatest monetary stability of the century.

NOTES

1. See Charles R. Geisst, *Visionary Capitalism: Financial Markets and the American Dream in the Twentieth Century* (New York: Praeger, 1990), especially Chap. 1 and 2.

2. Clay Anderson, *A Half-Century of Federal Reserve Policymaking, 1914–1964* (Philadelphia: Federal Reserve Bank of Philadelphia, 1965), p. 68.

3. For a further discussion of the Federal Home Loan Bank Board and the Reconstruction Finance Corporation, especially during the Roosevelt administrations, see Geisst, *Visionary Capitalism*, especially Chap. 2 and 8.

4. In the course of its early history, the Eximbank performed functions other than simply funding imports and exports. One of its original functions was the purchase of notes payable by China to the Reconstruction Finance Corporation and the Farm Credit Administration. This useful operation coordinated and consolidated the foreign notes due to various U.S. government agencies. It was truncated by the overriding financial needs caused by World War II.

5. U.S. Department of Commerce, *Foreign Investments in the United States* (Washington, DC: 1937), p. 14.

6. Ibid., p. 32.

7. Ibid.

8. Federal Reserve estimate from Federal Reserve *Bulletin*, December 1936, reiterated in U.S. Department of Commerce, *Foreign Investments in the United States*, p. 28.

9. U.S. Department of Commerce, *Foreign Investments in the United States*, p. 64.

10. Ibid., p. 60.

11. Ibid., p. 50.

12. The term *depression* was still used during this and previous periods to describe severe economic slowdowns. Recession had not yet become a popular term. Thus, in 1920–21 the slowdown was referred to as a depression rather than the more contemporary recession.

13. Cited in Herman Krooss, ed., *Documentary History of Banking and Currency in the United States*, Vol. 4 (New York: Chelsea House, 1969), p. 2811.

14. See Geisst, *Visionary Capitalism*, especially Chap. 8.

15. George L. Harrison, "Some Essentials of Monetary Stability," delivered to

the Academy of Political Science, New York City, April 1936, and reprinted in Federal Reserve Bank of New York *Quarterly Review*, May 1989, pp. 15–20.

16. U.S. Department of Commerce, *Foreign Long-Term Investment in the United States* (Washington, DC: United States Government Printing Office, 1940), p. 6. The lack of interest in corporate bonds was suspected but not proved by survey because, after the debt-payment moratorium, adequate records were not maintained again until the 1940s.

17. Paul Studenski and Herman Krooss, *Financial History of the United States* (New York: McGraw-Hill, 1952), p. 393. As they note, the American Stabilization Fund, actually in existence since 1934, was successful, managing during that time to turn a profit of some $21 million.

18. U.S. Department of Commerce, *Foreign Long-Term Investment*, p. 34.

19. Ibid., p. 41.

20. Roger Ibbotson and Rex Sinquefield, *Stocks, Bonds, Bills, and Inflation: Historical Returns (1926–1987)* (Homewood, IL: Dow Jones Irwin, 1989), p. 58. Annual return is stated as a combination of capital appreciation, income return, and reinvestment return.

21. See Geisst, *Visionary Capitalism*, Chap. 3, for a more comprehensive explanation.

22. U.S. Treasury Department, *Census of Foreign-Owned Assets in the United States* (Washington, DC: U.S. Government Printing Office, 1945).

23. Ibid., p. vii.

24. Ibid., pp. 14–15.

25. According to the census of foreign-held assets, certain nationalities had more of a penchant for nominee-held securities than others. For instance, of a total of $587 million in securities of all types held by British investors, $149 million were in registered form while the balance were in nominee or custody name of one sort or other. Canadians, on the other hand, showed the opposite tendency. Of a total of $543 million held, almost $400 million were registered. See U.S. Treasury, *Census of Foreign-Owned Assets*, p. 24.

26. Paul Einzig, *The History of Foreign Exchange*, 2nd. ed. (London: Macmillan, 1970), p. 292.

27. Studenski and Krooss, *Financial History of the United States*, p. 454.

3

The New Monetary Order

In the relative tranquility of Bretton Woods, New Hampshire, the international monetary conference which convened in 1944 sought to restructure the international financial system. The conference had been planned since 1941, and the dates illustrate that it was as much a product of the monetary turbulence and exchange problems of the 1930s as a direct response to the economic and financial chaos created by World War II. The immediate task was to remove financial obstacles that might lead to further political and economic strife. The agenda included many complicated and revolutionary items, but its basic purpose was to fashion a new sort of global Tripartite Agreement. Additionally, the conference framed two institutions that would successfully become mainstays of the international financial system: the International Monetary Fund and the World Bank. Through these it would create a relatively stable foreign exchange environment and construct mechanisms to help further Third World development. The idea of stability and order necessarily would have to extend outside the industrialized countries to the developing countries if it were to be more than a temporary fix for international financial problems.

FINANCIAL RECOVERY FOLLOWING THE WAR

The Bretton Woods Conference, held for three weeks in July 1944, produced the institutional framework for both the International Monetary Fund (IMF) and the International Bank for Reconstruction and Development, or World Bank. Both institutions were constructed to promote economic and

financial harmony—the IMF to stabilize exchange rates and the World Bank
to provide financing for postwar reconstruction and eventually to foster
north-south trade between rich and poor countries. But in the beginning it
was exchange-rate problems that required immediate attention. The years
since 1936 had proved that unilateral pronouncements about exchange rates
were of far less efficacy than international agreements, and the IMF was
founded to expand upon that principle. The purposes for which the IMF
was constructed were deemed matters of international concern. The agreement was considered "the law of the land" for countries that signed it.[1] This
meant that IMF decisions concerning exchange rates were of international,
not national, importance, although exchange-rate stability was essential to
every country's domestic politics and economic growth. Only ten years before, Italy and Germany had embarked on military expansion when their
domestic monetary policies failed to produce growth and stability. The new
monetary order envisioned international growth and stability, with all sig-
natory nations acting in tandem.

In addition to the financial significance of the conference, important political precedents were also established. Whether IMF decisions concerning
exchange rates would be legally binding or whether they would be international guidelines was less significant than the fact, at least at the time,
that twenty-two countries ratified the IMF agreement and brought it into
force by December 1945. Congress ratified U.S. participation in July 1945
and contributed $2.75 billion as its original subscription. At the same time,
the United States contributed an initial $3 billion to the World Bank. A
desire for both international political cooperation and growth and reconstruction underwent a resurgence not seen since the League of Nations had
been founded thirty years before.

Of all the technical aspects of the IMF's charter, the exchange-rate mechanisms are of most importance for present purposes. The new exchange-rate
regime used the dollar as its numeraire, finally supplanting sterling as the
official reserve currency. As discussed in the earlier chapter, for decades
the pound had been the currency most central banks held as their chief
foreign-reserve asset. But with continued financial pressures, over the years
Britain had erected a series of exchange and capital controls that made the
reserve nature of the pound more formality than fact. By the end of World
War I, the dollar had assumed a premier position in international finance.
Finally, with the Bretton Woods Agreement, the dollar rose from de facto
status to official recognition. Now, the IMF exchange-rate regime called for
currencies to be stated in terms of par value against gold or the U.S. dollar.
Once that par value had been established, the central bank, or appropriate
monetary authority of the country, had to endeavor not to let it deviate from
that value by more than 1 percent. This required countries to intervene
daily in the foreign exchange markets in order to keep their currencies within
the prescribed bands. In the past, intervention had occurred somewhat

haphazardly, only when a country wanted to change its exchange rate for its own purposes. Under this new system of daily monitoring, disequilibria could still occur, forcing a devaluation or revaluation, but the IMF had to be consulted before any new par values could be established.

The par value established by the IMF was considered the safeguard ruling exchange-rate stability. The assumption was that all countries would eventually establish convertibility for their currencies, although it was recognized that this goal could not be established strictly by the stroke of a pen. In some cases, convertibility was still not established when the system began to collapse, during the summer of 1971. However, this new exchange-rate regime produced order out of what had previously been chaos and helped many European countries lift their capital controls, which had been implemented during and after the war. Once those controls were lifted, investments again began to cross the Atlantic, and the United States again benefited, although the inflow was not as great as the dollars flowing into Europe to help the reconstruction effort as well as to establish direct U.S. investments abroad.

The United States was able to record favorable trade balances over the next several years because the Marshall Plan provided aid to European countries. Named for Secretary of State George Marshall, the plan was proposed in 1947 as a blueprint for recovery that would take approximately five years. Congress passed it as the Economic Cooperation Act and allocated about $6 billion in aid. But the Marshall Plan was not the only relief that America extended to Europe. Aid in one form or other was made available by the World Bank shortly after its inception at Bretton Woods, and by the Export-Import Bank as well. Between 1946 and 1951, the aid had resulted in net U.S. exports in each year, totaling as much as $42 billion in 1947 alone. This was also the greatest period of sustained exports in postwar U.S. history to date.

As Europe began to rebuild and the foreign exchange markets again opened for trading, investments flowed again to the United States from their traditional sources. British and Canadian investments began to increase as they had after World War I, distributed in much the same way. As to direct investments, British money again found its way into U.S. manufacturing and financial services, while Canadian funds were invested in the railroad industry and manufacturing, notably whisky and other spirits. In both cases, this was not so much fresh investments as continuing investments in favorite industries that had been interrupted by the war. As might be expected, most long-term direct investments established before 1940 remained in the U.S. unless liquidations were required. While it is true that there were many voluntary and forced liquidations during war time, nevertheless a great percentage of these investments remained and continued to earn a return.

By 1950, total foreign direct investment in the United States had risen to about $3.5 billion, an increase of about $100 million per year from 1940 to

1950. Common stock investments totaled almost $3 billion with another $1.5 billion in bonds, preferreds, and real estate.[2] The traditional discrepancy between direct and portfolio investments had begun to disappear, although stocks certainly remained the favorite investment overall. This was due to the market's performance after the war: in 1945 the Dow Jones Industrial Average began to rise, reaching a high of 235 in 1950, its highest level to that time. Interest rates continued to remain low, since the Federal Reserve maintained the peg on the yield curve.[3] But the late 1940s also brought a resurgence of demand for goods and services, many of which had been unavailable during the war. As a result, inflation surged from a reasonable 3 percent in 1946 to almost twice that level a year later. That made fixed-income investments less attractive than stocks, a phenomenon seen many times since the crash. But the United States was not alone in suffering postwar inflation. Most industrialized countries experienced even worse bouts during the late 1940s, especially those countries that had sought to make cheap money available in order to finance reconstruction and growth.

The attractiveness of U.S. investments in the postwar period was not a contentious issue among foreign investors. But as discussed in Chapter 2, during the war the intrinsic investment qualities and opportunities afforded by U.S. investments were overshadowed by the more urgent need to find a safe home for hot money during the war. Most short-term deposits in U.S. banks after 1938 were placed by governments or other official bodies, not by private investors or companies. After the war, most European governments were slow to relax capital restrictions on private investment, and the value of much common stock held by foreigners increased because the existing holdings rose in value. Fresh funds were only slowly finding their way back into the market.

During the immediate postwar period, U.S. investment abroad increased at a much faster rate than did foreign investments in the United States. While exports boomed from 1946 to 1951, foreign investment opportunities lured U.S. investors. At the end of 1950, foreign direct investment in U.S. manufacturing totaled approximately $1 billion, while U.S. direct investments in foreign manufacturing totaled almost $4 billion. Other industry groups showed the same sort of ratios, with the exception of finance and insurance, where the foreign amount was greater than similar U.S. investment abroad.[4] As will be seen later in this chapter, these proportions continued until the 1960s, even though the gross amounts increased dramatically on both sides.

By the 1950s it was becoming clear that the trends of the 1920s and 1930s were not interwar phenomena but rather were indicative of how foreign investors viewed investment opportunities in the United States. While direct investments were, for the most part, long-standing and grew every year, the amount of U.S. assets under foreign control was not significant. The Canadian preference for railroads and spirits production was as ingrained as the British penchant for financial services and certain types of manufacturing. But also ingrained was the foreign preference for common stock investment and speculation. For the next thirty years portfolio investments would continue to surpass direct investments as the investment choice for foreigners. In large part this preference was because portfolio investments came under less scrutiny and fewer official sanctions than did direct investments and, as a result, lured foreign investors into more speculative and short-term investing.

The popularity of the U.S. stock market was due to the fact that it was the only secondary market available to foreign investors free of most restrictions placed on international investors during this period. Its major rival, the London stock market, continued trading but there were restrictions on non-residents. The other European markets were quite small or insignificant after the war and would not develop into significant arenas for foreign investment for another twenty years.

After the Korean War, the United States would again enjoy a period of prosperity unlike anything since the 1920s. Political attitudes had also changed by then. Republicans occupied the White House for the first time since 1932, and the environment was popularly thought to be more conducive for business than at any other time in recent memory.[5] And in the 1950s, another international development occurred that had a significant impact on economic and political affairs in the next thirty years. In 1957, six European countries signed the Treaty of Rome, establishing the European Economic Community (EEC).[6] The structure of the new community was a direct descendent of another European institution established six years earlier, the European Coal and Steel Community (ECSC). The ECSC became an integral part of the European Community after 1957, but in its original form it represented in microcosm what the EEC would attempt on a much broader scale: economic integration of the coal and steel industries in its original six members in order to rationalize production and compete with the community's major foreign competition in domestic and world markets.

The EEC adopted the unified concept of the ECSC and carried it forward to the broader concept of European economic and political integration—a process that had many interim phases during the following forty years. In financing, the EEC also adopted techniques that had been deployed by the ECSC to raise external funds for community use, helping to create what had become known as the "supranational" agency borrower. The model that the ECSC and later the EEC employed was the same as used by the World Bank and, earlier, the Federal National Mortgage Association (Fannie Mae). While the supranational twist was new to financing—and for that matter, to international law—its borrowing techniques were similar to the methods used by the U.S. federal agencies to finance their needs.

The two main architects of the idea of the European Community were Robert Schumann of West Germany and Jean Monnet of France. Of the two, Monnet was the more involved in the financial aspects of the new supranational bodies. Immediately after the war, it was recognized that closer economic—and eventually, political—integration between France and Germany was needed in order to rebuild Europe and avoid future conflict. As just mentioned, the ECSC was fashioned to integrate the coal and steel production of the member states. The organization was truly supranational in the sense that it had a legal personality in its own right, had the ability to tax the member states to be paid by the industries involved (the levy), and had ultimate authority to make decisions concerning coal and steel production and marketing as well as retraining of workers who may have been displaced by community decisions. In a limited sense, the ECSC had assumed sovereignty in those limited cases where the power of the community superseded the powers of individual members.

Although the new body was novel and innovative, it was an unknown entity to the financial markets where it had to raise funds. The ECSC—and the EEC after it—raised money on the bond markets for long-term objectives, with obligations backed by the member states. In the event of default, the member states would honor any of the obligations. The members backed the borrowings according to their respective GNPs within the community. This supranational nature gave the new body a high credit rating in the financial markets. But despite this guarantee, and the fact that ECSC had its own seat in the United Nations, the U.S. bond market still required some European salesmanship before accepting it as a borrower. True to form, the bond markets in general looked askance at new borrowers, regardless of their genealogy.

The first U.S. loan to the ECSC came in 1954, when Jean Monnet negotiated a $100 million facility from the Export-Import Bank of the United States. This loan helped establish a precedent in the banking community, and three years later, Rene Meyer, Monnet's successor as the community's finance minister, negotiated the first ECSC bond denominated in dollars in the Yankee bond market.[7] That bond became the first in a long line of ECSC borrowings in New York. They were followed in later years by similar borrowings by the EEC and its long-term credit institution, the European Investment Bank, both of which bore identical guarantees.

Without access to the U.S. capital market, the early growth of the European institutions would have been impaired until indigenous European markets were reestablished. The entrepôt nature of the Yankee bond market suited the new borrowers well, although the borrowed funds were undoubtedly going to help finance competition with the U.S. steel industry. But the early borrowings of the European institutions and the World Bank also represented one of the rare U.S. financial exports of this postwar period—the idea of a financial agency as an independent borrower in its own right, using the Yankee bond market in much the same way that U.S. domestic agencies used the New York bond market. Bonds of those institutions, plus similar ones developed in time, employed the agency concept that had been used successfully by the Depression-era agencies of the Hoover and Roosevelt administrations. If the agency failed to honor its obligations, its guarantor would assume them to avoid a default. In the case of these European borrowers, the guarantor was not a single country but the treasuries of all the members of the European Community.

Supranational agencies were only one type of borrower tapping the Yankee bond market and, later, the eurobond market. European equivalents of the Eximbank established profiles in the Yankee market as borrowers of high standing, and they used the dollars for lending to buyers of their domestically produced goods. For example, the export credit agencies of Canada, Denmark, Sweden, Norway, and later Japan all used the markets extensively, especially after the Bretton Woods system collapsed. Even when U.S. capital controls were in force (see next paragraph), these agencies continued to borrow in the Yankee market, creating the curious situation whereby foreign borrowers were using dollars to compete with U.S. companies. As will be seen later, capital controls were of no consequence in this instance.

During the period leading to 1960, the foreign exchange market was dominated by controlled currencies. For instance, sterling was under exchange controls, although foreigners were allowed to buy and sell on the markets more freely than British residents or companies. Immediately after the war, an Anglo-American agreement was reached whereby the United States established a credit line of almost $4 billion for Britain. The money was to be used to stabilize sterling and to help lift exchange controls. But despite the assistance, sterling was devalued in 1949 and remained under immediate controls until 1959. IMF rules concerning a return to full convertibility were interpreted somewhat liberally during this period. The pound was not free of exchange controls until 1979, and did not join the other EEC currencies in the European Monetary System, itself established in 1979, until 1990.

The years following the Korean War were among the most notable for the U.S. capital markets. After decades of poor publicity and Justice Department and SEC investigations and litigation, the new issues market emerged to rally substantially and register large gains. The stock market especially flowered during the two-term Eisenhower presidency, and the Dow Jones Industrial Average rose from 293 in 1952 to 685 eight years later. Interest rates also increased. Less optimistically, yields on government bonds rose from about 2.5 percent to about 4.5 percent after the peg was lifted. Money market yields rose from about 2 percent on Treasury bills to about 4 percent before dropping back into the 2 percent range in the later 1950s.

Foreign direct investments in 1959 showed a substantial increase over their values in 1934, but the increase was less than the growth rate in the stock market index. In the twenty-five intervening years, total investment grew from $1.5 billion to $6.6 billion while total net worth of those companies controlled by foreign interests rose from $1.2 billion to $5.3 billion. The bulk of this increase was due not to increased investment in common stocks of companies on a controlling basis, but to increased surplus accounts of those companies under foreign ownership. On aggregate, that amount climbed from $400 million in 1934 to $2.9 billion in 1959.[8] If compared with the growth rate in the Dow Jones Industrial Average, the total increase in value was equal to the market, which moved from 110 to 660 during the same period. But the total value of the residual investments still legged the market index overall.

During the Eisenhower presidency and the years immediately following, operations and policies at the Federal Reserve affected both the foreign exchange markets and the inducements that normally attract or dissuade foreign investors. The beginning and end of one particular policy—using Treasury bills only when performing open-market operations—coincided with abolition of the peg in 1953 and restoration of convertibility in the international financial system in 1959–60. When combined with the Fed's policy of performing open-market operations using foreign currencies as well as Treasury securities, the new procedures signaled a dramatic change in the way the central bank approached the balance of payments problems and the matters of capital inflow and outflow.

For instance, prior to 1953, the Federal Reserve used a combination of Treasury bills and longer-dated Treasury bonds when conducting its open-market operations, buying and selling these securities in the markets in order to influence yield levels and the levels of bank reserves as well. But beginning in 1953, it moved to a "bills predominantly" policy, arguing that its immediate actions would affect the level of bank reserves in each Federal Reserve district. Buying and selling bills was the most efficient way of meeting its objectives. This change in policy direction was coeval with a long-standing law restricting the Treasury's financing needs by placing an interest-rate limit of 4.25 percent on long-term bonds. That restriction plus the bills policy during the 1950s had caused the Fed to conduct its open-market operations using both short- and longer-term securities. By swapping securities on the yield curve the Fed could affect the slope between the short and long end of the yield curve—for instance, by selling Treasury bills and buying bonds, or vice versa. Beginning in 1953, after the peg was phased out, the Fed shifted away from trying to alter the shape of the yield curve and centered its activities solely in the money market.[9]

The "bills predominantly" policy was terminated in 1961. One of the major reasons for the return to using all maturities of Treasury securities was the balance of payments problem that had been developing during the 1950s and the accompanying outflow of gold. In 1960 and 1961, yields on three-month Treasury bills were in the 2.3 to 2.6 percent range, causing an outflow of hot money. As foreign capital departed, there was selling pressure on the dollar and gold balances also declined. Until that time, Federal Reserve monetary policy focused on bills, but this was useless in the face of a desire to raise interest rates a bit to stem the capital outflow. By returning to the older policy, and also by adopting a new stance concerning the foreign exchange value of the dollar, it was hoped to change the flow of capital.

In 1962, the Federal Reserve intervened in the foreign exchange markets on behalf of the dollar. The program was designed in collaboration with the Treasury, whose resources for intervening in the market were limited. The Federal Open Market Committee emphasized that the intervention would offset any political or economic disturbances that might arise because of pressures on the currency.[10] It was not assumed that market intervention could remedy structural imbalances in the balance of payments, but it might help smooth out short-term disturbances that might arise. But the intervention itself was confined to what are known as swap agreements between central banks on behalf of their respective currencies.

Swap agreements exist when two central banks agree to swap, or exchange, their currencies at the prevailing rates for a specific period of time. The Fed could then use the currency acquired to buy dollars from those central banks with an excess, thus stabilizing its value. At the end of the swap period, the two central banks would unwind the arrangement or extend it, depending upon the success of the swap up to that time. Swaps became popular very quickly and were used extensively. On the day President Kennedy was assassinated, the Fed moved quickly in this manner to stabilize the dollar. By the end of 1964, the outstanding volume stood at $1.3 billion.[11] Since that time, they have been used in varying degrees, depending upon the economic ideology of the Fed and conditions in the foreign exchange market. But after 1961 it became clear that the Fed, not the Treasury, was the main operator in the markets since the value of the dollar was considered an integral part of monetary policy.

The international status of the dollar was not challenged during the 1950s and mid–1960s, although U.S. authorities worried about a continuing flight of capital in the early 1960s that would lead to a devaluation. With U.S. interest rates relatively low compared to European rates, both hot money and U.S. direct investments searched for investment opportunities outside the United States. The balance of payments problems that developed were due to massive U.S. direct foreign investments abroad, as opposed to foreign investments in the U.S. Between 1950 and 1960, the amount of direct foreign investment in the United States doubled while U.S. foreign direct investments tripled, eventually becoming five times as large as the value of foreign investments in the U.S. Despite the increases, the nature of the investments remained remarkably consistent with patterns developed in the past. British, Dutch, and Swiss investment centered on financial services and manufacturing, while Canadians remained involved with spirits production and transportation. U.S. investment abroad, however, was much broader and structurally different. Over 50 percent was invested in the development of resources and processing of one sort or other, and it was much more geo-graphically diversified than foreign investment at home.[12] Financial-service firms did not expand much overseas with the exception of U.S. commercial banks, which continued to open foreign branches and subsidiaries. The effects of the war were still being felt; having emerged stronger than its allies, the United States was in a better position to invest abroad than vice versa. Foreign markets were becoming increasingly attractive as new sources of labor, commodities, and raw materials as well as markets for goods, many products at least partly produced at a foreign address.

Because so much foreign investment in the United States came from traditional sources, in good part the value of direct investment was long standing despite the fresh funds that arrived in the 1950s. In 1959, total direct foreign investment stood at $6.6 billion, representing 1,170 industries under foreign control. Of that total, over $5 billion had already been estab-lished before the outbreak of World War II, totaling about half the value. Two-thirds of the balance was added in the 1950s, with the 1940s contributing a small amount, normally the reinvestment of retained earnings.[13] Ameri-cans, on the other hand, were quick to exploit their political strengths and postwar financial prowess by expanding abroad rapidly. Direct foreign in-vestment in the United States would again increase, but time and foreign exchange market conditions had to be favorable. And this resurgence came in familiar areas by the beginning of the 1960s.

GROWTH OF INVESTMENTS TO 1971

Within a decade, the amount of foreign direct investments in the United States again doubled in value. Foreign banks, for example, made great inroads in New York, adding many branches and subsidiary and agency operations. Equally, U.S. banks continued to expand abroad, making liberal use of the new euromarket that developed in London and other offshore financial centers. But at the same time, the horizon for foreign investment was clouded by new U.S. regulations seeking to limit both investment abroad and foreign borrowing in the United States. Wall Street continued as a magnet for funds, as price-earnings ratios rose to levels not seen since the 1920s. Bond prices began to fall and yields rose as inflation became a major factor in calculating investment returns.

The latter part of the twentieth century has become known as a period of internationalization of the world's financial markets, leading to greater com-petition among the leading commercial banks and securities houses. Gen-erally, this phenomenon traces back to the deregulatory actions of the United States, and to a lesser extent Britain, in the early and mid–1980s. But there was an important earlier event, in 1961, that was hardly interpreted as revolutionary at the time—the decision by New York State to allow branches of foreign banks to operate in New York City.

Foreign banks had maintained a presence in New York City since the nineteenth century, and they had been allowed to operate by the Federal Reserve since its inception in 1911. But those offices were banking agencies, rather than branches per se. Being the financial capital of the country, New York City was seriously limited by this restriction. Several of the major New York City banks, including Chase Manhattan and First National City Bank, actively lobbied for the 1961 banking bill, under the assumption that enhanced status of New York City as an international financial center was worth the increased competition that foreign branches would bring. Soon after the act became law, numerous foreign banks opened new operations. Their activities were no different from those of domestic banks—taking deposits, making loans, trading foreign exchange, and investing in short-term Treasury securities. But the growth these foreign banks experienced was dramatic. In 1950, total assets of the foreign banks were $758 million; by 1960, they stood at $3.4 billion and in 1972 the total had risen to $20.3 billion.[14] This growth was proportionately higher than the increase in direct foreign investment during the same period, although it should be noted that acquiring financial assets in the form of loans is not in the same category as direct foreign investments.

What the foreign banks were able to exploit was the growing domestic demand for funds, particularly acute in the 1960s. Especially after 1960, U.S. banks in general, and New York City banks in particular, underwent a funding crisis that accompanied their expansion into other areas of their respective states. By expanding geographically and diversifying their product portfolios, commercial banks often found themselves in need of funds but lacked the sources to satisfy demand. While New York City banks had determined that the pastures were equally green in the suburbs, foreign banks took the opposite view. They were in a sense filling the vacuum left by the city banks. Since domestic banks concentrated more of their efforts on retail banking, that meant following the population exodus to the suburbs. The foreign banks naturally remained in the city, concentrating their efforts on corporate, or wholesale, banking for their multinational clients. In essence, foreign bank operations in New York City and the immediate environs remained almost purely wholesale for the next twenty-five years.[15]

The increase in size of the New York City banking community came about at the same time as moves were afoot in London to enhance that city's role as an international capital center. In the case of London, it was the Bank of England's tacit approval of establishing an offshore entrepôt capital market for international companies and other borrowers—the euromarket—that came to overshadow the domestic developments in New York City and lead to what eventually became the world's largest offshore capital market. More will be said concerning this in Chapter 5. As will be seen, the British move proved much more successful than the American in providing entrepôt facilities. Successful courting of this new market meant that a substantial portion of the entrepôt business established in the New York capital market before the Depression now shifted offshore.

During the 1960s, the United States enacted three different forms of control to prevent an outflow of capital and protect the balance of payments from further deterioration. The three measures were not enacted at the same time, but rather, were phased in over a period of several years. They were a curious combination of a tax on the export of capital, voluntary restraints on U.S. companies' funding overseas operations with domestic dollars, and mandatory restrictions on the export of capital by multinational companies. The combined effectiveness was the subject of much debate at the time, but inadvertently the controls helped inject life into the emerging euromarket.

The first control was the Interest Equalization Tax (IET), introduced in 1963 during the Kennedy administration. The tax was a circuitous attempt to prevent the export of capital through the Yankee bond market and the market for listed foreign stocks; it taxed the interest and dividends on those instruments received by U.S. investors. As will be seen later, the usefulness of the IET was at best limited, but it had a positive effect on the development of the eurobond market.

The IET was only a limited response to the capital-export problem. The situation was more directly addressed in two measures introduced later. First, in 1965, the Johnson administration asked U.S. corporations with direct foreign investments to voluntarily limit their capital outlays abroad in order to lessen the capital exports problem. But the request did not address financial institutions; the Federal Reserve Board requested they limit their activities abroad. In both cases, multinational companies were urged but not actually restrained from using U.S. dollars to expand their overseas operations. The part of the program aimed at financial institutions was known as the Voluntary Credit Restraints Program, while the part aimed at nonfinancial multinationals was known as the Voluntary Restraints Program. Both existed in voluntary form for three years; in 1968, both were replaced by a mandatory program.

The Voluntary Credit Restraints Program actually was part of a calculated plan to contain foreign short-term credits granted by U.S. banks. The IET, on the other hand, was aimed at long-term credits through the bond and stock markets. Of the two, the long-term program was the more successful. After it was introduced in 1965, both long- and short-term claims by foreigners against U.S. banks (their branches abroad) decreased. Of the two, the long-term decreased much more significantly and continued to decline while the short-term quickly moved up again after 1965 as banks and their customers found ways around the program by using euromarket banking facilities.[16] This meant that banks and other financial institutions reduced the number of short-term loans they made to non-U.S. persons or institutions, and did not extend new credits for long-term loans coming due. While this appeared to have been successful, banks then switched to the euromarket, where such restraints were not binding although the Federal Reserve did make attempts to control bank euromarket activities in 1969.

Other corporations were also asked not to export capital to their overseas operations. This was aimed deliberately at direct investments abroad rather than portfolio investments, which the IET and the Voluntary Credit Restraints Program addressed. Replaced by mandatory restraints in 1968, the program restricted the amount of capital that U.S. companies could invest in overseas operations, using as a gauge a certain percentage above a base year previously established. The actual amounts depended upon the part of the world where the investment was to be made. But almost as soon as statistics began to be recorded, it was apparent that the program was not particularly effective. From 1965 to 1970, direct investments by U.S. companies in Europe continued to grow almost unabated.[17] Obviously, financing was being obtained but not by direct transfer of funds from parent companies in the United States. Corporations and their bankers were able to avoid the restraints with few problems.

Capital controls helped spawn a bevy of financing techniques that could be employed when governments made it difficult to transfer funds. U.S. companies made full use of these techniques between 1965 and 1973, when President Nixon finally lifted the IET and mandatory restraint programs. The first source of funds was retained earnings from overseas enterprises— a natural internal source since the overseas operations of many U.S. companies were particularly successful during this period. Retained earnings had simply been left abroad rather than paid to the parent company in the form of dividends. Also used were the bond sectors of foreign markets that permitted tolerable amounts of foreign borrowing. And one of the more clever and widely used techniques was the parallel, or back-to-back, loan arrangement whereby two companies, each with operations in the other's country and constricted by capital controls of one or more governments, privately loaned each other funds in the required currencies. When the loans matured, they simply repaid each other in the borrowed currency. The benefit of such an arrangement was that the money never actually crossed a border, so capital controls technically were not circumvented. American and British companies especially engaged in these arrangements during periods of capital controls in both countries.[18]

Beginning in the early 1960s, traditional problems were met with what were by that time traditional remedies. President Nixon lifted controls in 1973, citing the improvement in the balance of payments in the years immediately prior. However, because vast changes were occurring almost simultaneously in the international financial system, these traditional remedies were not particularly effective. For the first time since the Bretton Woods Conference, the amorphous grouping of institutions and markets thought of as the international financial system was undergoing a functional change so dramatic that it was almost structural in nature. Much of the change was brought about by continuing development in the capital markets. With the emerging eurobond market a new international capital market along with the foreign bond markets of the major industrialized countries, it became apparent that capital flows would be difficult to control. There was now a vast supply of money, denominated in the major currencies, available for lending outside the control of domestic banking authorities.

During the period 1962–71, direct foreign investments in the United States increased in value from $7.6 billion to $13.7 billion. Yet that increase represented only a fraction of both the total and the rate of increase in U.S. direct investments abroad. The nature of the foreign investments in the United States changed somewhat during this period. Manufacturing increased in importance from 38 percent of total investment to 49 percent. Insurance and finance declined by 8 percent. But despite the change in emphasis, ownership of investments remained remarkably the same. The United Kingdom owned 33 percent of the total in 1962 and maintained its share, holding 32 percent in 1971. Canadian ownership decreased from 27 percent to 24 percent, while Dutch and other European investment increased by 2 to 3 percent. Non-European direct investment remained nominal, actually declining from 4 percent of the total to 3 percent.[19] This overwhelmingly European influence had remained intact since the earlier part of the century, but would begin to be challenged in the next twenty years.

U.S. direct investments overseas outnumbered foreign direct investments in the United States by 5 or 6 to 1 during the period 1962–71. The late 1950s through the late 1960s became known as the decade of U.S. influence abroad. Once the supplier of capital, the United States now was also an investor in overseas production and distribution. But this growing influence had a negative cultural side. In 1958, the novel *The Ugly American*, by Lederer and Burdick, portrayed Americans living and working overseas as unaccustomed to foreign mores and culture. The title was used as a reference to the boorishness of U.S. tourists and businessmen traveling abroad. Later, during the Vietnam War, the pervasive U.S. business presence in Europe was again a topic of intense discussion, especially with the 1967 publication of *The American Challenge*, by J.-J. Servan-Schreiber. The book became an immediate bestseller, first in France and later in the United States. It warned of increasing dominance of European industry by U.S. multinational companies, and called for dynamic European political leadership, preferably within the European Community. In the late 1960s and early 1970s, the term *multinational*, almost exclusively denoting U.S. multinational companies, would become a favorite catchword of the New Left as it criticized the major agents of U.S. business imperialism. As little as twenty years after World War II, U.S. foreign direct investment was receiving often bitter criticism in addition to reaping the economic rewards of overseas operations.

Foreign portfolio investments in the United States remained quite thin in the late 1950s, and did not increase until the latter 1960s. For instance, in 1959 net foreign purchases of corporate securities was $435 million, $363 million in stocks and the balance in bonds. The Swiss were the largest investors, accounting for two-thirds of the total. When compared to total volume on the New York Stock Exchange, the number was insignificant. By 1968, that amount had risen to $4.2 billion, with the Swiss accounting for some 20 percent of the total. While the number was still insignificant on a total basis, it did nevertheless show a gain. What the net figures do not illustrate is the amount of trading that occurred in order to produce those net numbers. In 1968, foreigners traded a total of $30 billion (purchases and sales).[20] Trading stocks for quick gain was still more popular among foreigners than were long-term portfolio investments.

Capital outflow continued to exceed inflow, only exacerbating the balance of payments problem. Much of the imbalance could be attributed to the value of the dollar. As the outflow problem became more chronic, investors and traders anticipated a devaluation. Multinational companies were already expanding abroad, and a potential devaluation would only help them speed their investment decisions. Foreign investors equally began to eschew domestic U.S. investments, since a devaluation would diminish their holdings. By 1971, interest rates were higher in Europe, providing additional incentives for banks and other investors to add overseas assets. Conversely, foreigners had the incentive to borrow dollars; a devaluation would make it cheaper to pay back these borrowings.[21]

As a result, the international capital markets experienced increased borrowing activity after 1971. Much Yankee bond market borrowing shifted to the eurobond market. U.S. banks increased their overseas assets by almost 75 percent between 1970 and 1972, and there was almost the same proportion in the growth of their nondollar assets.[22] The period of diversifying out of dollars began, and the U.S. capital markets and the foreign exchange market started to feel the pinch very quickly. But despite conditions in the financial markets, foreign investment in the United States continued to grow, becoming more and more a topic in both the press and official circles. U.S. investments, especially direct investments, had an ideological and commercial side that many foreign companies felt mitigated the risks they faced.

INCENTIVES AND DISINCENTIVES FOR FOREIGNERS

Having relied on foreign investment in varying degrees in its past, the United States had never erected barriers to foreigners, instead adopting a pragmatic line except in times of war. However, over the years certain federal policies evolved to protect U.S. industry from foreign control, especially in sectors considered strategic or vital to defense. But for the most part, the business environment was remarkably free of controls. For years, the prevailing attitude was that the U.S. marketplace was large enough to withstand any sort of competition.

The size of the U.S. marketplace was the greatest incentive for foreign companies as they debated the advisability of direct investment. In sheer size and numbers, no other single market could match the United States for per capita income and consumption. Since the 1920s, about 66 percent of the gross national product (GNP) had been driven by consumer spending, and that fact was not lost on European companies, especially British, Swiss, and Dutch firms whose own countries had a lower per capita income and higher household savings rate. For example, the largest British-controlled companies in the early 1970s manufactured oil products, tobacco, foodstuffs, household detergents, and man-made fibers, while the Swiss were involved mainly in foodstuffs and pharmaceuticals. The Dutch penchant was for consumer goods such as foods and detergents, electronics, and man-made fibers. While each had its wholesale nature, there was obvious emphasis on consumer nondurables. This influence had evolved over time to the point where many consumer items that had become closely associated with everyday American life—Lipton tea, Nestle chocolate, Bayer aspirin, Shell gasoline, Grand Union supermarkets, and Norelco appliances—were produced by foreign-owned companies. Keeping that fact out of the public view was an important element of producing and selling in the United States.

The size of British investment in the country dovetailed with the large market. From a British vantage, the common language and traditions expanded the market more than fivefold. This was especially useful, since as just noted North American per capita income was higher than that in the United Kingdom. Equally important was the labor situation in the United States (and Canada). U.S. productivity was higher, fewer hours were lost to industrial actions by unions, and working conditions and standards were higher, leading to fewer labor complaints.[23] While these conditions had not always prevailed in the same proportions as they did in the 1970s, it was still clear that the United States was the most sophisticated market for British investments, followed closely by Canada.

The United States actively courted foreign direct investment, although this was usually left to the states rather than done by the federal government. Various (but not all) states had development agencies that sought foreign investment by offering state tax incentives, support in setting up physical operations, or offering advantageous financing. The obvious incentive for the states was increased employment. But occasionally states could also impede foreign investment through punitive state tax laws or by regulating the number of foreign banks operating within their boundaries. New York State banking law prior to 1961 was one example. But on balance, federal and state regulations were favorable to foreign direct investment.

On the negative side was the amount of public disclosure required by U.S. authorities when a foreign company acquired controlling interest in a

U.S. company. According to the Securities Exchange Act of 1934, acquisition of a U.S. company or going public in the U.S. stock markets required full disclosure of a company's financial position, including the parent company. These tight disclosure rules were something many foreign firms were not accustomed to, and meant they would have to disclose much more than their domestic shareholders might ordinarily know about them. However, this sort of disclosure was required of all issuers of corporate securities in the United States, and was absolutely necessary to acquire controlling interest in a public company. It was also necessary if the usual institutional investors were to be kept on the rolls. Fiduciary investors such as pension funds, insurance companies, and mutual funds could only invest in a company that registered its securities with the SEC.

Foreign portfolio and direct investment grew after the two devaluations of the dollar that stemmed from the breakdown of the Bretton Woods system in 1971. But at this time foreign portfolio investment was stable. In early 1972, net purchases of all U.S. securities by foreign investors totaled $7.4 billion. But that number is somewhat low when compared with gross activity at the time. Foreign gross activity in U.S. corporate bonds was $7.6 billion, gross activity in Treasury bonds $5.4 billion, and gross activity in equities $26.5 billion.[24] Out of the total of $29.5 billion, only $7.4 billion represented net purchases. The large difference is due to selling or short-term speculation. In this respect, it appears that foreign investors were adhering to the pattern that had been established several decades before: speculation and short-term profits remained a strong motivating factor. But within the next several years, foreign investment in U.S. securities would explode exponentially for the same reasons that U.S. foreign direct investment had grown so rapidly in the 1960s and early 1970s: investors were seeking currency diversity. But before that occurred, the world was turned upside down again by the breakdown of the exchange rate system that had sought to correct the mistakes of the 1930s and 1940s.

THE DEMISE OF BRETTON WOODS

The obvious risk to the international financial system constructed at Bretton Woods was structural reliance on the dollar and its convertibility to gold. If the dollar came under pressure, and convertibility to gold was more theory than reality, then the system's central numeraire would not withstand selling pressure. This is what occurred in 1981, when the balance of payments deficit of the United States forced many investors to sell dollars and buy the other major currencies as a defensive measure against capital loss. As previously seen, investors had already reacted to a potential dollar devaluation in the late 1960s and in 1970 by diversifying their assets away from dollars, sometimes incurring liabilities in the currency, hoping to lower borrowing costs. Capital controls had not been particularly effective in curbing the deficit, and there was a dollar selling spree in 1971 as a result.

Domestically, inflation had intensified during the late 1960s during the Vietnam War. After rejecting a tax increase in 1966, Lyndon Johnson requested one a year later, but Congress did not pass the enabling legislation until 1968, by which time inflation had continued to move ahead substantially. When combined with capital outflow, inflation put more pressure on the dollar. At the same time, the foreign exchange market had its adherents to the theory of purchasing power parity. The foreign exchange environment that had existed since 1947 was conducive to that theory, since the band of parities established by the IMF invited speculation based on inflation as the prime factor in establishing exchange rates. Thus a resurgence of inflation would lead to selling of the dollar because it signaled a realignment in other foreign currencies that would be expected to appreciate.

The storm clouds beginning to surround the dollar only grew heavier with the memory of the sterling devaluation in the 1960s. After an especially strong showing in the early and mid–1960s, Britain's economy experienced increased inflation, imports grew, and the pound began to look suspiciously overvalued at $2.80. The Labour government of Harold Wilson resisted devaluation on several occasions, but by 1967 the force to devalue had become irresistible and the pound was devalued by about 15 percent. Investors lost a fair amount of money in that devaluation, as well as in the sterling panics of the years immediately preceding. The problems surrounding the dollar were not that different and would be even more pronounced because of the dollar's role as the major reserve currency.[25]

European interest rates continued to create an outflow of dollars from the United States, and the balance of payments deficit continued to exert pressure on the Nixon administration. On the foreign exchange markets in mid–1971, the Swiss franc, Canadian dollar, Japanese yen, English pound, Dutch guilder, and Deutsche mark all were trading at premiums to their par value against the dollar, despite the fact that U.S. interest rates had begun to rise in 1969–70. The balance of payments had become news in the United States and Wall Street reacted badly. The Dow Jones Industrial Average dropped to a ten-year low of 631 in the second quarter of 1970, before rebounding in the latter part of the year and continuing to rise in 1971. Dollar investments were now certainly less attractive to foreigners than financial assets in the European markets, especially after the Deutsch mark was revalued in 1969. Pressure was mounting for the United States to do something. It was clear that the dollar needed to be devalued, but the methods to be employed engendered significant debate.

The final blow for the Bretton Woods system came on August 15, 1971, when President Nixon appeared on national television to announce a series of economic measures designed to help curtail unemployment, inflation, and the balance of payments problem. Among his recommendations were, *inter alia*, a three-month wage and price freeze, an increase in personal income tax exemptions, a cut in federal spending, a 10 percent tax surcharge on imports, and a cut in the convertibility of the dollar into gold. The suspension of convertibility was to be only "temporary" until necessary reforms could be carried out in the international monetary system.[26]

There was a fair amount of political content in the announcement because alternative measures had been suggested in the past for dealing with the problem of dollar devaluation. An option would have been to ask the IMF and the major trading partners to revalue their currencies, letting the dollar devalue indirectly. But Nixon's message and method of delivery suggested that some political mileage was being sought as well. Regardless of intent, the international monetary system underwent a metamorphosis, leading to a decade of increasing monetary and financial turbulence. The major intent of the August 15 speech was packaged with other economic measures and probably appeared, at least to the uninitiated, as nothing more than a temporary palliative to ease pressure on the dollar. But the suspension of convertibility proved to be permanent. What appeared to be nothing more than a readjustment of the Bretton Woods system became a milestone in international finance. Events following hard on its heels changed attitudes toward international investing and helped redirect the investment flow back into the United States. After 1972, realizing the American Dream meant relying more and more on foreign investment—perhaps more so than at any other time since the expansion of the railways in the nineteenth century.

NOTES

1. Hans Aufricht, *The International Monetary Fund: Legal Bases, Structure, Functions* (New York: Praeger, 1964), p. 10.

2. Samuel Pizer and Zalie V. Warner, "Foreign Business Investments in the United States," *Survey of Current Business* (Washington, DC: United States Department of Commerce, 1960), pp. 4–5.

3. Although the peg was still maintained after the war and lasted for several more years, the Fed raised interest rates above their wartime levels by about 0.5 percent, on average.

4. Pizer and Warner, "Foreign Business Investments," p. 24.

5. See Charles R. Geisst, *Visionary Capitalism: Financial Markets and the American Dream in the Twentieth Century* (New York: Praeger, 1990), Chap. 8. By this time, various investigations of the securities industry by the Justice Department were settled and the atmosphere on Wall Street was better than at any other time since the 1929 crash.

6. France, West Germany, the Netherlands, Belgium, Luxembourg, and Italy. Denmark, Britain, and Ireland joined in the early 1970s.

7. The ECSC passed on the borrowed money to its various enterprises through the Bank for International Settlements in Basle, which acted as its banker in the

early transactions. The BIS had acted in this capacity before; passing through German war reparations to the Allies is one example.

8. Pizer and Warner, "Foreign Business Investments," p. 13.

9. On this topic see Milton Friedman and Anna Schwartz, *A Monetary History of the United States, 1867–1960* (Princeton: Princeton University Press, 1963), Chap. 11; and Clay Anderson, *A Half-Century of Federal Reserve Policymaking, 1914–1964* (Philadelphia: Federal Reserve Bank of Philadelphia, 1965), Chap. 10.

10. See Anderson, *A Half-Century*, p. 135.

11. Ibid., pp. 137–38.

12. Pizer and Warner, "Foreign Business Investments," p. 24.

13. Ibid., p. 40.

14. Francis A. Lees, *Foreign Banking and Investment in the United States: Issues and Alternatives* (New York: John Wiley & Sons, 1976), p. 25.

15. On the topic of New York City banks expanding, see Geisst, *Visionary Capitalism*, Chap. 2. This was generally the period of New York bank expansion, whether it be by geographical expansion of branches, mergers, or the opening of international offices.

16. See Alec Cairncross, *Control of Long-Term International Capital Movements* (Washington, DC: The Brookings Institution, 1973), p. 40.

17. Ibid., p. 47. Investments in the United Kingdom not included in these statistics.

18. British controls lasted, in one form or other, from the 1920s until 1979, when sterling was allowed to enter and leave the country free of restriction or limitation.

19. Robert B. Leftwich, "Foreign Direct Investments in the United States, 1962–71," *Survey of Current Business*, February 1973, p. 32.

20. Federal Reserve *Bulletin*, December 1960, p. 117, and January 1970, p. A84. The Swiss influence is somewhat suspect since many foreign investors funneled money through Switzerland to benefit from discreet Swiss banking laws. Nevertheless, those investments were still labeled Swiss by origin.

21. Federal Reserve System, *Annual Report*, 1971, p. 56.

22. See James C. Baker and Gerald Bradford, *American Banks Abroad: Edge Act Companies and Multinational Banking* (New York: Praeger, 1974), p. 2.

23. Comptroller General of the United States, *Controlling Foreign Investment in National Interest Sectors of the U.S. Economy* (Washington, DC: General Accounting Office, 1977), p. 32.

24. Securities Industry Association, *The International Market: Growth in Primary and Secondary Activity* (New York: Securities Industry Association, 1987), p. 12ff.

25. See Robert Solomon, *The International Monetary System, 1945–1976* (New York: Harper & Row, 1977), Chap. 5. Sterling was devalued to $2.40, where it remained until the dollar crisis of August 1971.

26. Ibid., pp. 184–87. Solomon notes the similarity of language used by Nixon then and Prime Minister Harold Wilson at the time of the sterling devaluation. Both blamed international speculators for the problems of their respective currencies, although both obviously realized that traders and investors would have little choice but to sell the currencies at different times, only adding downward pressure on their exchange rates.

4

The Decade of Crisis

In the months immediately following the end of the Bretton Woods system of fixed parity exchange rates, several attempts were made to patch together the foreign exchange trading system that had worked effectively since the end of World War II. But all attempts quickly failed and the markets poised to enter a phase of floating exchange rates that would add an element of volatility to foreign exchange not witnessed since the Depression. The hard currencies now floated against each other; their values were determined by market forces of supply and demand rather than by predetermined parity values. While the foreign exchange markets grew substantially after 1972, many of the old techniques practiced by central banks and commercial banks required refinement so as to adapt to this new, fast-moving market environment.

Foreign investment in the United States began a new era after 1972, although it would take almost ten years before the effects of the new currency environment and the resulting changes in investor behavior were fully felt. The U.S. decision to effectively devalue the dollar in August 1971 was followed by OPEC's first oil price rise. That decision in itself was based on the devaluation of the dollar, which had eroded the cartel members' revenues since oil sales were billed in dollars. As a result, these two factors ushered in a period of market uncertainty and volatile hot-money flows not previously experienced.

Immediately after the August 1971 dollar devaluation, attempts were made to give the parity system increased flexibility, but the juggernaut to float became too great to resist. In December 1971, the major trading nations met in Washington, D.C., and developed a new plan to modify the IMF agreements with respect to parity values. The dollar was devalued to $38 per ounce of gold from its previous level of $35. The other major trading countries, the Group of Ten, agreed to revalue their currencies (set their values higher), and the trading band was moved from plus or minus 1 percent to plus or minus 2.25 percent. But even this new range did not prove sustainable because the United States continued to run a balance of payments deficit and pressure developed again for a realignment of exchange rates.

Actual floating of currencies did not begin until the second half of 1972. The pound was floated in June of that year, and the other major currencies followed suit within the next six months. Another devaluation followed in early 1973, with the dollar marked against gold at $42 per ounce. Fixed parities were no longer of any practical use, and by March 1973 most currencies were floating against each other. The dollar and the pound found themselves floating downward while the Deutsche mark, Swiss franc, Dutch guilder, and Japanese yen grew stronger. The European currencies in particular also came under additional pressure in having to maintain values within the European "snake," a system whereby the EC currencies plus several other currencies of prospective members traded in a prescribed band against each other while maintaining a band against the dollar at the same time. This pressure on the competition, plus the continuing weak balance of payments experienced by the United States, led to an additional 10 percent loss for the dollar in the summer of 1973.

Within a year, the IET and mandatory controls programs were lifted, with the United States citing an improvement in the balance of payments. Another strong, and perhaps more compelling, reason for lifting the ten-year experiment in capital controls was a desire to attract some of the dollar balances held by the oil-producing nations. OPEC raised the price of oil later in 1973 and quadrupled it within a year. Therefore, any attempt to bring some of those dollars back to the United States banking system was welcomed, although as will be noted in Chapter 5, the attempt met with only limited success since most petrodollars were held in the eurobanking system. The entrepôt market would not easily come home. Although capital controls had a great deal to do with its leaving originally, abolition of those same controls would not necessarily bring it home quickly.

The post–1972 era was one of great suspicion about the ultimate destination of OPEC surpluses. What OPEC members and other oil producers did with their increasing riches became the popular financial question of the decade. In the mid–1980s, that question would be asked again concerning Japanese investments. As it turned out, most OPEC balances were kept on short-term deposit in the euromarket rather than in the United States. But at the time, there was fear that U.S. property and direct investments would be bought by foreigners. The fear was real enough, but the reality did not amount to significant investment, as time later proved. But the fear was not without foundation. For instance, the foreign exchange reserves of Saudi Arabia increased twelvefold between 1972 and 1977 while its oil exports increased by only 50 percent. Similarly, the reserves of Kuwait increased ten times while its oil exports tripled. As a result of those newfound Arab riches and the fear they instilled, Congress passed two bills—the Foreign Investment Study Act in 1974 and the International Investment Survey Act in 1976—requiring the Department of Commerce to survey foreign direct investments in the United States to determine whether vital industries had fallen into, or were vulnerable to, foreign ownership. While the motives may have been political, the results were also practical since these studies gave a clearer profile of foreign investment than had ever before existed.

In the late 1960s and early 1970s, foreign portfolio investments were dampened by two events that unraveled, showing the vulnerability of U.S. markets to the occasional, but not insubstantial, financial fraud. The first case of fraud occurred during the late 1960s, when the IET was in force. Dishonest operators of unknown (or undisclosed) origins bought certain popular foreign stocks listed and trading on U.S. markets, and forged evidence of U.S. ownership before selling them to unwitting investors, many of whom were foreign. The ploy was to sell a stock at a premium to other foreigners by faking U.S. ownership, required by the provisions of the IET. Estimates of the amount bilked from investors ranged from $100 million to $1 billion. Prior to 1967 (when postal regulations changed), the fraud could have been committed simply by picking up a tax form at a U.S. post office and registering the beneficial owner of the security as American.[1]

The second fraud was named after the company, the Equity Funding Corporation of California, which cooked its books in order to defraud its stockholders. Operating as a seller of insurance and mutual funds, Equity Funding was able to record exponential growth each year for about nine consecutive years. An informant finally revealed that the company was in the habit of recording insurance on persons who never existed in a continuing attempt to report increased earnings. When the scandal was exposed, many insurance stocks fell drastically on the New York Stock Exchange. Investors' actual losses were estimated at about $300 million. Both frauds illustrated that the U.S. markets, although well regulated for the most part, were still vulnerable to fraud and that investors could not be fully protected.

These factors, plus the volatile performance of the stock market in 1972 and 1973, dissuaded many foreign investors from equity investments, as noted in the previous chapter. Interest in domestic bonds was also low, especially since the eurobond market had become a growing favorite among international investors. The new game for investors was playing currencies against each other in anticipation of devaluations or revaluations, as circumstances might dictate. After it became apparent that the United States would not resume convertibility, the markets became even more volatile with additional emphasis on short-term trading profits.

After 1972, the emphasis on short-term trading and speculation on the one hand, and the need for long-term investors to hedge their securities holdings on the other, was quickly recognized by the financial community. New exchanges organized to trade options on equities and financial futures products were introduced over the next several years, mainly in Chicago and New York.[2] While those new products would have a profound impact on the U.S. financial markets over the next twenty years, the initial response was muted. Domestic investors required several years to familiarize themselves with these new instruments and understand the risks and rewards associated with them. Foreign investors had little use for them, at least initially, because they were not capital market instruments but rather derivative instruments basically unknown in overseas markets.

While portfolio investment remained on the moderate side, foreign direct investments began to increase substantially after the demise of the Bretton Woods system. Between 1975 and 1979, the U.S. share of total world inflow of foreign direct investment funds amounted to about 24 percent. By 1982, the share had increased to 35 percent. That inflow made the United States the world's largest single recipient of foreign direct investment. The largest single contributor was Canada, contributing 19 percent of all transactions, while Britain ranked second with about 16 percent. The other three traditional investors—France, the Netherlands, and Switzerland—contributed about 5 percent each, while West Germany and Japan contributed about 11 percent of the total. But the rates of increase as measured by the number of transactions completed each year was remarkably the same for most major investors. Between 1976 and 1983, they increased the number of investments in the country by four to five times their original number recorded in 1976.[3]

Manufacturing experienced the largest number of transactions with about 32 percent of the total, while finance and wholesale trade industries registered about 10 percent. Real property transactions totaled some 28 percent of the total, while mining and retail trade businesses totaled slightly less than 5 percent each. Geographically, the Mideast and Southeast were recipients of about 50 percent of the investments while the Rocky Mountains region gained the least, only 3 percent. But despite the impressive number of new investments realized after 1972–73, the total number of Americans employed by foreign-owned or controlled firms was only 3 percent in 1981. Manufacturing had the largest proportion of Americans employed, accounting for almost 7 percent of the industry. Wholesale trade was second with about 4.5 percent, and mining third with about 3.5 percent. But in terms of sheer numbers, the companies acquired or started by foreign investors was more impressive than the number of people employed.[4] Most foreign-owned companies tended to remain rather small.

Valuing these foreign direct investments was another matter. The dollar amounts of these investments was and is difficult to value precisely and even the official statistics vary in their estimates. Between 1974 and 1980, a conservative estimate of the value is about $15 billion per year in the mid–1970s, rising to about $30 billion by 1980.[5] The total amount of investments by country of origin became a more standard measure of reporting in the 1980s, as it had been earlier in the century and in the nineteenth century as well. Despite the number of acquisitions by foreigners, their value and the number of people employed were not particularly significant. Particularly important was the fact that little if any OPEC money found its way into direct investments—most of it was in portfolio investments.

The same generalization concerning the size of investment holds true for portfolio investments by foreigners between 1972 and 1975. Net purchases of all U.S. securities remained about the same, $7.5 billion per year. Most of that was investment in equities, since bonds remained out of favor until the early 1980s. While that number remained constant in terms of the value of stocks held by foreigners, it rose above 1920 and 1930 levels as a percentage of all NYSE-listed shares, remaining in the 4 to 5 percent range until the 1980s. At the same time, the U.S. stock exchanges were capitalized at between $700 billion and $1.2 trillion from 1975 to 1980, about four times the value of their nearest competitors in Tokyo and London.[6] Of these two, only the London exchange was a serious competitor for money; the vagaries of dealing in the Tokyo market were still befuddling investors. But even London retained some practices, such as the stamp (turnover) tax levied by the government, that made dealing in London-listed equities somewhat expensive, especially since fixed commissions were in use until 1986. New York remained the dominant stock market for foreign investors, although withholding tax still applied to dividends paid to foreign investors.

The performance of the dollar in the immediate post–Bretton Woods years was the major impediment to portfolio investment funds flowing more quickly into the United States. From 1972 to 1981, the dollar depreciated against the major currencies by about 23 percent. During that same period, the yen appreciated by 13 percent, the Deutsche mark by 10 percent, and the pound by 15 percent. The dollar was out of favor among international investors, and although it continued to account for about 70 percent of all international financial transactions, the other major reserve currencies became more popular alternatives than they had been in the 1960s.[7] The dollar's role in international finance could not be disputed. Oil, among many other international commodities, was priced and billed in dollars, regardless of the producer's nationality. But the revenue that oil generated was often invested in other currencies, given the desire of major oil producers to diversify owing to the dollar's demonstrated weakness on foreign exchange markets.

Complicating matters was the role that the Deutsche mark and the yen played in international finance. As the dollar slipped in value, the major currencies that provided the greatest competition to the dollar in international trade experienced the most interest among international investors. Sterling remained one of the major reserve currencies, although its status as a favorite was fading quickly. Neither the West German or Japanese monetary authorities wanted to see their currencies assume a more central role, for fear that further demand would only weaken their domestic monetary policies from the outside. As a result, the dollar retained its preeminence but continued to deteriorate in value during the mid- and later 1970s.

The decade of financial crisis continued to be marked by rises in the price of oil, but it was equally influenced by the structure of the U.S. banking system, which was proving to lack resiliency in the face of rising interest rates. Interest rate ceilings remained in place on domestic deposits as mandated by Regulation Q, and for that reason alone, much of the OPEC surplus remained offshore, along with other eurocurrency deposits. But the major worry of Congress and policymakers was not the short-term capital flow toward the euromarket; instead it was the long-term portfolio investments that potentially could be made with this burgeoning surplus of dollars. There was a strategic concern that had not been seen since World War II. Would this rapid accumulation of dollars lead to increasing ownership of U.S. assets by foreign investors or, perhaps more appropriately, by new investors whose investment patterns and motives were not necessarily clear?

Prompted by this concern, Congress passed the Foreign Investment Study Act of 1974. Introduced by Senator Daniel Inouye of Hawaii, this legislation required the Commerce Department and the Treasury to study the patterns of both direct and portfolio investments, and to issue their findings within two years. This act was an admission that, despite various surveys done over the years, an inadequate picture prevailed of exact ownership of foreign assets in the United States. Immediately after the breakdown of Bretton Woods, the number of companies under foreign control, the book value of the assets involved, and the number of persons employed by foreign-owned companies were all under a cloud of uncertainty and became the subject of considerable scrutiny among statisticians.[8]

One of the major causes of concern was the shift in foreign investors from the traditional European and Canadian, who had dominated direct investments for over a century, to the more apparent *nouveau riche* of the international investment community, namely from the OPEC states and Japan. While it became apparent that oil money was being deposited in the euromarket, Japanese preference was for direct investments in manufacturing and real estate. In the survey completed and published in 1976, strong Japanese investment in resorts and real estate was found in Hawaii especially, the home state of the senator who had introduced the 1974 bill.[9] The reasons for this growing trend in direct investments was not directly apparent; instead, it was a combination of currency factors, comparative labor costs, and a desire to circumvent import duties and quotas.

In the 1960s, U.S. labor costs generally were higher than those in Europe and Japan. On the surface, this appeared to be a disincentive for foreign firms. But the desire to sell in the domestic market was too strong, and foreign firms continued to open manufacturing operations during the 1970s, especially after the demise of the fixed parity system. The foreign exchange system provided the incentive, and that helped the United States in the long run. As the dollar weakened after 1971–72, foreign imports were naturally expected to fall as foreign-produced manufactured goods rose in value. The instinctive business reaction was to open U.S. manufacturing operations, taking advantage of the weak dollar to purchase dollar long-term assets and produce products in the United States that previously were made in Europe or Japan. At the same time, this move enabled the manufacturers to avoid duties or quotas that normally applied to imports. Financially, the United States benefited, as would any host country that had witnessed a shift in locale by its competitors. What were once foreign goods were now, at least in some cases, domestic goods for balance-of-payments purposes.

The actual cost of producing those goods was also lower than might have been expected, although the United States has never been known as a market for cheap labor. For example, in 1973 hourly earnings in the United States were higher than in any other major manufacturing country. But when defined in unit labor costs (the ratio of hourly labor costs to output per hour), U.S. costs were lower than the major European countries or Japanese. Using 1967 as a base of 100, U.S. unit labor costs were about 14 percent higher in 1972. West German costs were about 62 percent higher, Japanese costs were 57 percent higher, and British costs were 29 percent higher.[10] When that factor was combined with the relative weakness of the dollar and the size of the potential market, it is not difficult to understand why the post–Bretton Woods 1970s became the period of intense foreign direct investment in the country.

But not all manufacturing enterprises opened by foreign companies during that period necessarily proved successful. Between 1965 and 1973, the growth in nominal wages, unit labor costs, and real wages in manufacturing was greater in West Germany than in the United States.[11] Although those discrepancies changed slightly in the period 1975–80, it prompted some German companies to open U.S. operations. Perhaps the most notable was Volkswagen's ill-fated manufacturing operation in Pennsylvania, opened in 1978 and closed in 1988. The problem for foreign manufacturers was one of quality: how to produce domestic goods with the same quality that the company had become known for when producing at home. In Volkswagen's case, the U.S.-produced car was considered of lesser quality and quickly fell out of favor, eventually hurting the parent company's market share in the United States.

The foreign direct investments prompted by these economic conditions in the 1970s began to turn the tables on the United States, which had long been an exporter of capital and investments abroad rather than a recipient of long-term direct investments. As foreign companies took advantage of favorable exchange rates and labor costs, the harsh political tone of the 1960s began to fade. Foreign commentators put less emphasis on U.S. economic imperialism, for example. Emphasis on the effects of business abroad did not necessarily recede, however. In the 1970s, attention was focused on the multinational corporation, whose activities could seriously affect the economics and politics of developed as well as developing countries. Since many multinationals were American, much of the criticism focused on U.S. investments abroad. The inroads made by foreign businesses in the United States during that time were mainly attributed to movements in the foreign exchange market. As the dollar declined, new U.S. direct foreign investment abroad also slowed somewhat, although it appeared not to affect investments made when the dollar was stronger. But the prolonged dollar decline after Bretton Woods caused other major developments in the markets, some of which were successful and others not. In all cases, they illustrated that the major trading nations were seriously contemplating alternatives to the dollar.

Throughout the 1970s, the dollar did not regain the stature it had lost in 1971–72. It retained its place as the major reserve currency and accounted for the majority of international financial transactions, but the volatility that had caused the breakdown of the fixed parity system only intensified under the floating exchange rate. As a result, governments and commercial enterprises took several measures to protect themselves from dollar volatility. The first occurred in 1979, when the European Monetary System (EMS) was born. The EMS was a currency system developed by the members of the European Community, using an artificial currency known as the European Currency Unit, or ECU. This artificial, or basket, currency consisted of the weighted average of the currencies of the member states (except Britain, originally) based on the size of each's domestic GNP in relation to the EC's total GNP. ECUs could be purchased or sold at banks, which converted a local currency into the hypothetical ECU and deposited the balance in bank accounts for their clients. Two EC members could then trade with each other in ECUs rather than being forced to buy or sell their own currencies on the foreign exchange market. The major advantage of the ECU currency was its purely European component; dollars were not used in calculating its central value. Although the ECU itself traded on the foreign exchange markets and was quoted against dollars, its value was more stable than any of its component currencies. In a period of dollar volatility, ECU holders were apt to gain or lose less by holding the basket currency.

The other measure tried during this period was the commercial use of special drawing rights, or SDRs, the currency used by the IMF in its own lending operations. The SDR is a basket currency that comprised more than a dozen weighted currencies of IMF members before it was readjusted to reflect the weights of the major European trading currencies, the dollar, and the yen. Although intended as an IMF tool for international lending, commercial banks saw the opportunity to use SDRs as a hedge against the dollar. As with the ECU, some banks created SDR accounts for their customers, touting them as a potential hedge against dollar decline. Briefly successful, SDR accounts became less popular in the early 1980s, when the dollar began to rise on the foreign exchange markets. Unlike the ECU, it never saw widespread use nor did it find its way into major capital market instruments and interest-bearing short-term securities.

These two measures, plus the general dollar divestiture in the 1980s, only served to underscore the central role that foreign exchange considerations play in determining foreign investment. The development of artificial currencies used for commercial transactions illustrated that investors still required protection against turbulent markets as worldwide interest rates began to rise and major stock market indices began to decline. Unlike the traditional hedging that occurs in the foreign exchange markets, the basket-currency approach provided ample proof that investors were now quite diversified and dynamic in their reaction to exchange rate developments. Although most were inextricably linked to the dollar for better or worse, they were not willing to see their holdings decrease in value owing to what most certainly appeared to be a whimsical market.

INVESTMENT SHIFTS CAUSED BY THE DOLLAR

The combination of Regulation Q and the weak stock market of the mid- and late 1970s provided a hindrance to foreigners who ordinarily invested a portion of their funds in U.S. portfolio investments. After touching its all-time high of 1050 in 1973, the Dow Jones Industrial Average retreated to a low of 632 in 1975, touched 1,000 again in 1976, and fell to the mid–800s by 1979. Yields on high-quality corporate bonds rose by about 200 basis points during the same period as inflation continued apace. The consumer price index continued to rise, and by 1979 it had almost doubled from the levels recorded in 1969. The largest increase came after 1973, as the oil price increases made themselves felt on the consumer as well as in the financial markets.

For investors who continued to buy bonds, eurobonds took preference over domestic U.S. issues because the former lacked withholding tax. (More will be said concerning this in the next chapter.) Because there were no tax factors in the euromarket, the real rate of return was higher. This simple fact proved to be a bonanza for the eurobond market, at the expense of the domestic fixed-income market.

The foreign investment patterns witnessed during the 1970s did little to further the political attractiveness of U.S. investments, especially portfolio investments. Political events provided more disincentive than incentive. Social security payments indexed to inflation, an indeterminate end to the Vietnam War, the Watergate affair, and the relative unwillingness of the Federal Reserve to combat inflation in any way other than to raise the discount rate all proved to be negative elements for foreign portfolio investors. The same factors that attracted foreign direct investment did not apply to portfolio investment because there were alternatives; the most notable being the euromarket. When these factors were coupled with the rigidity of the U.S. banking system and occasional financial scandals, it is not difficult to see why portfolio investors preferred other pastures.

The rigidity of the banking system did, however, provide an incentive for foreign banks to open U.S. offices during the period leading up to 1980. Ironically, the federal constrictions that prohibited U.S. commercial banks from expanding into other states did not apply to foreign banks. Since 1927, the McFadden Act had prohibited commercial banks from opening *de novo* branches outside their state of domicile, and state banking laws continued that practice. Effectively, this meant that true national banking, as in the Canadian or European sense, could not be conducted in the United States. But these constrictions did not apply to foreign banks that used a combination of branches and subsidiary operations to operate in more than one city and/ or state, serving their own domestic customers' needs as well as competing for domestic U.S. business.

Foreign banks in the United States were required to organize as state-chartered banks rather than as federally chartered institutions, since the Glass-Steagall Act did not recognize alien banks. To operate as a federally chartered institution they would have had to been incorporated under federal law. As a result, the operation of foreign banks in the United States was left to the individual states to decide.[12] Thus, there were foreign banking operations in states with the most conducive atmospheres. In 1973, foreign banks had established 58 branches in the country, with all but 5 in California and New York. Within two years, the number had proliferated to 107, with most of the branches in the same two states and in Illinois. But while the growth in the number of branches was substantial, the amount of deposits held by them was not. For instance, in 1973–74, foreign banks in California held about 3 percent of the state's total deposits, mostly in institutional deposits rather than retail deposits.[13]

The various state and federal regulations governing banking were indicative of the obstacles host governments could and still can place in the path of foreign direct investment. In the case of banking, most state and federal regulations do not appear to have been aimed at a particular nationality but served as across-the-board restrictions for all foreign banks.[14] In some cases, the exclusionary restrictions on foreign banks took many twists, all usually aimed at precluding the banks from doing business. For instance, some states required foreign banks to be members of the Federal Deposit Insurance Corporation (FDIC), a provision that excluded them from doing business in that state, since FDIC insurance was not available to alien banks at that time. Other states required foreign banks to hold a specific amount of assets exceeding liabilities, while still other states set special capital or other ratio requirements.

The rapid growth in the number of foreign branches also led to political problems in the banking sector. In 1980, the New York State banking commissioner refused to consider Hong Kong and Shanghai Banking Corporation's purchase of the Marine Midland Bank, citing the need to protect the integrity of New York banks from foreign interference. Although Hong Kong and Shanghai did gain control of Marine Midland after several years of jurisdictional disputes, the original refusal was nevertheless in step with the times, in that it reflected suspicions that foreign money was being used to purchase U.S. assets.

In the early and mid–1970s it was apparent that the United States was feeling vulnerable to the increasing dollar balances held by OPEC producers, as well as the increasing Japanese investment in U.S. manufacturing and real estate. Several measures in addition to those studies already mentioned were introduced, with the intent of controlling foreign ownership of U.S. assets. In 1973, a proposal was made in Congress to limit the foreign holdings of a public company to no more than 5 percent of the voting stock. Another proposal was for a foreign investment control commission in the executive branch to monitor and control foreign ownership of real property in industries considered vital to national defense and security. Yet another suggestion advocated regulation of foreign ownership in the energy and defense industries. These were in addition to the 1974 Foreign Investment Study Act passed by Congress to study the level of foreign direct investment. In 1976, more than forty bills were pending in Congress concerning foreign investment. But in a revealing study appearing in 1977, written by the Comptroller General, it was found that direct foreign investment in the United States was administered by no less than twenty different agencies or offices, in an uncoordinated fashion. In some cases, more than one definition of foreign control was used, and no uniformity in terminology existed in official bureaucratic terms to define foreign investment and the potential problems it could create.[15]

This report was prompted by the International Investment Survey Act, passed by Congress in 1976. That legislation stated the need for further study in order to determine the precise extent of foreign direct investments in areas deemed vital to national security. The major fear addressed on both occasions was that of hidden interests controlling certain sectors of the economy. Because of the vast discrepancy in reporting, it was considered possible that foreign interests could gain control of vital industries and remain unnoticed by regulatory authorities. Perhaps at no time since the 1957 Sputnik crisis had such an integral part of the American Dream been so closely linked to defense. In 1957, higher education became the beneficiary of government largesse through the National Defense Student Loan Program.[16] In 1976, the result was less coordinated. Despite the need to know about foreign investment, owing to what the comptroller general called America's "open door" investment policy, no clear set of guidelines emerged from this flurry of legislative activity.

Although there was a trend toward foreign direct investment in the early

1970s, portfolio investments still outnumbered direct investments by a ratio of about 2.5 to 1. At the end of 1974, direct investment was estimated at $26.5 billion while portfolio investments were about $67 billion. At the same time, U.S. direct investments abroad totaled some $119 billion.[17] Portfolio investment accelerated with the improvement after 1975 in the Dow Jones Industrial Average, but an unmistakable long-term trend was emerging. Before World War I, portfolio investments accounted for about 90 percent of all foreign investment. Sixty years later it had fallen to about 70 percent of the total. While portfolio investments had not lost their appeal, direct investments were gaining because of a combination of factors not previously witnessed.

The mid–1970s were not a period of great confidence in the financial markets. The OPEC-induced price rises following the Arab-Israeli war of 1973 produced a recession that lasted until 1975. President Nixon lifted wage and price controls in 1974, at the same time consumer prices were rising. He resigned the White House in 1974, and unemployment peaked at about 9 percent before receding in 1976. Rumors circulated in Washington about contingency plans to seize the Saudi oilfields if OPEC continued to raise the price of oil. Under such circumstances, Gerald Ford succeeded Nixon as president, proclaiming inflation to be domestic enemy number one. While determined to get the inflation rate down from its level of almost 10 percent, Ford was less than successful in dealing with the Federal Reserve, led by Arthur Burns. Although avowedly determined to reduce inflation, Burns presided over annual growth rates in the money supply (M1) of about 8 percent, and bore the brunt of much public dissatisfaction with the recovery from the recession. In 1978, Burns was replaced as chairman of the Fed by William Miller, whose tenure lasted only about a year and a half. While high U.S. interest rates attracted some foreign portfolio investments, it was not until Paul Volcker assumed the chairmanship of the Fed that foreign portfolio money began to return, albeit slowly.

During this period, foreign direct investments began to increase on the back of more uncertainty than had been seen since the 1930s. The reasons for this surge in investment are as diffuse as the nature of the investments themselves. But one fact became clear and had a profound effect on U.S. perceptions of its own economic and industrial strength: the relative "open door" policy so often cited in official literature had created an environment that inadvertently fostered a new competitiveness in foreign trade that Americans were unaccustomed to coping with. This new environment was caused, not by OPEC oil investments, but by the ever-increasing Japanese direct investments in U.S. manufacturing facilities.

COMPARATIVE TRADE DIFFERENCES

As the United States became a host country in the 1970s, its trade and investment policies came under intense scrutiny by foreign investors. But the United States was not singled out for unusual treatment. After the breakdown of Bretton Woods—indeed, even before it—there was an international explosion in foreign direct investment and it was increasing at an unusually high rate. Between 1972 and 1979, total global gross direct investments increased from $13 billion to $36 billion. The flow of money into the United States increased from $949 million to $9.7 billion. During the same period, investment flows into Western Europe increased from $5.9 billion to $9.4 billion. While the United States experienced the largest percentage of growth in direct investment among the developed areas, the phenomenon was not local: it was an international occurrence.[18]

But what exactly caused the United States to enjoy such popularity? It appears that the weakness of the dollar encouraged foreign companies to use their revalued currencies to purchase U.S. assets—the statistics tend to confirm this. The heavy inflow came after 1972. Looking back, we see that the flow diminished significantly when the dollar was temporarily strong in 1970–71 before the August 1971 crisis. European countries, many of whose currencies were revalued after 1972, tended to discourage investment and, as a result, Western Europe enjoyed the smallest rate of increase of all industrialized countries.

While a comparison of trends confirms the same currency phenomenon had been occurring since the nineteenth century, a further qualification is required. In several studies completed about ten years after this investment trend emerged, many Japanese companies in particular claimed that, while exchange considerations were obviously important to their investment decisions, the foreign exchange rate was not of paramount importance when investment decisions were made.[19] Other factors, such as unit labor costs, access to local markets, tax considerations, and the sophistication of the local workforce were of equal, if not more immediate, importance than the value of the dollar. What was of great immediate importance was the exchange rate and its effect upon the cost of capital. This meant that the start-up costs in a local currency were not as important as the costs associated with borrowing that currency in order to finance a particular project.

In this respect, the United States had an enormous advantage over most other countries: it possessed the largest capital market in the world, although the euromarket was providing competition, especially since the early 1970s. The Yankee bond market was able to provide large amounts of debt capital to foreign companies seeking dollars to fund expansion in the United States. When the Yankee market was not able to provide these funds, the money could always be obtained in the eurobond market and repatriated without penalty or fear of capital blockage by U.S. regulatory authorities. Though the foreign borrower would be subject to whatever was the market rate for coupon interest at the time, a declining dollar would only help by making the eventual repayment cheaper than the initial cost. The old adage held true: borrowing a declining currency will lower the borrowers cost of funds in terms of its native currency.

The effects could be seen quickly in the bond markets. Between 1970 and 1972, international bond issues more than doubled, from $4.5 billion to $9.7 billion. By 1977, the total had increased to $32 billion. Of the totals, borrowings in the international market by U.S. companies actually declined from $2.2 billion in 1972 to $1.3 billion in 1977. In the Yankee sector, foreign corporate bonds accounted for $1 billion in 1972 and climbed to $8.4 billion in 1976, before declining to $4.0 billion in 1978.[20] After the recession was over and the markets rebounded, the dollar became more stable and the incentive to borrow became less attractive. But borrowing in the Yankee market in 1976 alone would have accounted for $500 million more than the gross foreign direct investment in the same year.

In a curious twist, the end of the fixed parity system ushered in a new era in the entrepôt nature of U.S. markets and foreign investment. The bond markets, both the Yankee market and the eurodollar market, were supplying capital for investment in the United States. Although it had been assumed that this was the case throughout the twentieth century, the 1970s was the first period in which there was hard evidence to prove the point conclusively. For perhaps the first time since the 1920s (and the evidence for then was somewhat dubious), foreigners were raising capital in the United States to be invested domestically rather than exported. It had been fifteen years since the entrepôt market had escaped to London; how long it would remain there depended to a large extent on currency and interest-rate conditions in the future.

Of the foreign companies that invested in new U.S. direct investments during the 1970s, the Japanese were perhaps the most prominent. From the mid–1960s to 1972, the value of Japanese direct investment had been running at about $100–150 million. Although the valuation figure represents investment far behind the British, Canadians, and northern Europeans, the Japanese penchant for producing consumer goods and investing in real estate brought their increasing investments under close scrutiny. But perhaps more important, the increase in Japanese investments in manufacturing brought to light a management and industrial style markedly different from the American. From the shop floor up to the level of public policy making, the Japanese style was, in many ways, diametrically opposed to the American style. In addition to providing manufacturing competition at home, the Japanese philosophy also flew in the face of the U.S. multinational corporations that had bore the brunt of social and economic criticism since the end of World War II. The U.S.-based multinational company was now seen as a behemoth, less efficient than its Japanese counterpart and less willing to leave a positive mark on the countries in which it operated.

The contrast in trading philosophies centered on what is known as the theory of comparative advantage. In its simplest form, this theory states that two countries trade with each other in those goods or services in which they have a comparative advantage; that is, they each produce those things which bring them profit, with one country allowing the other to dominate because of higher quality or better production techniques. But comparative advantage was meant to be beneficial to both parties, since the country that did not benefit from producing one particular good would concentrate on another good that it did better, gaining an advantage in that area.

Prior to the 1970s, U.S. direct investment overseas exceeded direct investment in the United States by a large margin, as mentioned earlier. Japanese international investment tended to be more trade related: Japan produced the goods at home and exported them, rather than produce them abroad. Using high-productive efficiency at home and an export-driven policy aided by the government, Japan was able to establish an enviable reputation without large amounts of foreign direct investment. When Japanese companies began to enter the U.S. marketplace after 1972, the philosophy had apparently changed somewhat, and U.S. businesses and politicians begin to take notice. Buying Japanese goods was becoming an accepted part of American consumerism, but the direct entry of Japanese subsidiaries into the United States brought the perceived problem closer to home. Shortly, Japanese companies operating in the United States would suffer the same criticism that U.S. multinationals had borne ten years before. Apparently comparative advantage had not been practiced. In response, many Japanese industrial companies and banks made a concerted effort to bring economic benefits to areas in which they manufactured or traded. In the 1980s especially, many Japanese banks loaned money and guaranteed loans in areas of the United States hard hit by both the 1980 recession and the lack of industrial competitiveness that had caused U.S. manufacturers to lose their market share.

The differences in foreign investment and trading philosophies between the Americans and the Japanese in the mid–1970s were striking. In 1975, U.S. investment abroad totaled about $133 billion, exceeding exports by a ratio of 1.2 to 1—equal to almost 9 percent of GNP. Japanese foreign investment, on the other hand, was about $15 billion, only 27 percent of exports and 3 percent of GNP.[21] But the strong yen and a favorable balance of payments created an atmosphere that induced Japanese companies to invest more abroad. The value of Japanese direct investments in the United States increased substantially after 1971. Between 1972 and 1974, the value rose from a minus $227 million (on a valuation basis) to $480 million while reinvested earnings doubled. Of the two major areas of Japanese interest at the time—manufacturing and financial services—manufacturing showed the largest increase, almost tripling in value from $129 million to $358 million.[22]

Despite the suspicion that the strong yen led to this increase in investment, many Japanese companies surveyed claimed that exchange rate considerations were not of primary importance when considering direct investment in the United States.[23] But in this instance financing costs in relation to exchange rate considerations were not of immediate concern, either. A more fundamental problem had plagued Japanese companies since World War II; it was related to foreign exchange but not immediately attributable to the yen-dollar rate. Since 1949, Japanese companies had been constricted by exchange controls limiting the amount of capital they could export for foreign investment purposes. Because of those restrictions, most companies remained export driven, and with the approval and assistance of the central government, they began producing the great discrepancy in trade statistics with the United States and the rest of the world. The exchange controls were not officially relaxed until 1980, at which time the United States and many other countries began experiencing increased investments, both direct and especially portfolio. But many of the controls officially abolished in 1980 were actually relaxed in prior years, and it was this relaxation that helped account for the increase in direct investments in the United States after 1972–73. While the actual exchange rates in the markets may have been of secondary importance, the ability to acquire foreign exchange certainly was not.

The structure of these new industries was also somewhat different. The assumption is that the Japanese penchant was heavily slanted toward consumer electronics and (later) automobiles. For instance, at the end of the 1970s, a total of 521 Japanese-owned manufacturing plants had been established in the United States. About half of them were involved in food products, metal products, chemicals, and nonelectrical machinery; only about 15 percent were involved in producing electrical equipment. Of the 521, about half were start-up operations and the other half were acquisitions. About 55 percent were wholly owned subsidiaries, while 45 percent were joint ventures with U.S. partners.[24]

Despite the inroads made by the Japanese, the overwhelming majority of foreign direct investments in the United States remained British. The long-standing investments of the British, Dutch, and Canadians remained in place, and certainly did not come under the intense scrutiny to which the OPEC and Japanese investments were subjected. But investments in the United States underwent an even more radical transformation in the 1980s which made the prior decade seem tame by comparison. In the midst of the currency turmoil following the end of Bretton Woods, an old chestnut finally bloomed after making several brief reappearances since the 1920s. In the world of currency volatility, methods of predicting future values made a resurgence.

STRUCTURAL SHIFTS IN INVESTMENT PATTERNS

While some foreign investors were claiming that exchange rates were not of primary importance in determining the extent of their new U.S. investments, the often-quoted theory of Gustav Cassel began to draw attention in the post–Bretton Woods era. Floating exchange rates were an ideal proving ground for the purchasing power parity theory. Their volatility was upsetting the foreign exchange market on the one hand and opening the possibility of trading profits, based upon that volatility, on the other. Intelligent estimations of future spot rates as well as forwards were necessary for both speculation and hedging.

The one factor that helped characterize the 1970s as the decade of crisis was the general volatility of the financial markets. The Dow Jones Industrial Average made no real gains between 1972 and 1979, although it did touch the historic 1,000 level several times before retreating in each instance. Money market and bond yields continued to rise throughout the 1970s. New financial markets and instruments gained significant ground in the investing community, a sign that times had become strained and new methods were certainly worth a try, although some innovations would not succeed in the long run. Nevertheless, the foreign exchange markets bred their own sort of volatility and that in turn made the search for new predictive methods more urgent. FAS 8, the new accounting standard adopted by the Financial Accounting Standards Board, proved to have a deleterious effect upon the income statements of many multinational companies. The rule applied two types of exchange rates when valuing a company's overseas assets and liabilities. Fixed assets and long-term liabilities were booked at the exchange rate at the time of booking; current assets and liabilities were recorded at the rate current at the time of the financial statements. Any ensuing gains or losses had to be taken to the income statement of the parent company in the quarter incurred. If exchange rates moved unfavorably, normally with the overseas portion in foreign currencies being valued lower, the parent company incurred a loss in that particular quarter. The earnings of U.S. multinationals thus began to swing, based on the changing values of the dollar. FAS 8 could not have come at a more inopportune time. As the dollar weakened against many other currencies, its current value was always, at least in general terms, below its historic value established several years before. That could spell a gain for a company in a quarter. Any subsequent gain for the dollar in the next quarter could effectively wipe out that gain, making it difficult to predict earnings in advance.

Many multinational companies sought to stabilize their overseas holdings by hedging their currency exposures in the forward market. They also employed other hedging techniques including money market hedges and overseas asset diversification. The intent was to hedge on a quarterly basis so that losses would not be incurred and reported on the income statement that would in turn cause investors to sell their shares. The intent was to hedge as much of the overseas balance sheets as possible, and the technique became known as balance sheet hedging. This behavior created even more volatility in the foreign exchange markets, since so many companies were seeking protection from the methods imposed by FAS 8.

The currency problem was somewhat more complicated than simply view-ing the dollar in deteriorating terms. While the weakness was attracting direct foreign investments, it was conversely dissuading portfolio investors, who would be slow in purchasing securities if they thought the currency would weaken further in the short term. The recently developed options and futures markets were of little help, since they were still in their early stages and their use had not become widespread, even among domestic investors. Market volatility tended to dissuade investors rather than attract them, especially when combined with an erratic currency. The combination of poor political and economic factors in the post-Watergate era created a climate of uneasiness about U.S. securities, regardless of their type. Between 1972 and 1975, net purchases of U.S. securities by foreigners hardly changed, increasing from $7.4 billion to $7.5 billion. Foreign holdings of stocks actually declined from $39 billion to $35 billion. The marginal increase was made up by a doubling of activity in net purchases of Treasury bonds.[25]

Between 1972 and 1980, foreign direct investments increased by almost six times, from $14.8 billion to $68.4 billion. While currency matters are sometimes discounted as primary factors in the foreign investment decision, there is little doubt that this massive amount of investment was generated in part by the relative weakness of the dollar. The distribution of the net increase in investment also displayed some telltale signs for the future. Japanese direct investments increased over thirty times, from an almost negligible $130 million in 1972 to about $4 billion in 1980. About half of that amount was in manufacturing facilities while the rest was concentrated in banking and chemicals. During the same period, the Dutch replaced the British as having the most valuable direct investments in the country. By 1979, the Dutch had forced the British into second place for the first time in the history of foreign direct investment, with $12.5 billion to $9.5 billion, excluding investments from the Netherlands Antilles.[26]

The weak dollar did not have as pronounced an effect upon U.S. direct investments abroad, however. After 1972, investments continued to increase at about 10 percent per year until 1980, when the rate of growth slowed considerably. But a radical change had begun. Foreign direct investment in the United States had started to gain ground on U.S. direct investment abroad, and the old ratio of five or six U.S. foreign investments abroad for every foreign direct investment in the United States began to slip. By 1979, the amount of U.S. overseas direct investments was $192.6 billion as com-pared to the $52.2 billion invested in the United States. Although the figures were still somewhat suspect, it was evident that political responses would be forthcoming in the 1980s, after the effect of the capital inflow had been absorbed and studied.[27] Within ten years, the amounts would be equal, as will be seen in the next chapter. Usually lost in the maze of statistics that normally accompanied increased investment from Europe and Asia, this phenomenon reversed a trend that had persisted since the 1920s. The United

States would no longer be a net exporter of long-term capital, through either the bond markets or direct foreign investment. The astonishing fact was that this reversal had been accomplished in an extremely short period of time.

Perhaps the most intriguing question that emerges from comparison of U.S. foreign direct investments and foreign investments in the United States is the reason why they both occurred. From 1972 to 1979, about 70 percent of U.S. direct foreign investments were concentrated in developed countries, and about half those investments were in manufacturing. At the same time, about half of the foreign investments in the United States were concentrated in manufacturing, with most originating from developed countries. Why were foreigners manufacturing in the United States while Americans were manufacturing abroad? Generally both were seeking to penetrate new markets with goods that could not effectively be exported from home. In many cases trade barriers stood in the way of what otherwise could have been profitable export ventures. Equally, the market for goods as well as the expanding market for services was becoming more international in scope, and many companies needed closer proximity to foreign markets in order to understand them better as well as to utilize the local labor force, physical resources, and local distribution facilities. Each factor taken by itself may not have been compelling enough to warrant direct investment but when taken in tandem proved to be irresistible.

Trade relations with the United States typified the desire to avoid restrictive practices, and were the ultimate reason for increasing Japanese investment in U.S. manufacturing. Since the late 1950s, U.S. objections to inexpensive imported Japanese goods had strained relations between the two countries. Many imports were fibers such as cheap cotton and synthetics. In 1972, the two countries signed a textile agreement after almost fifteen years of voluntary Japanese restrictions on exports to the United States. Shortly thereafter, similar self-imposed quotas were placed on steel exports. Later, agreements concerning the orderly marketing of specialty steels and color televisions were also concluded, followed in the 1980s by voluntary Japanese export restraints on automobiles. Given that trade tensions were gaining strength almost yearly, the Japanese sought to manufacture many of these goods in the United States rather than be subject to trade restrictions or punitive tariffs.

MARKET CONFIDENCE AND HIGH INTEREST RATES

While it would be incorrect to assume that foreign direct investment in the United States always takes advantage of a weak exchange rate, nevertheless there is an inextricable link. A clear relationship also exists between political and economic confidence and the level of foreign portfolio investments that a country is able to attract. When exchange rates are unfavorable, foreign investments in securities fall; when the currency appears to be recovering, they increase in order to take advantage of it, seeking a gain in either the currency, the investment itself, or both. As already mentioned, the 1970s were not noted for increases in foreign portfolio investments in the United States. But after 1980, the markets in general began to see a strong demand for dollar-denominated securities, despite the fact that the recession of 1980–82 was accompanied by persistently high inflation in the United States. Ordinarily, high inflation deters investors from buying a currency for fear of future depreciation. In this case, the opposite occurred. The dollar began its meteoric rise after 1981 partly because of the high interest rates accompanying inflation. But another less tangible factor entered the picture, a factor that had its origin in the late 1970s during the Carter administration.

In the autumn of 1979, Jimmy Carter appointed Paul Volcker to replace William Miller as chairman of the Federal Reserve Board. Miller had succeeded Arthur Burns and had served for only a year and a half. During his tenure, the Fed had adopted a somewhat cautious policy of combating inflation, and discontent surrounded Miller, who had no previous central banking or commercial banking experience. One of appointee Volcker's major attributes, as president of the New York Federal Reserve Bank at the time, was his popularity among both domestic and foreign investors.[28] The idea was to select a banker whom the investment community trusted to combat rising inflation and its attendant problems.

The effects of Volcker's tenure at the Fed were not immediate, by any means. It took several years of tight monetary policy and a worldwide recession in 1980–82 to reduce inflation and slow growth of the monetary aggregates. One of the immediate effects of Volcker's appointment was a precipitous fall in bond prices in October 1979, after the Fed announced a renewed commitment to lowering inflation by paying closer attention to bank reserves and the monetary base. While the changes in Fed leadership and policy were welcomed, several years would elapse before the markets would rally, bringing interest rates down and sending stock prices sharply higher.

A similar set of circumstances in Great Britain in the mid–1980s proved a harbinger for the dollar's later performance. The Conservative government taking office in 1979 also committed itself to strict monetary control in order to bring down British inflation. This policy translated into higher domestic interest rates and eventual stagflation, but its immediate effect on the pound was somewhat unexpected. Almost at once sterling began to rise on the foreign exchange markets, and by the middle of 1979 it had gained almost 15 percent against the other major currencies, reaching a level against the dollar not seen since the Bretton Woods days of 1971. The trend lasted for another year, in which the gain was almost 30 percent, before the dollar began its own rise and the pound subsided. The rise of both currencies at different times gave ample proof of the markets' favorable view of strict monetary control as applied by the central banks, especially when that control spelled higher short-term interest rates as well.

Ironically, the decade of crisis ended with perhaps the most traumatic year—1979—since 1971. The inflationary pressures that had crept into the economy since the beginning of the Vietnam War, and had been fueled by the OPEC price rises, began to gain momentum by the end of the decade. Money market and bond yields began to rise and the stock market indices fell, all reflecting a loss of investor confidence in monetary policy and growing discontent with the policies of the Carter administration. While the Dow Jones Industrial Average remained relatively stable in 1979, reflecting levels of the previous year, the price-earnings ratios of major stocks in the indices recorded their lowest levels in twenty years. Bond yields began an inexorable rise that by December put them in double figures for the first time in the twentieth century. Similarly, yields on Treasury bills rose to about 12 percent by December, creating a negatively sloped yield curve. At the end of 1978, the dollar had also sunk to its lowest point in the decade.

In purely financial terms, the period from 1972 to the end of 1980 was perhaps the worst time for attempting to achieve the American Dream since the late 1930s. The rise in interest rates to historically high levels, the volatility of the stock markets, and the weak dollar began to alter the perception of the United States as an economic locomotive for the world. Indeed, during the recession of 1980–82 pressure was put on both West Germany and Japan to act as the engine of renewed economic growth. After all, the United States was wrestling with inflation, high interest rates, unemployment at unacceptable levels, and growing levels of corporate debt. Undoubtedly, economic conditions had changed radically and quickly. Long insulated from foreign influence, at least the visible sort, the United States was now having to cope with foreign direct investment that was both substantial and visible. No longer were the names of foreign companies associated with traditional American products. Being Japanese, many were clearly new and represented a perceived threat to U.S. industry and management styles. While the American Dream was obviously still intact, it would now have to be more accommodating. Pressure was being put on the industrial infrastructure, with results that would not be clear for another decade. The "open door" investment policy practiced for so many years would now have to be reconsidered. One other fact was also rapidly becoming clear; the entrepôt market structure practiced and encouraged for so long had changed substantially. But any conclusions drawn at that time about its future direction would be incomplete, since further developments would quickly follow in the 1980s.

NOTES

1. A new regulation introduced in 1967 sought to tighten the simple method that had been used as a loophole for the fraud. See John F. Chown and Robert Valentine,

The International Bond Market in the 1960s: Its Development and Operation. (New York: Praeger, 1968), p. 83. This was the second financial fraud of the twentieth century perpetrated through the U.S. Postal Service. The other was the Ponzi scheme, devised by Charles Ponzi after World War I, which defrauded investors in and around Boston, using international reply coupons sold by post offices. See also Chapter 1.

2. See Charles R. Geisst, *Visionary Capitalism: Financial Markets and the American Dream in the Twentieth Century* (New York: Praeger, 1990), Chapter 7, for a more detailed description of the new hedging products and the exchanges on which they traded.

3. U.S. Department of Commerce, *Foreign Direct Investment in the United States, Completed Transactions, 1974–1983.* (Washington, DC: U.S. Department of Commerce, 1985), pp. 11–22.

4. Ibid., p. 12.

5. For example, in 1977, 198 cases were also identified but the value reported, $2.087 billion, was attributable to only 114 of them, leaving 84 completed acquisitions not valued. See U.S. Department of Commerce, *Foreign Direct Investment in the United States, 1976, Completed Transactions* (Washington, DC: U.S. Department of Commerce, December 1977), p. 7. In the 1985 study by the Department of Commerce cited in note 4, the number was estimated to be 198 known cases in 1976 but no value was placed upon them.

6. Securities Industry Association, *The International Market: Growth in Primary and Secondary Activity.* (New York: Securities Industry Association, 1987), pp. 9–20.

7. The strength of sterling was not uninterrupted during this time. The pound declined during 1973 and 1974 as a result of a British banking crisis, and again during 1976 when the United Kingdom received a loan from the IMF. On the banking problems, especially see Margaret Reid, *The Secondary Banking Crisis, 1973–75* (London: Macmillan, 1982).

8. Simon Webley, *Foreign Direct Investment in the United States: Opportunities and Impediments* (London: British–North American Committee, 1974), p. 7.

9. U.S. Department of Commerce, *Foreign Direct Investment in the United States,* Vol. 3 (Washington, DC: U.S. Department of Commerce, April 1976).

10. Leonard Yaseen, ed. *Direct Investment in the United States* (New York: European-American Banking Corporation, 1974), p. 10.

11. Linda A. Bell, "Wage Rigidity in West Germany: A Comparison with the U.S. Experience," Federal Reserve Bank of New York *Quarterly Review*, Autumn 1988, p. 15.

12. See David M. Phillips, *Legal Restraints on Foreign Direct Investment in the United States*, Vol. 7, Appendix K. In U.S. Department of Commerce, *Foreign Direct Investment in the United States* (Washington, DC: U.S. Department of Commerce, 1976), p. 168.

13. Francis A. Lees, *Foreign Banking and Investment in the United States* (New York: John Wiley & Sons, 1976), p. 31.

14. Phillips, *Legal Restraints*, p. 171.

15. Comptroller General of the United States, *Controlling Foreign Investment in National Interest Sectors of the U.S. Economy* (Washington, DC: General Accounting Office, 1977).

16. See Geisst, *Visionary Capitalism,* Chap. 6, for the background on educational loans.

17. Comptroller General, *Controlling Foreign Investment,* pp. 2, 41.

18. The Study Group on FDI, *Foreign Direct Investment 1973–87* (New York: Group of Thirty, 1984), p. 4.

19. Ibid., p. 36. See also Mamoru Yoshida, *Japanese Direct Manufacturing in the United States* (New York: Praeger, 1987), p. 45.

20. J. P. Morgan & Co., *World Financial Markets,* various issues; and Salomon Brothers, *Prospects for the Credit Markets in 1978* (New York: Salomon Brothers, 1978).

21. Kiyoshi Kojima, *Direct Foreign Investment* (New York: Praeger, 1978), p. 9.

22. Robert P. Leftwich, "Foreign Direct Investment in the United States in 1973," *Survey of Current Business,* August 1974.

23. See Yoshida, *Japanese Direct Manufacturing,* p. 45.

24. Ibid., pp. 189–90.

25. Securities Industry Association, *The International Market: Growth in Primary and Secondary Activity,* pp. 12–19.

26. U.S. Department of Commerce, *Survey of Current Business,* various issues.

27. Ibid. The number can be considered suspect depending upon how foreign direct investment is calculated. In a benchmark survey, *Foreign Direct Investment in the United States, 1980,* published in 1983, the Department of Commerce estimated the amount of direct investment at $521.9 billion, about ten times the official estimate from their usual *Survey of Current Business* estimates, published annually. The discrepancy can be explained by the more ambitious scope of the 1983 publication. That study listed as foreign direct investment all U.S. companies that had a modicum of foreign ownership, not just the book values of foreign parents' equity in, and net outstanding loans to, U.S. affiliates. The indirect political implication of this counting is that while the strict definition of controlling interest indicated that $52.2 billion was owned by foreigners, ten times that amount could be said to be influenced by foreign investors.

28. See William Greider, *Secrets of the Temple: How the Federal Reserve Runs the Country* (New York: Simon & Schuster, 1987), Chap. 1, for the background on Carter's nomination of Volcker.

5

The Rise of the Eurobond Market

As seen in Chapter 3, the balance of payments problems that the United States suffered in the late 1960s and early 1970s finally led to a break in the convertibility of the dollar into gold. One of the contributory factors to the financial turbulence was the presence of an offshore market for dollars and other hard currencies that had developed in London and other financial centers. These offshore centers made it possible for banks, corporations, and sometimes even governments to circumvent domestic banking restrictions and generate credit somewhat independently of the wishes of monetary authorities. In a manner reminiscent of an earlier era, this offshore activity helped generate capital exports in much the same manner as the Yankee bond market had prior to the 1929 crash.

Taken in aggregate, these offshore centers became known as the euromarket. Originally, the market was located mainly in London and other European money centers, but eventually the term was applied to any center that practiced offshore banking, including such far-flung financial outposts as Singapore, Hong Kong, and Bahrain. The idea of a euromarket has always been somewhat difficult to comprehend because it is a large, amorphous over-the-counter market for currency deposits, bonds, and money market instruments conducted primarily between banks in the major money centers. Its history is a peculiar blend of politics, banking, and secret investing. It has played a central role in the Third World debt crisis, the financial deregulation in the United States and Britain, and much of the financial innovation characteristic of the 1980s. All the while it has remained remarkably free from regulatory interference.

The euromarket has grown at an exponential rate since the mid–1960s. Within fifteen years of its inception, it established itself as a major source of funds for many different sorts of borrowers. But it got its start in an ad hoc manner, a characteristic that prevailed for the next thirty years. Sometime in the early 1960s, a French commercial bank was said to have taken a dollar deposit from the Soviet government. Unwilling to deposit the money in the United States for fear of political repercussions during the cold war, the Soviets opted for an offshore depository willing to pay interest in dollars. That relatively simple yet original bit of banking created what became known as the eurodollar market—that is, the market for dollars outside the territorial United States.

A market as such actually developed when the bank accepting the deposit had to book a corresponding asset yielding more than the interest it was paying for the money. Since eurodollar deposits yielded more than comparable domestic U.S. deposits, they could not simply be invested in domestic U.S. short-term assets because the bank's return would not be high enough to produce a profit. As a result, the bank had to develop its own market for lending the money, usually at rates higher than a U.S. bank would charge. Ordinarily, higher loan rates dissuade borrowers from using these loan funds, but times proved not to be ordinary. Once a eurodollar deposit was accepted, it was only a matter of time before the eurodollar loan market developed.

The advantage to banks willing to accept such deposits was obvious from the outset. Since these banks were offshore, they were not restricted by the Federal Reserve or the Comptroller of the Currency. Essentially, this meant that they were not bound by domestic U.S. reserve requirements. If the country in which the banks was located did not require reserves on foreign currency deposits, then the bank was engaging in a banker's dream—reserve-free borrowing and lending. Any dollar deposit taken in could be loaned at its full value. By not having to sequester reserves, banks quickly recognized that loans of this nature potentially could be more profitable than domestic loans. Also, loans could be made to willing borrowers anywhere in the world, as long as the borrowers would accept eurodollar rates of interest rather than loans based upon the prime rate of interest.

What that effectively meant was that borrowers were willing to accept floating rates of interest rather than rates fixed for short periods over the domestic prime rate. Eurodollar loans were normally fixed to three- or six-month deposit rates, better known as the London Interbank Offered Rate (LIBOR), and a risk spread is added on top of this reference rate. The bank then readjusts the rate of interest at the appropriate interval at an agreed-upon spread over LIBOR. This loan adjustment period was something new to borrowers of U.S. dollars. Ordinarily, this sort of floating rate was found on sterling loans made by British banks. But a bit of European influence crept in to what was otherwise an adjunct of the U.S. domestic dollar market.

This British influence was not unusual, since Britain was at the time the major international financial center. In essence, the entrepôt market of the nineteenth and early twentieth centuries had reemerged in almost classic form, again serving as a market for foreigners using a foreign currency.

British tax and monetary authorities were happy to see this market develop in London as long as it did not interfere with their domestic policies. As long as the dollars and other foreign currencies were borrowed and loaned to foreigners for use outside Britain, then there was little harm to the domestic financial structure. The invisible account would benefit and London's international standing would only be enhanced. Ironically, the entrepôt market had reappeared in dollars, for those wanting to do business with the United States or others in dollars, but the venue had changed. The real question was whether the functional side of entrepôt capitalism had changed with it.

The name *euromarket* was something of a misnomer when used to describe the short-term side of this new financial sector, since it did not originally trade short-term securities or financial instruments but comprised mostly nonnegotiable term deposits. But what made the term *market* somewhat applicable was how deposit and lending rates were established. Since the vast majority of banks operating in London and other offshore financial centers were not American, the only way they could effectively lure depositors was by bidding for funds. Therefore, the rate at which they were willing to pay for funds became known as the London Interbank Bid Rate, or LIBID. The offered side of money, at which they loaned funds, was normally one-eighth of a percent higher.

This market element meant that borrowers who agreed to floating interest rates were subject to the full range of market changes when a loan came due for its periodic adjustment. Since there were no caps on the maximum amount of interest charged, the potential for an escalation of interest was theoretically unlimited. When U.S. domestic rates went above 20 percent in 1981 and 1982, eurodollar loans were adjusted upward, many reaching 25 percent. That escalation in interest rates was one of the prime factors in the Mexican debt crisis of October 1982. Because of this risk factor, there were caps placed on both eurodollar and domestic adjustable loans by the mid- and later 1980s.

The real euromarket in the strict sense of the term was the eurobond market that began developing rapidly in the mid–1970s, after having grown at a moderate rate for about ten years previously. The first eurobond per se was a fifteen-year issue floated in 1964 for Autostrade, the Italian highway system. Besides having the distinction of being the first eurobond, the Autostrade issue was a good case study of how the eurobond market was able to emerge at the expense of New York's traditional Yankee bond market. The issuance of this first eurobond was a combination of relative costs and market prejudices. The ordinary alternative to dollars for any European borrower would have been the Yankee bond market, but Autostrade was not a recognized name in the capital markets. It would have been difficult to sell the bond to Americans for that fact, plus there was the inhibiting factor of the Interest Equalization Tax. As a result, the new eurobond market became a natural stalking horse for the new sort of bond that did not have a traditional market home.

The eurobond market emerged shortly before the United States imposed its Interest Equalization Tax (IET) in 1963. This tax was aimed at dissuading foreign borrowers from borrowing and exporting dollars from the United States in order to improve the balance of payments situation. The tax was a one-time excise tax leveled on the purchase price of long-term securities of foreign origin. The net effect was to reduce the yield on those securities so that they equaled, but did not exceed, yields on comparable domestic U.S. securities. The idea behind the IET was simple: in order to dissuade capital exports from the United States, the investors would be targeted instead of the foreign issuers of securities. By taxing the traditional yield premium that investors demanded from Yankee bonds, the major incentive for investing in them would be removed and the new-issues market would become moribund. In the ten years that the IET was in place, it succeeded in curtailing the number of foreign issues but inadvertently gave impetus to the offshore market where the IET had no effect.

Within the next ten years, activity in the Yankee bond market remained at moderate levels while the eurodollar bond market benefited from the increasing demand for dollar financing. From 1963 to the end of 1972, new eurobonds increased from $75 million to almost $5 billion—business that certainly would have been realized in the New York market if not for the IET. This was a major about-face from the 1920s, when new-issue activity was sought actively by the Republican administrations and the Federal Reserve alike. Concern about the balance of payments and the actual destination of exported dollars was now more important than the investment banking commissions that were lost in the process. But the possibilities were not lost on British politicians and central bankers, just as they had not been not lost on politicians forty years before. Lord Cromer, governor of the Bank of England in 1962, anticipated the U.S. move toward some form of capital controls when he stated,

The time has now come when the City [London] once again might provide an international capital market where the foreigner cannot only borrow long-term capital . . . but will once again wish to place his long-term placement capital. This entrepôt business in capital . . . would not only fill a vital and vacant role in Europe mobilizing foreign capital for world economic development. It would also be to the advantage of British industry in financing our customers.[1]

The entrepôt market in dollars was set for a major shift away from the United States. The British motive for wanting to attract the nascent euromarket business was similar to Benjamin Strong's reasons for wanting to develop the Yankee market in the mid–1920s: the commissions that investment banking institutions would earn, plus the ability of international customers to raise funding for their purchases of domestic goods and services, added up to a potential boom for the visible and invisible trade balances. But one crucial factor could not be anticipated in the early 1960s. As the new euromarket developed into a full-fledged capital market, the behavior of its major participants was not easy to gauge or predict because of the disparate nature of the market and the institutions operating within it.

The financial turbulence produced by the breakdown of the Bretton Woods and Smithsonian agreements benefited the euromarket because the lack of political consensus necessary to maintain the fixed parity system was accompanied by the first round of OPEC price rises. The oil price rises put pressure on U.S. domestic prices since the United States was a net importer of oil. As prices and interest rates began to rise in the 1970s debt financing also began its rise internationally. And the phenomenon was not confined to the United States. Many oil-producing countries began to borrow against their downstream oil revenues. At the same time, many countries borrowed to help pay their increasing import bills. The debt explosion began and the eurodollar market was the direct supplier of funds as well as a major source of profit for banks operating within it.[2]

Both the short- and long-term sides of the euromarket witnessed their most dramatic growth between 1972 and 1982. The amount of deposits accumulated offshore in dollars was estimated at $200 billion in 1972, rising to about $850 billion in 1982. Similarly, the amount of new eurodollar bond issues rose from $6.3 billion to $42 billion. Syndicated bank loans rose from $6.8 billion to $98 billion during the same period.[3] While the domestic U.S. market grew at a similar pace during this time, many of the funds borrowed in the euromarket were put to use outside the United States. Long-term money borrowed from the eurobond market could be used by U.S. companies to finance domestic U.S. investment, but repatriation of eurodollars by U.S. banks through short-term loans to U.S. companies for use at home was partly blocked in 1979 by the Federal Reserve.

Although the IET was lifted in 1974, investment in U.S. securities was still encumbered by a withholding tax levied on foreigners receiving either interest or dividends. The rate was 30 percent, withheld at the source by the paying agent bank; the tax greatly reduced the yield received by foreign investors.[4] The only way that foreign investors could get relief from the tax was if their resident country had a double-taxation agreement with the United States. Otherwise, the tax reduced the yield without any relief. The tax made investment in eurobonds even more attractive to non-U.S. investors. Eurobond interest (in any currency) was usually made by a paying agent located in a tax haven—that is, a country that withheld no tax at source. This effectively meant that eurobond interest was tax-free to many investors, since many countries did not tax the offshore holdings of their residents, but rather, only those funds that earned a return in their domestic market system. U.S. investors, on the other hand, had no particular incentive to invest in eurobonds. Most fiduciary investors were bound to invest in registered securities only. And even if they did invest in a foreign security, any unearned income was taxable by the Internal Revenue Service, since the United States practices what is known as universal taxation—residents must pay tax on any income, earned or unearned, regardless of where it was derived. Even after the IET was lifted, the eurobond market continued to flourish because of this factor.[5] Although these taxes appeared to be only minor annoyances, foreign investors voted with their money and usually chose the euromarket over the domestic market except for U.S. Treasury bonds.

The eurobond market developed in this relatively brief period to become an integral part of the capital market in U.S. dollars, as well as in the other currencies available for long-term lending. Dollars, however, were the mainstay and accounted for between 70 and 80 percent of all eurobonds issued in the primary market. Although it maintained its own characteristics, the eurodollar sector was functionally if not structurally integrated into the U.S. capital market. The one factor that continued to distinguish between a eurodollar bond and a domestic, SEC-registered bond was the nature of the investors purchasing it: eurodollar bonds continued to be bought by foreign investors, usually seeking to avoid withholding tax. Domestic bonds, especially corporates and Treasuries, continued to appeal to investors subject to the full panoply of domestic investment regulations.

After the dollar began its meteoric rise on the foreign exchange markets in the early 1980s, eurodollar bonds reached the height of their popularity, for reasons that are discussed in Chapter 6. During the 1970s, the main function of the eurobond market, as well as the eurodollar market as a whole, was to recycle dollars from surplus countries to deficit countries, in addition to the usual borrowing and lending activities of more traditional investors. Clearly, the institutional side of the entrepôt market had been lost by the United States, even though many U.S. commercial and investment banks acted as underwriters in the eurobond market. The Yankee bond market remained ensconced in the New York capital market but it had certainly taken a back seat to the euromarket.

Unlike many responses to past practices in the Yankee bond market, there was little that the U.S. regulatory authorities could do to curb the growth of or regulate the eurobond market. Given the dollar's preeminent role in international transactions, little could be done to curb the use, or appetite, for the currency outside the territorial United States. But the new entrepôt market did not necessarily help facilitate trade with the United States, that often-quoted ideal used to justify borrowing, especially by foreign companies. Between 1960 and 1979, the United States ran a trade deficit in all but four years (1964, 1974, 1975, and 1979). While it would be reasonable to assume that some of those dollars borrowed by foreigners were used to purchase U.S. goods and services, many of them were also borrowed by U.S. companies and repatriated for domestic investment uses or kept abroad because of the restraints programs. And interest paid to foreigners only helped exacerbate the balance of payments problem, even though many U.S. companies paid the interest through offshore finance subsidiaries established for the occasion. On the surface, the entrepôt concept would have worked reasonably well but for one exception. Using the borrowed funds to buy U.S. goods or services was a part, but only a fraction, of the potential use of the money. The same problem that plagued the capital markets in the 1920s had returned, but this time in a more complicated guise: much of this money was also being raised by foreign companies in order to compete directly with the United States. The avenues used to raise the money were now very complicated and sometimes quite convoluted. The relatively simple days of the 1920s, when benefits and disadvantages were much more clear, were certainly gone forever.

The offshore capital market became the *bête noire* of domestic regulatory authorities, in part because it helped develop financing features deemed inimical to monetary policy. As will be seen later, the floating-rate note denominated in U.S. dollars was an invention of the eurobond market and was used extensively by commercial banks with international branches needing funding. Eventually, the concept found its way into the U.S. domestic markets. But in the 1970s, adjustable interest rates were frowned upon by U.S. bank regulators and would probably have violated the usury laws or interest-rate ceilings of many state banking authorities or the Federal Reserve. The West German Bundesbank equally distrusted floating-rate securities and effectively forbade them to be denominated in Deutsche marks, whether issued domestically or in the eurobond market.

Frowned on by some monetary authorities and impractical for many traditional investors, the eurobond market nevertheless carved a niche for itself in the financial world. As the 1980s began, the market became known for financial innovation, much of which would eventually find its way to the United States through what has become known loosely as the "internationalization" of the capital markets in general. It also became known as a place where cheap capital could be raised, at interest rates lower than those in the domestic markets.

The euromarket did complement monetary policies, although the benefits were rarely mentioned. Every dollar that escaped from the domestic financial system and shifted to an offshore bank or a bond investment was one less dollar to be counted in the domestic U.S. money supply. This became especially important after 1979, when the Federal Reserve, under Paul Volcker, shifted its focus of control to the monetary base in an attempt to control inflation. Officially, these dollars were said to have "leaked" from the domestic banking system and therefore would no longer be counted in the official money supply. Although eurodollar rates of interest were usually marginally higher than U.S. rates, the two did nevertheless move in tandem. As U.S. interest rates moved steadily upward in the late 1970s, the prospect of no reserve requirements caused many banks to shift balances to the euromarket. Equally, corporate depositors actively sought those marginally higher rates on their deposits and, in short, a great deal of money escaped from the domestic system. But after 1980, the behavior of U.S. banks changed because the Fed, using the authority of the Monetary Control Act, imposed the same reserve requirements on eurodollar deposits held by the overseas branches of U.S. banks as it did on domestic corporate time deposits. At the same time, the central bank also gained the power to prevent foreign banks abroad from repatriating reserve-free eurodollars for domestic U.S. lending. The Monetary Control Act also gave the Fed regulatory authority over all branches of foreign banks in the country, whether they were federally chartered or not.

While the eurobond market developed into a significant offshore source of capital for U.S. and foreign borrowers, it did not contribute much to the U.S. balance of payments. Its major contribution was to act as a mechanism for transmitting financial techniques not yet tried in the United States into the domestic capital market. As an entrepôt, its effects were difficult to gauge because, as with the traditional Yankee bond market, it was not easy to predict the behavior of foreign companies or governments borrowing dollars. The postwar process whereby U.S. financial practices were exported to the rest of the world, especially the agency practices mentioned in Chapter 3, was now coming full circle: the United States was becoming an importer of new financial concepts.

CONCEPTUAL IMPORTS

The eurobond market grafted new concepts onto traditional debt instruments. The result made eurobonds somewhat different from their domestic counterparts, whether they were dollar bonds or denominated in other hard currencies. No traditional feature of a bond was considered inviolate, and experimentation covered all features of bonds—coupons, maturity dates, interest payment dates, and call features. As mentioned earlier, the variations from long-established tradition were mainly designed to accommodate the borrower of funds, but investor acceptance was also required if anyone was to buy these new instruments.

When many of these innovations began, mostly in the mid–1970s to mid–1980s, no one could have foreseen their import into the domestic U.S. capital market, to become part of the financing of the American Dream. It would have been difficult to imagine that the way expatriate U.S. and foreign bank branches funded themselves would lead to a revolution in U.S. mortgage financing. Even more far-fetched would have been the idea that these innovative products would lead foreign portfolio investors back to U.S. dollar-denominated assets because these assets could protect investors from capital loss in times of interest rate uncertainty or foreign exchange fluctuations. But one fact did become clear very early in the history of the market: investor acceptance of these new vehicles meant that finance was about to become much more complicated and sophisticated.

The major houses in the eurobond market years up to about 1980 were mostly British and European merchant banks, commercial banks, and investment banks; U.S. investment banks played a smaller role. U.S. commercial banks were represented by merchant banking subsidiaries organized as Edge Act companies specifically to engage in investment banking, an activity they could not engage in at home because of the constrictions of the Glass-Steagall Act of 1933. But the market remained dominated by the Europeans and the British, both of whom understood the intricacies of international finance better than the Americans. As a result, many of the eurobond issues they underwrote, while denominated in dollars, bore close resemblance to bonds issued in the German, Swiss, and British bond markets.

Companies wishing to tap the eurobond market had to adopt features on their bonds suggested by the investment bankers if they hoped to sell them successfully to the international investor. But in many cases these features also proved attractive to borrowers as well. Perhaps the best known eurobond feature involved the coupons (interest payments) attached to a particular issue. Most domestic dollar bonds bore semiannual interest so most borrowers had become accustomed to paying in that manner. Investors equally had become accustomed to calculating interest on a semiannual basis. But the eurobond underwriters were able to sell bonds with annual interest payments only, a radical switch from American practice. This was in keeping with the German and Swiss tradition of paying interest once per year. That feature alone attracted numerous borrowers, American and otherwise, who quickly recognized that the method allowed them opportunity use of the money for six months in every year.

Investors were willing to accept payment in this manner because the bonds were normally kept in bearer form at a depository in their names—a manner similar to the nominee method discussed in Chapter 1. The depository was usually in Luxembourg, which imposed no withholding tax on foreign investors. This effectively meant that eurobonds were tax-free to investors unless they were compelled to claim the interest earned on their domestic tax forms. For the benefit of anonymity, the trade-off was annual interest. Since the market grew exponentially between the mid–1970s and the late 1980s, this factor hardly proved a deterrent.

The payment of annual interest proved that investors were willing to accept unconventional features on dollar bonds if there was a benefit. Building quickly upon that simple principle, underwriters introduced a myriad of new bond features on eurobonds, some of which would prove successful while others would fall by the wayside. But few would have thought that the international capital markets, and ultimately domestic U.S. financing, would be changed in the process. The other features introduced were far from simple, however. Each had its own geneology, depending upon the financial system from which it was adapted. In the twentieth century, European experiments with bonds had included issues indexed to inflation; bonds with variable, or floating, interest; issues with no defined maturity date, or perpetuals; and tap issues that could be increased or decreased according to market conditions. Once the euromarket had successfully experimented with them and they were subsequently imported into the United States, the face of the debt markets was substantially changed.

The floating-rate note was the one innovation in financing that particularly suited the commercial banks operating in the euromarket. It was used by many banks, U.S. and foreign, to fund their overseas branches with dollars. Basically, a bank would borrow, on average, for a period of ten to fifteen years. The interest paid was to be calculated on a floating rather than on a fixed coupon basis. Underlying this floating rate was a reference rate—the rate that the coupon would actually be set against. The coupon would then be adjusted at a specific spread above the reference rate and would be readjusted every three or six months. Normally the reference rate was LIBOR, and these bonds were said to be floating above LIBOR. The borrower exposed itself to variable rates of interest in this case. More worrisome was the fact that LIBOR had a relatively short history and no one could predict the range in which it could fluctuate, especially during the general interest rate spiral of 1979–84.

This new type of bond proved novel in more than one respect. First, it combined the long-term nature of a bond with the interest-rate features of a money market instrument since it was based on a short-term interest rate. Second, it presented the borrower with a risk never before faced by long-term borrowers: not knowing the cost of funds in advance. Third, it offered investors a hedge against inflation that could not be obtained with a normal bond investment. As interest rates rose following inflation, so too would the interest on these bonds since they were readjusted periodically. Fixed bond interest had been a hallowed tradition, at least in the United States; these new instruments offered both borrowers and investors a new wrinkle.

Floating-rate notes became one of the major tools international banks and their branches used in funding themselves in dollars. The bank was free to loan the borrowed money to others in turn at a higher spread than it paid on the floating bond. This was little different from taking in a variable rate deposit and lending to others at a higher variable rate. Being free of reserve requirements, the floating-rate bond quickly became a natural source of funds for banks; any other business enterprise would not find them natural in the slightest. Nonfinancial companies usually continued to opt for fixed-rate money so that they could adequately budget capital for their investment plans. Banks, on the other hand, used the notes to augment their lending business. As long as the interest-rate elements on both the asset and liability side were coordinated, adverse interest-rate movements would have minimal effect on the return, at least in theory.[6]

While innovative and practical, floating-rate bonds were more trouble-some economically. Instruments of this nature had been discussed period-ically in the United States for at least twenty years prior but had never been implemented, at least by government or government-sponsored borrowers, because of the inflationary impact they might have as well as their potential threat to monetary policy. By offering the investor interest rates that could rise with the market, these bonds offered capital protection against loss at the same time. Widespread use could offset Federal Reserve policy by keeping investors abreast of inflation, especially when tighter monetary pol-icy was desired. For the same reasons, the Bundesbank of West Germany refused to allow floating-rate bonds to be denominated in Deutsche marks, either domestically or in the euromarket.[7]

Another reason that floating-rate bonds were not able to make inroads into the U.S. capital markets was the presence of interest-rate ceilings. In this particular case, the logic of the market, so successful offshore, worked to its detriment at home. In order to market these bonds successfully, most issuing banks had to classify them as deposit notes or something similar, indicating that the bonds ranked equally with deposits in the event of the bank's liquidation. This made the bonds first-tier liabilities. If these instru-ments had been sold in the United States, they would have come under the aegis of Regulation Q of the Federal Reserve—a vestige of the banking regulations of the 1930s that allowed the central bank to impose a ceiling on interest rates paid on deposits. It was not until interest-rate ceilings were abandoned in the early 1980s that floating-rate bonds found a niche in do-mestic financing.

In a sense, it could be said that floating-rate bonds indexed both investors and borrowers to the inflation rate if there could be a correlation between interest payments and the actual dollar inflation rate. While not indexed officially in the same manner that many developing countries linked financial instruments to domestic inflation, the floating-rate note was a step in that direction. In the early 1980s, the British Treasury took a first step closer to the concept by issuing an obligation (gilt) directly tied to the British consumer price index. It would pay 2 percent more than the inflation rate, calculated periodically. Bonds of this type had the advantage of using a broad basket of goods as their reference rate rather than simply relying on a money market rate such as LIBOR. Usually this meant that indexed bonds were less volatile, and costly, to the borrower of funds. Despite its novelty, the indexed bond per se never caught on in the euromarket, which continued to rely on the proven standby, the floating-rate note.

Another British invention, the perpetual bond, also made a resurgence in the euromarket in the 1980s, after a hiatus of 150 years. Issued at the time of the Napoleonic wars in order to consolidate borrowings, the perpetuals, or war loans, were fixed-coupon bonds that bore no maturity date, meaning that they would never be redeemed unless the British Treasury decided to do so by calling them. While something of an accounting nightmare, the perpetuals made good economic sense since they were callable. As it turned out, many were not called because interest rates never moved substantially below the 3 to 4 percent coupon levels at which these bonds were issued.

The euromarket experimented with these issues by combining them with floating interest rates to create the perpetual floating-rate bond. Borrowers paid periodic interest at a distinct spread over LIBOR for an indeterminate time. The major borrowers using these instruments were commercial banks and certain governments accustomed to borrowing in the euromarket. While their natures may have been different, their motives for using such an esoteric form of borrowing were remarkably the same. Borrowers would borrow at a specific spread over LIBOR and then pay interest until the rates moved even lower or they thought they could borrow at an even smaller spread than the original. Since the form they borrowed in was perpetual, there was no particular timetable for this and the borrower could afford to wait for the right conditions. In theory, this technique enabled borrowers to take advantage of the lowest interest rates possible. But what spelled trouble for U.S. banks that borrowed in this fashion was not market conditions or investor disfavor. The Internal Revenue Service ruled that such instruments were not actually bonds but rather equity, more properly resembling preferred stock. And since the bonds had to be reclassified, the interest paid could not be termed interest as such and claimed as a tax deduction. Because of that ruling, the process was halted for U.S. banks and the market for these somewhat peculiar instruments became much more limited.

Widespread success of the perpetual floating-rate note would have solved a major problem for commercial banks with extensive overseas and euromarket exposure—perpetual funding. Without it, banks operating in the otherwise regulation-free market had to resort to other methods of funding their lending operations. The decline of this novel method also illustrated that domestic authorities could and did have an effect on euromarket developments, despite the visible absence of traditional regulatory authorities.

One of the best-known techniques imported from the euromarket was the zero-coupon bond, an instrument that substantially changed financing and investing practices. Essentially, this is a bond that bears no interest coupons, and as a result is sold at a deep discount from par. The investor's return is the capital appreciation, or the difference between the purchase price and maturity (redemption) price. From the buyer's point of view, these instruments answer an age-old problem facing investors everywhere: how to adequately compound a bond's interest to ensure a definite future value. Since interest is not received, it does not have to be reinvested. Being discounted from the redemption price, interest is effectively in the hands of the investor from the outset. Zero-coupon bonds are the only investment vehicles that can be valued in two dimensions. Investors know both the current and the future value if they hold them to maturity.

The first borrower of zero-coupon bonds was the U.S. retailer J. C. Penney, which borrowed in the euromarket in 1981. The strategy became a prototype in international finance, and amply illustrated the entrepôt that the eurobond market had become—for U.S. borrowers as well as foreign. The techniques employed were complicated, but they brought together the various markets in a manner that was unheard of ten years before. Zero-coupon bonds were used so often in the years immediately following that they became fairly standard if market conditions were favorable.

Zero-coupon financing brings together the most confusing set of market conditions and exploits them equally to the benefit of the borrower. The company borrowing in this manner raises an amount of money that is less than par or face value but must pay back the full amount upon maturity. The amount raised depends upon the bond rate used to establish the discount. For instance, a 10 percent twenty-year traditional bond bears coupons amounting to 10 percent per year. A zero-coupon bond bearing a rate of 10 percent for twenty years is discounted at that rate for the time period; in either case they are both 10 percent bonds. The traditional bond borrower raises the full amount; the zero-coupon bond borrower raises only a fraction of it.

While the source of funds is the same, the uses of the borrowed funds could be quite different. In most cases, the zero-coupon borrower uses the money to establish what has become known as a *defeasance*. The funds are used to purchase an asset costing less than the amount raised or, put another way, yielding more on a discount basis. The asset purchased then retires the zero-coupon bond at maturity. In such a manner, the original bond is defeased, or preretired, by the newly purchased asset. The difference between the discounted amount raised and the cost of that asset is considered a profit. If the difference between the two is too small to benefit a company, the operation can be postponed until market conditions change in favor of the deal.[8]

The zero-coupon concept became quite popular in the 1980s, but the U.S. Treasury zero-coupon issues were the most popular of all because they lacked a default risk factor. The early eurobond zeros showed that a demand existed for these instruments, ranging from insurance companies to individual investors who purchased them for individual retirement accounts.[9] They also benefited the investment banks that underwrote them for corporations or stripped the Treasuries in order to create the Treasury zero. For instance, an investment bank could strip a bond and then charge customers slightly more than the mathematical sum of the two parts, increasing their commissions and creating the unusual situation whereby the value of the parts is slightly greater than their sum. This can be justified in some cases by pointing to the innovation and work involved in creating these new investment vehicles.

Of all the innovations from the euromarket during the 1970s and 1980s, the swap concept was perhaps the most far-reaching and helped revolutionize the capital markets. At first glance, the concept is so complicated that it seems it would have been doomed before it actually began. Previous experience in the capital markets proved that complicated investment vehicles found small audiences and failed for lack of investor interest. But within three years of the emergence of this new market, the number of outstanding swaps exceeded the number of outstanding municipal bonds in the United States. The reason for the obvious break with tradition can be found in the nature of the market. Swaps were designed for, and traded by, corporations and merchant banks seeking to change the cost of debts they had previously incurred. The traditional investor played little or no part in this market.

The professional investors who participated in this market understood the complex issues at stake. Essentially, a swap involves two parties exchanging either interest payments on bonds or the currencies in which the bonds were originally borrowed. The former is referred to as an *interest-rate swap* while the latter is a *currency swap*. The two parties are normally brought together by a merchant banker who knows their financing needs, although the parties may not know each other during or after the transaction. They must have different types of debt outstanding and different needs. For instance, in an interest-rate swap, a party with fixed-coupon debt may seek a swap with another that has floating-rate debt payments. The intermediary banker arranges a swap deal whereby they agree to exchange the payments in terms suitable to both parties. The idea is to produce a new cost of borrowed funds for both parties that is somewhat better than the traditional bond market could have provided.

One of the major reasons swaps succeeded so quickly is the involvement of commercial banks. In order to be successful, swaps require a third-party guarantor—a role commercial banks were more than willing to assume. For an annual fee, they guarantee a swap transaction in the event one party defaulted. The fee they receive is relatively small, so swaps quickly became a volume business—the more swaps that were guaranteed, the more fees that were earned. Banks were especially eager to increase their fees since the Third World debt crisis unraveling at the time had seriously eroded their profitability. Swaps came along at the right time, as far as the commercial banks were concerned.

While growth in the eurobond market had been significant, the exponential growth in the swaps market was a phenomenon heretofore unwitnessed in twentieth-century finance. In 1983, the market was literally in its nascent stage, but by 1990 the number of outstanding swaps was estimated at around $1.5 trillion, counting the debts of both parties in that amount.[10] Swaps were conducted between outstanding bond issues of many international borrowers, and also involved transactions using combinations of bonds along with syndicated bank credits and other types of loan arrangements. Although complicated, the usefulness of swaps was evident: they helped reduce the cost of funds to both parties or otherwise helped tailor borrowing needs that could not be easily met in the traditional markets. While they did raise a plethora of regulatory questions concerning capital adequacy of the guarantor banks, swaps perhaps did more to internationalize the capital markets in the 1980s than any other single development.

These innovations in the bond markets all owed their raison d'être to interest rate developments and funding problems encountered by banks in the 1970s and 1980s. Foreign banks operating in the eurodollar bond market required a source of funding for their loans that was not necessarily short-term. Floating-rate notes provided a simple but stable source of long-term funds based on short-term adjustable interest rates. In the early and mid–1970s, they were particularly important because of the increasing competition among banks for eurodollar business. Also, by being long-term, these funds were not subject to withdrawal, as were deposits. Banks able to borrow on this basis, therefore, had a distinct advantage over smaller institutions that had to rely solely on deposits.

Interest-rate swaps and currency swaps owed their existence to the historically high U.S. dollar interest rates that prevailed between 1979 and 1984. Interest rates began an inexorable rise beginning in October 1979, based on the Federal Reserve's continued tightening of the monetary aggregates as well as on the oil-based inflation created by the OPEC price rises of the 1970s. Although the yield curve between short- and long-term interest rates hit its most negative slope in 1981, and began to correct itself gradually thereafter, interest rates remained high until the summer of 1984, when they finally began to fall back to single digits. The actual drop into a permanent, positive slope took an additional two years, however. During that six-year period, the financing behavior of many organizations had changed from what had seemed the halcyon days of the early 1970s. Borrowers of money had been especially hard hit by the sudden changes in interest rates, since the constant uncertainty put many capital spending plans in doubt. The market for swaps thus had a vast potential audience, all of whom had a distinct desire to lower or change their cost of borrowed funds.

Although floating-rate bonds, zero-coupon bonds, and swaps were the major innovations in the eurobond market, they were by no means the only ones. Bonds were issued on a *tap* basis, employing methods similar to those used by the British Treasury to sell new issues. If market conditions were not deemed wholly suitable for a new issue, the borrower reserved the right to hold back a portion of it rather than sell it at a low price. Later, when conditions improved, the remainder could be "tapped" into the marketplace at the price originally envisaged. Also used was another British progeny, the partly paid issue. This required investors to pay a portion of the bond's selling price at issue, with the remainder due within a short period of time, perhaps six weeks to two months. If interest rates moved down in the interim, the bond would be trading at a premium at final payment date, allowing the investor to make an instant profit should he decide to sell them after he had paid the balance. This feature appealed to investors' speculative nature. In reality, both devices were nothing more than marketing techniques designed to sell bonds under less than optimal conditions.

Finally, another new wrinkle was the fungible issue, a bond that could be traded with previous issues of the same borrower, ensuring greater liquidity and trading possibilities than if it were a separate issue. This device was an acknowledgment that bond investors were concerned about the secondary market for their issues and about the reliability of market prices and market liquidity. Issues that become larger in point of time, at least in trading terms, stood a better chance of appealing to investors than those that might suffer lack of liquidity or an adequate number of secondary market makers.

Not all of these bond innovations became standard fare in the eurobond market. Some were designed for certain types of markets or interest-rate conditions and would not appear until those conditions were present. This flexible approach became the hallmark of the eurobond market and was perhaps its greatest contribution to development of domestic U.S. capital markets in the 1980s. When compared with the euromarket, the domestic market appeared rigid and inflexible. The standard fare was the straight, fixed-coupon bond that had taken a battering in the interest rate rise of the late 1970s. The most vivid example was the original IBM debt offering syndicated simultaneously with the change in monetary policy announced by Paul Volcker in October 1979. Issued at a coupon rate appropriate before the rise in interest rates, the bond was still in syndication with its many underwriters when the interest rate increase came, and it subsequently lost almost 8 percent of its value in one week as yields adjusted in the market. While that sort of event benefited the borrower of funds, it left many unhappy investors and underwriters, underscoring the need for some innovation in the bond market if money was to continue to be provided to companies for capital purposes.

INSTITUTIONAL SIDE OF THE MARKET

Much of the innovation in the eurobond market was directly attributed to the banks that served as underwriters. Most of these were based in London, and regardless of their original nature, acted as investment banks when operating in the offshore market. Eurobond underwriters came from several distinct domestic backgrounds. They were either subsidiaries of European commercial banks, securities houses in their own right at home, or Edge Act subsidiaries of U.S. banks operating in the eurobond market in a manner that was otherwise prohibited domestically by the Glass-Steagall Act.[11]

While the eurobond underwriters were of many different nationalities, all acted as investment banks nevertheless. Their reasons for participating in the market were somewhat different, depending upon their lineage. The continental European investment houses were, for the most part, subsidiaries of commercial banks that functioned at home as universal banks, performing commercial and investment banking under one roof, unrestrained by domestic banking regulations. The British underwriters were usually the major accepting houses or merchant banks, practicing investment banking for international clients. The U.S., Japanese, and Canadian underwriters were subsidiaries of commercial or investment banks, operating at arm's length from their parents, especially if a commercial bank parent, since all were constrained either by the Glass-Steagall Act or a domestic variant of it.

Underwriting profit was the major motive for participating in the market, but in the case of Edge Act subsidiaries, not the only one. Throughout most of the 1970s and 1980s, the full underwriting fee on a eurobond issue denominated in dollars was about 2 percent of the issue price. Thus, on an issue of $100 million, the underwriters stood to earn $2 million if market conditions were favorable. On average, that fee structure was about 0.375 to 0.5 percent more than the fees on a domestic U.S. bond. In addition, the behavior of syndicates was somewhat different in the eurobond market than in the United States, giving underwriters more latitude in selling the bonds.

Underwriting agreements in the eurobond market were between lead underwriter and the other members of a syndicate. If a syndicate member's behavior was less than ethical, any violation of the terms in the underwriting agreement was between the investment bankers themselves. Normally, lead managers turned a blind eye to the behavior of junior underwriters. But in the United States, the agreement was between the borrower of money and each underwriter individually. Underwriting behavior tended to be more on the straight and narrow, lest the client learn of an underwriter's practices and act against it by refusing to do business in the future.[12] As a result, the eurobond market became known for loose behavior on the part of investment bankers when it came to selling new bond issues. Price cutting was the norm on new issues, something that domestic underwriting practices tended to discourage and later rules prohibited. While the primary motivation was originally profit, many market participants in fact made little if any money underwriting issues. Instead many recorded losses in most years and eventually left the market to the coterie of continental and British houses that were successful. Many of the unsuccessful were Edge Act U.S. subsidiaries. But one thing that the latter group did gain was investment banking experience in bond underwriting—something that certainly could not be gained at home. As early as the mid–1970s, many U.S. commercial banks began to anticipate the demise of the Glass-Steagall Act, and opened investment or merchant banking subsidiaries abroad. In fact, that was one of the prime reasons many subsidiaries entered a market where profit was uncertain at best.

Some of the later entrants into the eurobond market were Japanese investment banking houses or subsidiaries. These large Japanese houses had limited success on Wall Street in the 1980s when trying their hand at underwriting domestic U.S. issues. But euromarket practices served their long-term philosophies. The price-cutting techniques common in the market dovetailed nicely with the Japanese corporate policy of offering services at the most competitive prices possible, at least until a market niche was achieved. But there was a distinction between this type of negotiated bidding for a new deal and the price cutting just mentioned. Given the flexibility of underwriters, deals were usually discounted after terms and conditions were set on the bond issue. The Japanese practice was to discount the cost of the issue to the borrower directly. For instance, a 10 percent bond issue with fees of 2 percent could be discounted by perhaps 1.5 percent to produce a yield higher than 10 percent to the investor. The alternative was to offer the borrower a lower coupon rate, perhaps 9.875 percent with a slightly thinner fee structure and then to insist on selling it at par, or issue price. This technique found great favor among clients, and Japanese houses had much new issue business but often with little profit to show for it. If this practice had involved selling a domestic good on a foreign market, it probably would have been objected to on the grounds of dumping, or undercutting the market. Many investment banks responded to the practice by simply refusing to become members of the Japanese-led syndicates.

U.S. investment banks succeeded much better in the eurobond market than did their Edge Act commercial bank subsidiaries. By being able to place one or two investment banks in the league table of top eurobond underwriters, U.S. investment banking provided contemporary proof of a recurring issue: investment banking relationships between securities houses and their corporate clients have been developed over many years so bankers knew their clients' international, as well as domestic, financing needs on the basis of experience.[13] Once established, those relationships were both difficult and potentially costly to break. U.S. investment banks were able to serve both their domestic and their international clients better than the commercial banks, and eventually served as the main transmitters of financial innovation in this rapidly increasing international marketplace, following the deregulatory legislation introduced in the United States in 1980 and 1982.

The eurobond market was useful for banks for both practical and planning reasons. But while many U.S. commercial banks used the facilities established in London to prepare themselves for a change in the domestic banking situation at home, the potential to make money in the euromarket was still the greatest lure. In addition to the bond business, the syndicated loan business was the most profitable for commercial banks, since the fees for large syndicated loans were not subject to market fluctuations, as were bond underwriting fees. Since many holders of dollars deposited funds in banks outside the United States, the vast pool of eurodollars presented the greatest bonanza for bank lending in years. The "jumbo" loans made by banks in the euromarket had a fee structure attached to them that was similar to bond underwriting fees: usually about 2 percent of the amount loaned plus the appropriate spread over LIBOR, the base rate charged on the interest. This potential for profit made the market irresistible for most banks with international operations or aspirations.

In addition to the fees charged for putting together a loan package, usually for a medium term of four to ten years, banks also profited by charging fairly high spreads over LIBOR. They could accomplish this by lending money to Third World borrowers whose credit standing was not of the highest order and who were thus willing to pay spreads over eurodollars that would have been considered excessive for most short-term domestic customers. This was a very crude form of risk adjustment to offset what was rapidly becoming declining profitability on the domestic side for most U.S. banks in the late 1970s and early 1980s. If a bank's domestic profit margins came under pressure, it was inclined to make more risky loans oversees in order to offset the negative effect. This exposed the bank to both counterparty risk *and* interest-rate risk, although the idea of floating-rate assets was to place the burden of changing interest rates on the borrower, not the lender. When interest rates began to rise in the late 1970s, many developing countries found it increasingly difficult to service the rising interest charges and went into technical default or rescheduled their loans. Until 1980, the banks were able to reap large profits on their lending businesses, but beginning in 1980, with the rescheduling of Poland's debts and the near default of Mexico in 1982, profitability began to erode and the banks sought other markets in which to lend or develop new products.

The U.S. banking enthusiasm for euromarket lending is normally cited as only a part of the explosion in lending that took place between 1975 and 1982, as a result of OPEC surpluses on the one hand and the deficits they created on the other. But if considered in broader terms, U.S. bank participation in the lending phenomenon was prompted in no small part by domestic problems that made new avenues of profit so attractive, even if the banks were short on the expertise necessary to make the new ventures successful. In the mid–1970s, commercial banks were hurt by a domestic recession and interest rates that continued to rise slowly. New types of financial intermediaries, especially money market mutual funds, were luring depositors by offering money market rates of interest while the interest rates offered by banks were still under the constraints of Regulation Q of the Federal Reserve. The investment bank corporate bond business was feeling severe pressure from the new type of agency bonds—mortgage-backed securities—that had been created in the earlier part of the decade and had found great favor with investors, mostly domestic. Thus both types of institutions had strong motives for expanding into various sectors of the euromarket.

By 1980, most of the major institutions operating in the euromarket had already been established, with the exception of the Japanese investment houses, which were later entrants. Almost all benefited from the economic climate between 1982 and 1987, when the market recorded its strongest growth and actually exceeded the U.S. bond market as the largest new-issues market for corporate and non-U.S sovereign issues. The phenomenal rise of the dollar beginning in 1981 and the international borrowing explosion that was already underway contributed to behavior in the capital markets that had never before been seen, or even contemplated. In many ways, the eurobond market served as the best barometer of 1980s finance, with its established penchant for arbitrage (in the form of defeasances), financial innovation, and healthy fees providing the capital markets worldwide with a big of unaccustomed flair.

THE MARKET'S BOOM YEARS

The 1980s were the decade of the dollar, with the currency rising to historic heights before dropping to unprecedented lows against the other major currencies. A more complete discussion follows in Chapter 6, but as imagined, those currency movements created investor reactions not unlike those that had occurred in the past. Both direct and portfolio investments in the United States would come under intense scrutiny by foreign investors, much as they had in years previous when currency realignments had clouded the investment horizon. In the international markets, events, products, and innovation were dominated by currency movements as never before. The new entrepôt market was poised to make a significant contribution to domestic U.S. finance.

Activity in the money and bond markets often now proceeds at a pace that confounds most textbook accounts of investor and borrower behavior. However, before 1980 there was little evidence to suggest that this would be the case. After the October 1979 rise in interest rates and the original IBM bond offering, most investors would have wagered that there would be a serious drop in new-issues activity as interest rates continued to rise in the last year of the Carter administration and the first year of the Reagan administration. The yield curve between short- and long-term interest rates had become distinctly negative for the first time in the twentieth century, and inflation had reached almost 15 percent, also a record. The credit-tightening activities of the Federal Reserve suggested that borrowing would eventually have to wane as the costs of capital became too expensive. But a glance at the new-issues activity in the bond markets painted a somewhat different picture. It continued at a brisk pace and the dollar began a strong advance on the foreign exchange markets.

The major reason behind the new-issues activity was the real rate of interest (borrowing rate minus the inflation rate). In most cases, it was flat or marginally positive, not the positive 2 to 3 percent investors in dollar bonds had become accustomed to. This prompted many companies to borrow because it fitted well into an inflation pattern. Even if the rate of inflation continued high, manufacturers or providers of services could always mark their products or services higher in the future. A low level of real interest rates benefited borrowers more than investors. Although this situation only persisted for about two years—until about mid–1982—it nevertheless began a trend that was continued by another set of economic factors equally compelling.

There was continued tightening of credit and persistant high interest rates as the inflation rate began to move lower. After late 1982, when the recession had finally ended, real interest rates ranging between 4 and 7 percent could be found in the markets as bond rates remained stubbornly high despite the drop in inflation. This created enormous demand for the dollar and dollar-denominated investments, especially bonds. As a result, the currency continued to rise on the foreign exchange markets, reaching its historic highs late in the winter of 1985. By that time, it had recorded a 40 percent rise against the other major currencies since 1980–81. With strong demand, investment bankers were quick to respond by developing bonds with features that would have been unacceptable to investors under more normal circumstances. At the time, investors did not seem to mind as long as the investment was denominated in their favorite currency.

Commercial banks were also quite keen to find new products that would bring them profits, because the Mexican debt crisis had made lenders much more wary and international lending through syndicated bank loans began to decline after 1982, in some cases by as much as 30 to 40 percent within one year.[14] High-margin loans would prove useless if the borrower was not able to make repayments in timely fashion. When the interest-rate and currency swaps were developed, the banks were quick to recognize the profit possibilities and began guaranteeing the swaps in large numbers and amounts. Swaps were considered less risky than loans because they involved only the guarantee of the bank to repay if one of the parties defaulted. Banks booked swaps as contingent (off-balance sheet) liabilities and were able to book the guarantee fees directly as income. Their balance sheet exposures were not affected by swaps, as they were by loans. In addition to helping the swap parties reduce their interest-rate exposures, swaps also aided the banks with their own exposures. In several years the swap market grew exponentially, as noted earlier in this chapter.

In order to perform swaps, the market had to have instruments that could actually be swapped, and this is where currency preferences played a role. The swap market owed its origins to aberrations in the eurobond market that allowed corporate borrowers of high credit standing to issue bonds that sometimes had coupons lower than U.S. Treasury bonds of the same maturity. In capital-market theory and practice, that sort of reverse-coupon gap was unthinkable because Treasury bonds were free of default risk and were the benchmark by which all other dollar bonds were measured. But structural market aberrations allowed this situation to develop nevertheless. Foreign investors in U.S. bonds were still subject to withholding tax on interest payments, and that simple factor made many look to eurobonds. Most important, the demand for dollar-denominated instruments was so strong that these investors were willing to overlook the original coupon yield in order to purchase dollar instruments. The combination of the two factors was powerful enough to allow bonds to be floated at yields unthinkable in the U.S. domestic market.

Some high-rated borrowers could thus borrow at a rate lower than the Treasury, and take the proceeds and buy a Treasury bond yielding a marginally higher return, pocketing the difference on a risk-free investment. At the same time, they could borrow funds cheaply and find that almost any investment would yield more than their costs. The basis for defeasances and swaps was laid, but this market peculiarity did not last a particularly long time. By mid–1985, the aberration had disappeared but the economic effects and financial possibilities lingered and became accepted financial practice.

During the last stages of the dollar's strength in 1985, the demand for eurodollar bonds, and the intense borrowing activity of borrowers willing to take advantage of it, created an enormous primary market. In 1985 and 1986, the gross number of eurobonds issued outnumbered the number of new corporate and Yankee issues in the domestic market. Technically, this activity caused the eurobond market to become the largest corporate bond market in the world, a distinction that disappeared during the period of dollar weakness in and after 1987. However, new-issues activity continued brisk, and the eurobond market rivaled the domestic market for new issues. Within twenty years, the market had risen from its fairly humble origins to be a major dollar market in its own right.

During its twenty-odd-year history, the eurodollar market was still perhaps better known for innovation than for any other single quality. It was the tinkering with bond concepts that had brought the market its stature, and it would remain the primary comparison with the domestic market. But innovation did not remain purely a eurobond market phenomenon; it was exported to the United States and became imbedded in the financial innovation of the 1980s. Within ten years, most of the concepts developed in London and elsewhere were taken for granted in the United States and were considered U.S. instruments without regard for their origins.

The floating-rate note was introduced into the domestic capital markets on a large scale after interest rates were effectively deregulated in 1980 and again in 1982. The Depository Institutions Deregulation and Monetary Control Act (DIDMCA) of 1980 and the Depository Institutions Act (Garn–St. Germain Act) of 1982 abolished interest rate ceilings on deposits as well as the amount of interest that could be charged on loans. As a result, banks and other mortgage lenders were able to borrow in floating rate, or adjustable, form and make mortgages on an adjustable basis with the proceeds. Even if the institution did not borrow in security form, the adjustable rate mortgage (ARM) proved more viable than a conventional mortgage because the rate paid on deposits now varied and the revenue streams derived from mortgages could be set according to the costs being paid out on deposit interest. Whether in actual bond form or conceptually, the floating interest rate had finally come of age.

The transition in the capital markets from traditional straight bonds to floating-rate instruments was fairly routine, since many U.S. banks had been borrowing in the eurobond market in floating form for some years. Now, rather than fund their overseas branches, banks were funding domestic assets, regardless of where the money was borrowed. The marketplace was becoming truly "internationalized" in that euromarket instruments and concepts had found their way into the domestic market. As a result, adjustable rate mortgages were offered on a large scale, and by 1986 they had become the most popular form of U.S. mortgage for new homebuyers.[15] While not necessarily a panacea for the U.S. mortgage industry ailments, especially the thrift institutions, floating-rate instruments proved their usefulness in the new deregulated environment—a market similar to that which had spawned these new instruments.

During the decade of deregulation, the U.S. capital market was a net importer of concepts and products from the eurobond market. Zero-coupon bonds, floating-rate notes, perpetuals, bonds that could be extended (extendables), and bonds that could be put back to the borrower at the investor's option (putables) were all euromarket ideas that gained quick, if not long-lasting, acceptance in the domestic market. On the other side of the coin, some U.S. capital market instruments were exported to the euromarket, where they had an impact on European finance. The most notable was the mortgage-backed security, normally issued in the United States by the government-sponsored mortgage assistance agencies. The mortgage-backed idea was used by several investment banks (U.S., British, and others) to float sterling obligations backed by a pool of British mortgages—the borrower in this case was a bank rather than an agency. Through this technique, some banks were able to offer fixed-rate mortgages in Great Britain on a limited basis, a market otherwise known almost exclusively for floating-rate mortgages. But, for the most part, the U.S. domestic market remained a net importer of ideas from the euromarket.

Responding to the budget deficit that had been building since the Economic Recovery Tax Act of 1981, in 1984, Congress relaxed the withholding tax on interest paid to foreign holders of U.S. Treasury bonds. Certain issues of Treasuries, usually new issues, were now exempt from withholding tax if purchased by foreign investors. This event appeared to provide serious competition for the euromarket, stealing a bit of the tax-free thunder that had helped it thrive over the years, but that was not the case. Another U.S. securities regulation in effect since the turn of the decade vitiated the overall benefit that lifting of the tax might have had. All U.S. bonds, regardless of type, were now registered in the name of the beneficial owner. Bearer bonds in the United States had become a thing of the past, but bearer bonds were still the norm in the eurobond market, where registered bonds were almost unheard of. Over the years, international investors had come to appreciate the anonymity of bearer instruments, and therefore many declined to buy U.S. domestic instruments. In effect, one regulation replaced another, and as a result, the euromarket remained an investor's favorite. That popularity translated into greater demand for eurobonds, attracting borrowers of many nationalities.

The eurobond market owed its vitality to legal and regulatory changes in the United States over the years that made offshore investing attractive. At first glance, withholding taxes, fear of capital blockages, or desire to remain anonymous hardly seem sufficient reasons to spawn a new marketplace that would grow large enough to challenge New York as the dominant corporate bond market. Individually, none of those factors was enough, but when combined they formed the raison d'être for the offshore market. The potential loss to U.S. investment banking was enormous. All banks operating in the eurobond market shared the fees on about $150 billion worth of new issues per year. At a 2 percent total fee structure, that amounted to about $3 billion charged by underwriters before calculating their actual profits based upon the selling prices of the bonds. Britain individually gained the most from the investment banking activity by taxing the profits of those securities houses earning profits in London. Between 1960 and 1973, Britain's invisible trade balance more than quadrupled, helping it become the second highest invisible earner in the world by 1971—earning about half of what the United States did through the selling of services.[16]

The new entrepôt market had certainly proved its worth, and U.S. companies nevertheless benefited by borrowing funds in the market at costs that were, in many cases, lower than the domestic market would have allowed. The euromarket as a whole developed because of the rigidity of the U.S. banking system prior to 1980. Even after the domestic system was deregulated, the market continued to thrive because of its ability to adapt to new economic conditions and to experiment with financial techniques not yet known or tried in the United States. Benjamin Strong would have recognized this as a serious loss to the U.S. balance of payments account. It was this sort of business that the Republicans had courted so avidly, and somewhat short-sightedly, in the years prior to the 1929 crash. A significant part of the entrepôt market had successfully moved overseas after 1963. Thus the financial vessel of the American Dream had lost one of its mainstays. But the foreign capital would return in a more beneficial form through portfolio and, more significantly, direct investments.

NOTES

1. Quoted in Charles R. Geisst, *Raising International Capital: International Bond Markets and the European Institutions* (London: Saxon House, 1980), p. 5.

2. For a more detailed explanation, see Charles R. Geisst, *Visionary Capitalism: Financial Markets and the American Dream in the Twentieth Century* (New York: Praeger, 1990), Chap. 3 and 7.

3. J. P. Morgan & Co., *World Financial Markets*, various issues; and Organization for Economic Cooperation and Development, *Financial Market Trends*, various issues. Eurodollars are on a gross basis.

4. The withholding tax was not levied against foreign holders of foreign securities trading in the domestic market. Thus Yankee bond interest and dividends on foreign stocks were exempt when paid to foreign investors.

5. The absence of compulsory withholding tax proved to be a stronger magnet than the lack of disclosure on most eurobonds. Unlike domestic corporate bonds, eurobonds obviously were not registered with the Securities and Exchange Commission, and as a result, their accompanying prospectuses tended to be much shorter. U.S. regulatory authorities were fond of pointing out that eurobonds did not afford as much investor protection as a registered domestic bond. However, as seen in Chapter 3, that perception proved mainly incorrect since stringent U.S. disclosure requirements sometimes proved a disincentive to foreign direct investors in U.S. assets as well as in this case, although for admittedly different reasons.

6. Put in language that was more popular in the 1980s, floating-rate notes were one of the early forms of liability securitization. What they actually represented was the conversion of a bank liability into a security, with all of the added advantages of marketability for investors that a traditional deposit or certificate of deposit could not offer.

7. The West German central bank was able to control issuing activity in the euromarket, where it technically had no official control, by forbidding any euromark bond from ever entering the country for purchase by German investors. The U.S.

authorities never imposed such a ban, only requiring eurodollar bonds to "season" for ninety days before being purchased by U.S. investors.

8. The classic form of a defeasance involves issuing a zero-coupon bond and using the proceeds to purchase a U.S. Treasury zero-coupon bond at a lower price. Thus at maturity the Treasury bond redeems the corporate bond and little, if any, risk is apparent to the borrower. But two problems still remained: that operation assumed that Treasury zeros existed in the first place and could be purchased at a lower price than the zero corporate issue actually raised. First, Treasury zero-coupons were in fact "stripped" bonds whose coupons had been removed by an investment bank technically able to do so. The Treasury did not have the authority to issue an original zero-coupon bond, so intermediaries such as investment banks performed the stripping. The closest that the Treasury actually came to this was the STRIPS program, more formally the Separate Trading of Registered Interest and Principal of Securities program, initiated in 1985. According to the provisions, it designated certain of its own issues for stripping, allowing the holder to create a zero-coupon Treasury bond. Second, zero corporates usually only yielded less than a Treasury zero when the corporate was issued in the eurobond market at a rate admittedly out of line with Treasury yields. The investor actually accepted this state of affairs because he did not have to pay tax on the zero-coupon eurobond. Domestic zero-coupon bonds, Treasuries included, carried a tax liability that could seriously have dampened an investor's enthusiasm for them.

9. See Geisst, *Visionary Capitalism*, especially Chap. 7 on financial innovation, for a more detailed discussion of the uses that these and other instruments had for individual investors.

10. The number of outstanding swaps is difficult to estimate because they are essentially private transactions on the books of their guarantor banks. However, a swap dealers' association was formed in the early 1980s, and is able to estimate the number issued in any given year because of standard procedures used by the organization's members.

11. U.S. banks often operated merchant or investment banking operations in London or other centers by organizing them as Edge Act subsidiaries. The subsidiary usually was owned by a Delaware corporation organized under the Edge Act of 1919, giving the parent bank the right to offer banking facilities to nonresident investors. Through that avenue, commercial banks could underwrite corporate securities in the eurobond market, something they could not do at home because of the provisions of the Banking Act of 1933. For a fuller description see James C. Baker and Gerald Bradford, *American Banks Abroad: Edge Act Companies and Multinational Banking* (New York: Praeger, 1974).

12. On investment banking practices in the market, see Samuel Hayes and Philip Hubbard, *Investment Banking: A Tale of Three Cities* (Cambridge, MA: Harvard Business School Press, 1990).

13. See Geisst, *Visionary Capitalism*, for a brief account of the original case, *U.S. v. Henry Morgan*, in which some U.S. investment banks were charged with price collusion in the formation of underwriting syndicates. The argument mentioned in the text is essentially the same as used by those banks in their defense.

14. See OECD, *Financial Market Trends*, October 1984.

15. The popularity of these mortgages depends upon interest rate conditions. If long-term rates are high, the adjustable is popular because it costs less initially than

conventional mortgages. This type of mortgage was not confined to U.S. homeowners, however. It was the norm for mortgage lending in Great Britain, although the adjustment mechanism and the funding methods were somewhat different.

16. See Brian Griffiths, *Invisible Barriers to Invisible Trade* (London: Macmillan, 1975), pp. 15–18.

6

The Rise and Fall of the Dollar

By the autumn of 1980, the U.S. economy had become a major issue in the presidential election in which Ronald Reagan defeated Jimmy Carter. High interest rates, unemployment, a growing budget deficit, and a recession had created the worst set of economic circumstances since the 1930s. The financial markets had been able to take heart with the appointment of Paul Volcker to the chairmanship of the Federal Reserve Board a year earlier, but the dollar continued depressed as did the stock markets and the bond and money markets. The seams of the financial system were not strong enough to withstand all the pressures, and a new financial being was in the making.

One of the legacies of the Carter administration was the Depository Institutions Deregulation and Monetary Control Act, known as the Monetary Control Act, or DIDMCA. Passed in 1980, this was the first significant legislation affecting the power of the Federal Reserve since the Eccles Act of 1935. As its name implies, the act had two sides, monetary control and deregulation. It gave the Fed greater control over reserve requirements by extending its regulations to all depository institutions, not just to federally chartered commercial banks. At the same time, it provided a timetable for dismantling Regulation Q, that regulatory hangover from 1933 that had kept a limit on the amount of interest paid on savings accounts.[1]

The Monetary Control Act had a significant effect on U.S. and foreign banking, as mentioned in Chapter 5, but it had little direct impact on foreign investors. Its indirect impact was to provide a more conducive investment environment by unshackling the credit markets from interest rate restraints, thus helping contribute to the "internationalization" of the financial markets.

As a result, the 1980s proved to be a watershed decade in terms of foreign investment. Both direct and portfolio investments increased to record amounts. Wide currency fluctuations and high real interest rates had produced phenomena not seen before in U.S. financial history. As inflation reached its twentieth-century peak and interest rates quickly followed, massive demand developed for U.S. portfolio investments, reversing most orthodox notions of what produces favorable investment climates. The question most frequently posed during the 1970s—how to stem the decline of the dollar—was readily answered by 1985: let interest rates rise to combat money inflation, and the high rates of return would lure foreign investors back to the dollar. But that would be difficult, if not impossible, to accomplish if the political climate was not conducive.

One of the major products of the battle to combat inflation was an increase in foreign investment, especially portfolio investment. As has been seen in previous chapters, portfolio investments, particularly stocks, had been the favorite U.S. investment of foreigners for most of the twentieth century, with the exception of the 1970s. Stocks represented the economic boom of the 1920s, the eventual recovery in the 1930s, a safe haven during World War II, and a way to participate in the bull market of the 1950s and 1960s. But when the investment gild came off the lily in the 1970s, direct investments supplanted stocks. During that decade, the only feasible way that foreign companies could participate in American prosperity was by selling goods in the domestic market, and the devalued dollar made that possible. But as the 1980s began, given the uncertain state of the economy, increased foreign direct investment would have been a safe bet but exponential growth in portfolio investments appeared remote at best. It appeared that conditions from the 1970s were continuing and with them the investment patterns established by foreign investors.

Although the Monetary Control Act continued the restraints on bank interest set by Regulation Q, the U.S. capital markets, and especially the bond markets, were somewhat simple when compared to their international counterparts, especially the eurobond market. Innovations such as floating-rate bonds, currency option bonds, and many other financing exotica that had appeared in the euromarket were not known in the domestic market. The withholding tax was still in place, and the markets were slowly being subjected to more regulation rather than less. Within a few years, all U.S. bonds would have to be registered in the name of the beneficial owner, doing away with bearer bonds. The discount that an underwriter could give a client buying a new issue was soon regulated as well, seemingly providing more disincentives for foreign investors. All of these developments were occurring at a time when the other major bond markets were becoming larger and more hospitable to foreign investors. The time did not appear right for an increase in U.S. fixed-income investments.

Of all the poor economic news confronting investors, inflation was probably the most disturbing. Inflation had raised its ugly head before, but not to the level experienced between 1979 and 1981. The annual rate of increase in the consumer price index (all items for all urban consumers) was 11.25 percent between 1978 and 1979, 13.80 percent between 1979 and 1980, and 10.25 percent between 1980 and 1981. Making matters worse was the compounding effect that inflation was having on wages and savings. By the end of 1983, consumer prices had almost tripled from 1967 levels. It was this effect that prompted Congress to pass the Economic Recovery Tax Act in 1981, lowering the tax on capital gains and adjusting tax rates to prevent "bracket creep inflation"—the effect experienced when inflation pushes wage earners into higher tax brackets. As early as 1979, the inflation rate was inviting comparisons with those in Third World countries. Cries of hyperinflation were often heard, although the inflation between 1979 and 1980 proved to be the record and began to subside in the years following.

During the early 1980s, the Federal Reserve attacked inflation by closely monitoring the monetary aggregates, strictly adhering to target ranges for growth in the money supply. It used its full complement of monetary tools, including widespread use of open market operations, to achieve its goals. The operations of the Fed were in addition to the special credit controls imposed by the Carter administration during the early months of 1980, which had a fast but short-lived effect upon the credit markets.[2] Short-term interest rates fell quickly and then rose again after the controls were lifted by the autumn of 1980. The Fed had a problem controlling the money supply, in that some of the financial innovations of the preceding fifteen years were distorting what was considered money. The widespread use of credit cards, checking accounts that paid interest, and money market mutual funds were all challenging the definition of M1 as notes and coin in circulation plus demand deposits. The control of credit soon required that these new instruments be redefined and reclassified.

As the 1970s ended and the new decade began, the regulatory authorities attempted to come to grips with the influence the euromarket was having on the domestic financial system and to compete with it at the same time. In 1978, New York banking authorities sought to recover some of the business and influence that had been lost when the entrepôt market shifted to London by proposing establishment of International Banking Facilities, commonly known as IBFs. These facilities resembled the tax-free enterprise zones that were being established in some states, allowing importation of some foreign goods for eventual sale in the United States or abroad, free of tax. These enterprise zones were used also in some foreign countries under the more common name of free port. New York authorities proposed that banks be allowed to establish IBFs in New York City in order to bring home certain banking activities. The IBFs would be allowed to accept deposits in dollars or other currencies, and make loans to foreign residents, free of local taxes. Reserve requirements and interest-rate ceilings would not apply, either.

The idea required approval by the Federal Reserve, and after lengthy discussion the central bank gave its permission. By late 1981 IBFs began to operate in New York and other locations.

Despite the complexity of the domestic financial system and the rapid changes it was undergoing, foreign investors were not dissuaded but rather were attracted to U.S. investments. Even the Third World debt crisis— begun "officially" when Mexico tottered on the brink of technical default of its external debt in the autumn of 1982—did not deter foreign investors from U.S. securities, especially Treasury bills and bonds. Interest rates fell immediately after announcement that a Mexican default was possible, owing to the Federal Reserve's temporary loosening of interest rates. This gave many international speculators the opportunity to buy Treasury bonds in a "flight to quality" and to benefit by having interest rates fall and bond prices rise. Beginning in 1980, U.S. investments became even more fashionable among foreigners, and they now began buying larger and larger amounts of Treasury securities and, after 1982, a record amount of equities as well. None of the investment motives was new or radical; they followed lines established over the years. The spector of high U.S. inflation prompted many investors to do exactly the opposite of what may have been expected; in the best investment sense, they set out to make a buck.

GROWTH IN PORTFOLIO INVESTMENTS

Overall growth in foreign portfolio investments between 1980 and 1986 was considerable, but could not be attributed to all securities nor did it occur evenly during that period. In 1980, net purchases of U.S. securities by foreigners was $13.2 billion, an increase of $5.7 billion from 1975. The number increased to about $24 billion in 1981 and remained steady until 1984, when it increased to $30 billion. Then in 1985 and 1986, the numbers soared to $74 billion and $86 billion, respectively.[3] While these figures were higher than previously witnessed, they paint only a partial picture of the condition of the financial markets at the time.

In 1980 and 1981, net activity in Treasury bonds and notes accounted for $5 billion and $15 billion of total net amounts. Net activity in corporate bonds accounted for only $3 billion and $3.50 billion, with the balance accounted for by equities. What was unusual about the figures was the historically disproportionate number of Treasury securities in the totals. Between 1972 and 1979, the amount of net Treasury bond investment was about the same proportion of the total as in 1980 and 1981, but the amount of gross trading that occurred was markedly different. For instance, in 1972, gross activity in Treasury issues was $5.4 billion with net activity at $3.3 billion. In 1975, the proportion was $2 billion net on a gross of $16 billion. By 1980, the net of $5 billion was produced by a gross turnover of $97.4

billion.[4] Obviously, investors were no longer content to hold Treasuries for the long-term.

To many investors, heavy trading and price volatility in Treasury bonds was not a familiar trend. But as inflation began to rise, turnover became much more pronounced and the price-yield swings were vast by traditional standards. A ten-year Treasury bond rose from an average yield of 8.86 percent in January 1979 to yield 12.30 percent in November 1980. On a bond bearing a 7.50 percent coupon, that change represented a price fall of almost 30 points—almost 30 percent of what the investor had paid for the bond at new issue. Although the trend between 1979 and 1982 was decidedly in favor of higher yields, the bond market occasionally rallied and short-term speculators were able to record gains found normally only in stock markets, which were assumed until this time to be more volatile than bond markets. One of the periods in which speculators took great delight was when the Credit Control Act was imposed by the Carter administration during the spring of 1980. Bond yields fell almost 3 full percentage points between March and late May, and ninety-one-day Treasury bill yields dropped as astonishing 7.50 percent, from 15 percent to 7.50 percent. After the controls were lifted, yields began to rise again, but the magnitude of the declines gives a clear picture of how volatile prices had become.

The secondary corporate bond market did not experience quite the same swings in prices and yields as did the Treasury market, although new-issue yields did reach historic highs. In this case, the U.S. Treasury paid the price for the efficiency of the secondary market. Most heavy bond trading continued to take place in the Treasury market, where price quotations were more reliable and dealer liquidity was greater than in other market sectors. Thus the Treasury market became the bellwether for the entire marketplace. One of the disturbing trends it indicated was an investor preference for short maturities of Treasury bonds during periods of uncertainty. By 1982, the average maturity of U.S. Treasury debt fell to about four years. Immediately after World War II it had been about ten years. The only other time it had fallen so short was after the OPEC price rise in 1974–75.[5]

The immediate effect of the heavy trading in Treasuries was that the yields quickly came to reflect investor expectations, and that translated into rapidly escalating costs of interest for new issues for the Treasury itself. After about two years of high coupon fixings on new issues, interest became the largest item in the U.S. budget, even exceeding defense spending. That condition persisted until interest rates began to fall back to single digits in 1985 and 1986. But as long as interest rates remained high, foreign activity in Treasuries increased. Gross activity increased in 1981 to $122 billion, continued to $175 billion in 1982, and reached $254 billion in 1983. But by then the astronomical growth pattern had set in. Turnover increased to $450 billion in 1984, went to $967 billion in 1985, and leaped to $2 trillion in 1986. The net activity figures were also impressive but were obviously less. If the 1986

gross sum had also been a net figure, it would have meant that the U.S.
Treasury was almost totally indebted to foreigners in 1986. The net numbers
were about 6 to 7 percent of the gross for most years with the exception of
1986, when foreigners held about $86 billion of the $2 trillion they turned
over.[6]

The phenomenal interest in Treasuries can be attributed to both interest
rates and political factors. In fixed-income terms, Treasury bonds provided
the best real rate of return, when there was one, of any domestic bond that
could be considered liquid. Bond yields did exceed inflation, especially after
1980, and that provided the major incentive for investors. Corporate bonds
proved less attractive, owing to spotty liquidity in the secondary market.
But more important, Treasuries provided for safety from default in a highly
volatile period, representing what is known in the markets as a "flight to
quality." That flight proved to be a good bet after 1982–83, when inflation
began to fall while yields remained stubbornly high for another two years.
In 1984, when yields again rose to almost historic highs before falling, the
real rate of return to investors was about 6 percent, the highest so far during
the twentieth century. That return confirmed the faith that many investors
had several years before about the ability of a "monetarist" Fed to conquer
inflation. Optimists were rewarded with the largest price gains ever in the
bond markets.

Interest rate movements also created massive currency speculation, a
phenomenon not unknown in the markets but perhaps occurring for different
reasons. As the real rate of return began to widen, foreign investors increasingly bought more dollars in order to purchase Treasury and other securities.
As a result, the dollar began its meteoric rise, beginning about the same
time that interest rates peaked in late 1980 and early 1981. Eurodollar deposit
rates touched almost 22 percent in the latter part of 1980, and the domestic
prime rate was also over 20 percent. In contrast, euro–Deutsche mark rates
were about 10 percent, eurosterling were 15 percent, and euroguilders were
about 12 percent. In all cases, the yields on dollar-denominated instruments
were the only ones in the hard-currency countries bearing a real rate of
return. In the midst of the worldwide recession that gripped the United
States and Europe, the dollar began its historic rise.

Political factors also aided the process. After 1980, the Japanese monetary
authorities began to loosen some controls on investing in non-yen-
denominated assets, allowing banks, insurance companies, and other fidu-
ciaries to add to their foreign currency holdings. Given the historically high
savings rate in Japan, many of these institutions were awash with funds and
eager to invest outside Japan. The eurobond market and the U.S. Treasury
market were the main beneficiaries, with Japanese institutions purchasing
most of their corporate holdings in the eurodollar bond market and Treasuries
in the domestic market. The eurobond market was especially useful since
new issues were bearing coupons of over 15 percent and no withholding tax

was applicable. The Treasury market benefited simply because of the instruments it traded were free of default risk. Its other major attraction was the bullet nature of the bonds themselves. Treasury bonds do not bear sinking fund or call provisions; investors could therefore be assured of the high coupon yield for the life of the bond without fear of an early retirement.

As can be seen from the gross and net numbers given, activity in Treasury bonds increased dramatically immediately after interest rates hit their peak in 1980–81. The next substantial rise in Treasury activity came between 1984 and 1985, when gross activity again doubled. In the summer of 1984, the U.S. Treasury announced that the withholding tax on new issues would be eliminated for foreigners; withholding tax on secondary issues would continue as before. That change was designed to help the United States fund its growing budget deficit by luring foreign buying power into the primary market from the secondary market. The change had its most pronounced effect beginning in 1986, when gross activity again doubled. Net activity declined, however. As interest rates declined, more short-term profit taking ensued, and the lure of fast trading profits temporarily overrode the desire to hold Treasury issues for longer than necessary.

The proportion of gross to net activity also illustrates the hedging techniques used by investors. A low ratio suggests that investors are willing to hold the securities—in this case bonds—rather than attempt to sell them for a quick profit. Equally, adequate hedging techniques allow the investor to hold the securities while adjusting his hedge position rather than buying or selling the securities themselves. The activity recorded from 1980 to 1986 suggests that investors did not employ hedging techniques to any great extent. While volume did increase on the futures exchanges during that time, the number of interest-rate futures contracts traded did not match the number of trades in the actual bond, or cash, markets. During periods of interest-rate volatility, institutional investors normally employ active bond management strategies that require frequent buying and selling, or combinations of the two, to achieve their ends. These active management strategies only helped to increase bond market volume in much the same way that FAS 8 had encouraged increased foreign exchange hedging in the spot and forward markets, creating increased volatility in the process.

During the period 1980–86, the largest investors in U.S. Treasury bonds on a gross basis were the British and Japanese. Japanese turnover began modestly in 1980 at $6.6 billion and increased to $572 billion by 1986. The British began with $33 billion in 1980 and increased to $444 billion by 1986. But neither country was a particularly large net investor in Treasury issues. On average, the Japanese and British retained only 1 to 2 percent of the issues they traded in any given year. The largest net investor in Treasuries was West Germany, which kept a much higher proportion (8 to 10 percent) of the issues it traded. The Canadians also remained traders rather than net investors.[7]

Much of the intense interest in Treasury bonds stemmed from the fact that they were noncallable. Interest in corporate bonds also increased dramatically after 1980, and especially after the recession ended in 1982, but the interest was less intense than it was for Treasury bonds. After interest rates began to fall in 1984–85, the corporate bond market witnessed the largest number of calls in its history, as many issues floated with high coupons were retired. High-coupon Treasuries, on the other hand, were able to record significant price gains since their prices fully reflected their yields and noncallable nature. Investor interest in corporate bonds increased for reasons slightly different from those for Treasuries but the net result was the same—significant activity.

As seen in Chapter 5, the mid–1980s were a period of intense activity in the eurodollar bond market. Borrowers were able to achieve a cost of funds that was lower than the cost for coupons in the domestic U.S. corporate bond market. The reason for the coupon dichotomy was currency speculation: as the dollar continued to rise prior to 1985, many investors were willing to purchase eurodollar bonds that bore lower coupons than their domestic U.S. counterparts. In some cases these coupons were actually lower than those on Treasury bonds of similar maturities. Between 1984 and 1986, currency speculation created a market segmentation effect in the eurodollar sector that borrowers rapidly seized upon. As long as international investors were anxious to purchase dollar bonds of quality borrowers, regardless of absolute yield level, borrowers and their investment bankers were more than willing to oblige.

It was this segmentation effect that had created the opportunity for zero-coupon defeasances as well as interest-rate swaps. This relatively short time produced more financial innovation than had been seen in the past fifty years. In a period of high interest rates and intense currency speculation, both the primary and the secondary sides of the bond markets fared well. The same could not be said of the U.S. equity market, however. Stock investors had to wait for the recession to end before realizing substantial gains.

Gross activity in equities by foreigners increased beginning in 1983. Between 1980 and 1982, the activity remained fairly constant at about $75–$79 billion. Then in 1983 it increased to $134 billion, and by 1986 increased again to $277 billion. This increase in activity followed the international trend for the same period. Foreign activity in stocks worldwide was approximately $400 billion in 1985 and increased to $750 billion in 1986. Thus approximately 37 percent of all international equity trading in 1986 was in U.S. equities.[8] Although the growth in the stock markets between 1982 and 1987 was the greatest since the bull market of the Eisenhower years, the U.S. stock market was not necessarily best in terms of return for Japanese or German investors—nor was it the best performing stock market of the period.

After the recession ended in 1982, growth in the market indices was certainly impressive in purely domestic terms. The average earnings per share of the 500 composite stocks that make up Standard & Poor's index increased from $12.64 in 1982 to $16.64 in 1984, before declining to about $14.50 in 1986. Dividends increased from $6.87 to $8.28 per share and price-earnings ratios increased from 11.31 to 17.54.[9] On a percentage return basis, common stocks registered some of their highest gains since the early Roosevelt and again the Eisenhower years, culminating in 1985 with a gain of 32 percent. But despite these gains, bonds provided stiff competition by registering their highest gains in the twentieth century. For example, between 1982 and 1986, long-term government bonds constantly registered gains of 24 to 40 percent on a total return basis, outperforming the stock market in several of those intervening years.[10]

The combined rally acted as a magnet for foreign capital. By 1986, 21.5 percent of net equity activity was attributed to foreigners, as compared to 28 percent of Treasury bonds and 50 percent for corporate bonds (including eurobonds). In 1986, foreign holdings of U.S. stocks were estimated at $163 billion, representing about 7.4 percent of the market value of all NYSE-listed shares.[11] Foreign stock holdings on this basis had reached their twentieth-century records. But on a total return basis, including currency movements, the U.S. markets lagged behind several other major markets in vying for foreign investment funds.

Calculating stock market returns on a currency basis, the U.S. markets did not perform as well as the German, Japanese, and British stock markets in the same period. For a yen investor, 1982 was the only year that the U.S. markets outperformed the German, British, or domestic Japanese markets. After 1982, the United States fell behind in most years. The same is true for Deutsche mark–based investors; 1982 again was a banner year for the U.S. stock markets. On an adjusted basis, some of the smaller stock markets had gains far in excess of the performance data for the major stock markets in the major currencies, but their relatively small economies or problems with exchange controls and local regulations made investing in them a marginal affair for most major investors.[12]

Many U.S. investment houses increased their overseas operations during the 1980s, and that expansion helped contribute to the increase in numbers of foreign investors in U.S. equities. The number of overseas sales offices doubled within a decade, and by 1986 some 280 sales offices of major brokerage houses existed abroad. The same phenomenon did not occur in reverse, however. Foreign investment sales offices were virtually unknown in the United States. The average U.S. investor has the smallest proportion of his portfolio holdings in foreign securities of any investor in the hard-currency countries. The brokerage houses quickly saw the advantage of selling a bit of the American Dream to foreigners by moving to their locales. Foreigners, on the other hand, were never able to achieve a similar result by selling directly to U.S. investors.[13] Those foreign banks and brokers that opened investment banking facilities in New York did so in order to compete in the New York markets more than to represent their domestic retail clients.

DIRECT INVESTMENTS TO 1986

Somewhat surprisingly, the amount of portfolio investments finding their way into the U.S. markets did not have a deleterious effect on direct foreign investments during the 1980–86 period. The major development was the increase in direct investment in the United States. In 1980, total foreign investment in the United States was $68.3 billion, while U.S. direct investment abroad totaled $215 billion. Over the next nine years, foreign investment in the country increased to $400 billion while U.S. investment abroad increased to $373 billion. Throughout the decade, British direct investments remained the most valuable, followed by the Dutch, Japanese, and Canadian. Only in 1988 did the Japanese displace the Dutch in second place. The 1980s were the Japanese decade nevertheless, since investment from Japan grew at the greatest rate of any major investing country. In 1980, Japanese direct investment stood at $4.26 billion; by 1989 it had reached $70 billion.[14]

On a valuation basis, much of the increased value in foreign investments was due to retained earnings left in the United States by foreign companies rather than being repatriated. As the dollar rose in value, more companies left their surplus behind in the hope that the dollar's rise would continue to benefit them. Although it can be difficult to gauge the precise effect of the retained earnings in all cases, they nevertheless did contribute to the totals and also illustrated that even direct investors behave as portfolio investors by seeking currency appreciation whenever the opportunity presents itself.

The increased figures can be somewhat misleading if understood solely in the context of the attractiveness of U.S. investments. In the case of Japan, the increase in investments also had strong political overtones. The friction between the United States and Japan that developed during the previous two decades continued well into the 1980s. In 1980, U.S. concerns were voiced over the number of Japanese-made automobiles sold in the country, and the United States imposed relatively high import duties on Japanese-made pickup trucks. Within a year, the Japanese began voluntary export quotas to the United States on compact autos. This voluntary restriction was initially to last until 1984. In 1983, import surcharges were placed on Japanese-made motorcycles as well.

Because of these export restrictions, voluntary and otherwise, Japanese manufacturers acted quickly to open more facilities in the United States in order to avoid further tensions. Japanese goods manufactured in the United States would be considered American-made for balance of payments purposes, and would not be included in restrictions placed on imports. At the same time Japanese product development aimed at circumventing restrictions by developing products that did not fall within the ambit of quotas or restrictions. One example was the development of larger cars for export, therefore outside the realm of the voluntary restraints program, extended until 1985 after it expired in 1984.

During the same period, the U.S. trade imbalance moved into sharp deficit, exacerbating trade relations with Japan especially. From about $25 billion in 1980, the deficit widened to about $125 billion in 1985. The deficit with Japan accounted for the largest portion, and was the primary cause of the trade friction. From the end of 1972 to 1985, U.S. imports from Japan increased almost ten times while U.S. exports to Japan barely tripled. This imbalance helped raise talks of even more barriers placed before a greater variety of Japanese goods as well as led to greater U.S. pressure on Japan to open its domestic markets to U.S. goods. But despite political and xenophobic arguments to the contrary, the imbalance with Japan could be traced to economic trends, one of which was the exchange rate between the two countries. Between 1980 and 1985, the yen had depreciated by almost 30 percent against the dollar, before recovering some ground toward the end of 1985. That dollar appreciation made Japanese goods cheaper in the United States, and when combined with widespread consumer concerns about the quality of U.S. goods, it led to an influx of Japanese goods.

On the other side of the coin, the exchange rate hurt the U.S. exports. The dollar's appreciation against the yen was somewhat more than its appreciation against other hard currencies. As a result, the cost of U.S. goods rose relative to Japanese-produced goods, even more relative to the other goods that competed in the Japanese market.[15] The exchange rate regime became the major stumbling block to improved trade relations between the two countries.

After the dollar's decline, which began in the late winter of 1985 and continued through the Plaza Agreement of later that year, the competitiveness of U.S. goods in the international marketplace began to increase. From 1980 to 1985, the price of foreign-manufactured goods fell about 5 percent a year when measured in dollar terms, making the goods attractive to U.S. consumers. But in 1986, U.S. prices fell 17 percent per year on average against foreign competition, allowing the United States to also recapture some of its lost trade advantage.[16] The decline of the dollar, given impetus by the concerted actions of the Group of Seven, helped shift the tide and reverse the effects of the early part of the 1980s.

Following the high inflation at the beginning of the decade, wage costs in the United States began to subside, proving to be a lure for foreign manufacturers seeking to set up shop in the country. U.S. wage growth remained significantly below that registered abroad. During the 1980–87 period, hourly wage compensation rates for manufacturing employees grew about 5.7 percent on average, as compared to about 8 percent for other foreign industrialized countries. This was similar to a trend in the early and mid–1970s that attracted many direct investors after the breakdown of Bretton Woods, as noted in Chapter 4. Capital costs were also cheaper in the United States, based upon the real rate of interest, which had dropped from historically high levels to equal other foreign levels by 1987.[17]

In the period 1972–1989, the dollar came full circle and then declined again, prompting foreign investment and subsequently protecting it by making it too expensive to liquidate depreciated dollar assets. This was true of both direct and portfolio investments. The period of exceptional dollar strength between 1981 and 1985 had hurt the United States trade balance while significantly strengthening others—those of Germany and Japan most notably. In terms of national accounting, this shift obviously hurt the U.S. trade figures but nevertheless benefited the United States. In addition to helping increase foreign investment, direct investments also helped influence competitiveness and product quality.

In December 1981, the Financial Accounting Standards Board (FASB) adopted an accounting change, replacing FAS 8, the older method of accounting for foreign exchange gains and losses, which had been used since October 1975. The new method valued all assets and liabilities of a multinational company located overseas in current terms. FAS 8 had used the monetary-nonmonetary method in valuations, valuing monetary items at current spot rates and noncurrent items at the rate in effect when they were acquired. While a variant of an older current-noncurrent approach, FAS 8 had been dubbed the temporal method, and it had required gains and losses to be taken to the parent company's income statement on a quarterly basis. After 1976, when the dollar was fluctuating on the foreign exchange markets, this method caused wide variations on the income statements and earnings of many multinationals. As a result, FAS 8 was widely disliked by many corporate treasurers and caused many companies to spend time and money on hedging techniques not required under the earlier current-noncurrent method. The latter allowed firms to set aside reserves against translation losses. Gains for a year could then be set off against losses before reporting foreign exchange gains or losses for the year. The new FAS 52 standard employed a variation of the older method by allowing translation gains or losses to be listed on a separate line of a company's balance sheet under shareholders' equity. When the item was eventually realized it was then to be taken to the income statement for the year.

During the ten-year period 1975–85, the U.S. economy experienced some structural changes that will be debated for years to come. The shift to a service economy had begun, whereby more new investment and employment were created in service industries than in manufacturing or farming. That gave rise to different financing needs that had both an effect on and were affected by the financial markets. At the same time, U.S. industrial productivity declined, and there were concerns about the quality of many U.S.-made products, especially in comparison to increased imports from Japan. Clearly, the rise and subsequent fall of the dollar by the mid–1980s had a profound effect on the financial markets, on production, and on quality control.

Comparisons of U.S. manufacturing labor productivity between 1974 and 1982 illustrate that both U.S. and Japanese rates of annual growth remained the same, with the Japanese growing at about 5.5 percent rate as compared to about 1.5 percent in the United States. West Germany suffered a decline during the same period. Equally, manufacturing productivity grew about 10 percent for the entire period in the United States as compared to about 67 percent in Japan and about 40 percent in Germany. When combined with higher unit labor costs for the United States in the latter 1970s, it was apparent that U.S. productivity was waning.[18]

With manufacturing productivity falling and the dollar rising sharply after late 1981, consumers were in a good position to purchase increasing numbers of foreign-made manufactured goods. The overall trend was combined with a generally low opinion of U.S. manufactured goods. Surveys taken in the early 1980s revealed that U.S. consumers were not confident about the quality of domestic consumer durables and automobiles. In 1973, some 12 percent of consumers questioned felt that Japanese cars were of better quality than their U.S. counterparts. Ten years later, the figure had increased to 40 percent.[19] The Japanese obsession with quality and quality control had developed exponentially since the 1960s, when the United States was complaining about the cheap textile imports from Japan and their relatively shoddy quality.

Those perceptions plus the strength of the dollar enabled consumers to vote with their pocketbooks and buy increasing numbers of European and Japanese imports. At the same time, many smokestack industries fell on hard times as companies found that foreign steel products were cheaper than American-made products. A similar trend had been seen in Great Britain about ten years before, inviting comparisons of both countries as declining industrial powers. The net effect of these trends could be seen in the mounting merchandise trade deficit, which reached an estimated $150 billion in 1985.

All of these economic consequences of the expensive dollar finally prompted central bank intervention after March 1985, designed to bring about a depreciation. The Plaza agreement, reached in New York in the autumn of the same year, officially acknowledged the need to bring the dollar down further, and the currency continued its fall to the point where, by the end of year 1988, it had given up most of its gains of 1981–85. The merchandise trade deficit persisted until 1990, when it started to diminish. The results for the economy were marked but did not occur immediately.

The dollar's strength had reduced farm exports to a fraction of their former levels, in turn forcing many bankruptcies in the agricultural sector and putting severe strain, *inter alia*, upon the Farm Credit System.[20]

Once the dollar had fallen, a lag effect took its tool on many manufacturers and financial institutions. However, U.S. competitiveness and productivity began to rise again following 1985, as the weaker dollar reduced the consumer penchant for foreign manufactured goods and prompted exports, albeit slowly. Between 1972 and 1990, the American Dream had undergone one of its fastest rewakenings as the economy had substantially changed. But one fact remained in the post–Bretton Woods era that was markedly different from anything preceding it: the markets and the economy had entered a new stage of volatility and uncertainty unlike anything experienced before, with the possible exception of the Depression years.

Productivity, efficiency, and capital investment all increased after the dollar's decline. Perceptions about the quality of U.S. manufactured goods remained low, although improvements in quality and reliability were made during the latter half of the 1980s. Foreign direct investment continued, however, even after the dollar's depreciation, as foreign companies continued to expand manufacturing and banking activities especially. The growing "internationalization," or globalization, of the world's major economies dictated that investment decisions be made as much on the basis of marketing and manufacturing potential as for foreign exchange considerations, especially since the foreign exchange market had become so volatile. That is not to suggest that foreign exchange played a lesser role in investment decisions. In 1985, sterling fell to its historic low against the dollar—$1.07. Between 1984 and 1985, British direct investment in the United States rose by about 10 percent. The following year, 1985–86, when the pound began to rise, investment increased by 20 percent. While currency considerations remained the primary motivation for investing abroad, the size of the U.S. market plus consumer taste for foreign-made goods suggested that foreign investment would continue even during less than optimal exchange conditions.

The Yankee bond market and the eurobond market provided much of the funds needed for these investments in the United States. In the absence of capital controls after 1973, the entrepôt market was again working at full throttle, especially in 1986, when the eurobond market had its record year for new issues. Many of the dollars raised abroad found their way back to the United States and into domestic capital investments. It is difficult to determine the precise amount raised by foreigners and invested in the United States during the boom bond market and investment years of the mid–1980s, although the dollar's behavior proved crucial. As noted earlier, a strong dollar ordinarily deters foreign investors unless financing is easily available at the same time. The new-issues market for eurodollar bonds flourished during the early and mid–1980s. As it became apparent that the dollar would eventually depreciate in the face of the growing U.S. merchandise trade deficit, its relatively high value at the time made capital acquisition expensive but acquisition via dollar financing viable. When the dollar depreciated to its 1980 level, more direct investment was engendered and dollar bond borrowing retreated after 1986. Direct foreign investment in the United States was able to benefit from either side of the phenomenon, and new investments continued apace for the rest of the decade.

Despite the ever-increasing amount of new money finding its way into U.S. markets, the actual economic impact of the direct investment was not as significant as might have been thought. In 1980, the $68.4 billion invested directly in the country generated less than 3 percent of nonbank employment, less than 1 percent of U.S. property holdings, and about 9 percent of total assets.[21] The furor in the 1970s, set off especially by the increases in Japanese investments in manufacturing and property, did not produce the controls feared by many. If the Japanese element is subtracted from the 1980 total (less $4.2 billion) the xenophobic fears are based more on myth than reality. In 1980, more than 50 percent of total foreign direct investment was still held by the British, Dutch, and Canadians.

The influence of foreign investments was given official, but unheralded, acknowledgment in the mid–1980s, when the Federal Reserve allowed several foreign securities dealers to become primary dealers in the Treasury bill and bond markets. Several prominent British, Japanese, and Swiss firms promptly applied for the official designation and began to participate in auctions along with their U.S. counterparts. Being designated a primary dealer also meant that the Fed would use those dealers' facilities in performing open-market operations as a part of its monetary policy. Admitting the foreign dealers was more than an acknowledgment of their financial prowess, however. In the case of the Japanese firms in particular, the intent was to pressure the Japanese government to admitting more U.S. securities firms into the Japanese financial markets, where domestic practices tended to discriminate against foreign brokers and dealers.

THE 1987 MARKET BREAK AND BEYOND

The events leading to and immediately following the stock market's precipitous fall in October 1987 illustrate both the sensitiveness of the world's stock markets in the 1980s and the impact that flows of hot money can have on domestic economies. Rather than use the term *market crash*, the presidential commission that studied the collapse coined the term *market break* to denote a temporary stoppage in the market's usual functions. This time the market's performance did not lead to bank failures or have a domino effect on the economy.

Viewed in purely mechanical terms, the market break showed great similarities with the 1929 event. After the initial round of price falls, many stocks continued to drop in price because of forced margin selling since many investors were not able to meet maintenance margin calls. That squeeze on investor liquidity eventually caused a drop in New York real estate prices and led to serious cost-cutting measures at many brokerage and investment houses, leaving the securities industry smaller. The Federal Reserve acted quickly on October 19, when the Dow Jones Industrial Average declined by 500 points, and added liquidity to the banking system to bolster the banks against any demand for funds.

Unlike the 1929 crash, however, the market break was much more of an international event than any market disturbance before it. Since the end of the 1981–82 recession, foreign investors had been integrally involved in the market's rise to its record of 2725 points prior to the October break. Because of their influence, the events cannot be viewed in a purely domestic context. As noted earlier, foreign interest in U.S. equities had increased each year since 1981, and represented a greater percentage of share ownership than at any time in the past. Since international equity diversification, especially among European investors, was a much greater percentage of resident financial holdings in Britain, West Germany, and the Netherlands than it was in the United States, and since many of those funds were invested in the U.S. stock markets, any negative interpretation of U.S. or international financial statistics by fund managers in those countries was bound to have a negative impact on the market indices.[22]

One of the major contributory factors to the market break was a fear of rising interest rates that was developing in the United States and Europe. U.S. interest rates had risen since the summer of 1987, as had those in Britain, Canada, France, and Italy; rates in West Germany and Japan had remained stable throughout much of the year. Between June and October, the prime rate had risen 0.5 percent while commercial paper rates increased by a similar amount. The most pronounced changes occurred in Treasury securities, with Treasury bills increasing about 1 percent and medium-term Treasury bonds rising by the same amount. In the bond market especially, the rise was most pronounced. Yields on thirty-year Treasury bonds had increased from a 1980s low of 7.25 percent in 1986 to about 9.60 percent prior to the market break. The anomaly was that these changes were occurring while the stock market indices were reaching new heights.

A fundamental indicator of the market's health was the amount of money loaned on margin to stock investors. Between January and September 1987, the amount of call, or margin, loans outstanding increased from $35 billion to $44 billion—an increase larger than that of the previous year.[23] The margin loan rate charged by brokers to their clients is based on the prime rate and also increased during that period. Since it became apparent that U.S. interest rates were rising, raising the cost of carry stocks bought or sold on margin, the rise in some—but certainly not all—foreign interest rates suggested that relatively low interest rates were gone and selling pressure developed in the markets. In essence, the direct foreign influence on the market break was more psychological than real.

There was a real fear centered on interest rates, but in this case it was the cost of debt for many companies that worried investors. After the recession ended in 1982, much of the merger and acquisition (M&A) activity was financed in part with original-issue discount bonds, or junk bonds. The attractiveness of junk bonds from the borrowing company's point of view was their tax advantage: interest was tax deductible, as it was on any corporate interest payment, regardless of the creditworthiness of the company. This deduction was preserved in the Tax Reform Act of 1986, which otherwise made drastic changes in both corporate and personal income taxes. But in the months preceding October 1987, the House Ways and Means Committee studied the deduction as it applied to companies with weak balance sheets, incurred either before or after junk-bond borrowing. The committee, as did the Federal Reserve itself, studied the matter in order to respond to criticism that the tax deduction was a government subsidy for borrowing in order to finance an acquisition. On another level, it was argued that when the Federal Reserve allowed massive borrowings for junk financings, especially at banks rather than in the bond market, it was effectively monetizing corporate takeovers in the face of its otherwise restrictive monetary policy. But regardless of how the trend was interpreted, fear that Congress would remove the deductibility of interest on mergers and acquisitions, thereby substantially weakening already weak companies, caused many investors to sell stocks of companies that were—or were rumored to be—involved in M&A activities. That selling was also characteristic of many foreign speculators, who were closely involved with many deals in the market. The suggestion that the market for junk financings might dry up caused much selling that helped precipitate the market break.

Once equity prices began to fall, all of the world's stock markets reacted negatively. The percentage change in stock market prices ranged from a fall of almost 60 percent in Australia and Hong Kong to about 12 percent in Japan and Denmark. The U.S., British, Canadian, and West German stock markets fell about 22 percent on average. No single economic reason adequately describes the price reactions across the board. Estimates of the losses vary considerably but, on average, about $1 to $1.5 trillion was lost in all the markets combined, on paper or in real terms. In examining the price falls after the fact, several points have become clear concerning the transmission of price movements. In general, it appears that when one market experiences volatility others quickly experience the same. In short, a "herd instinct" transcends individual markets and spreads selling panic to all.[24]

Mass market psychologies require their own transmission mechanisms in order to spread. In the Anglophone economies, the mechanisms had been in place for decades and had been seen before, if not in such a pronounced manner. Even after British regulation passed in 1986—the inelegantly named "Big Bang"—overhauled the British stock market and its trading mechanisms, many U.K. stocks were traded in New York to avoid local U.K. securities taxes and take advantage of the economies of scale that London was unable to offer. As a result, some of the British secondary turnover originated in New York and panic spread quickly between the two markets as a result. Equally, some U.S. secondary stocks traded in London through multiple listings, and erratic price movements in one market affected the other in turn.

On the new-issue, or primary, side, the effects were also felt. Some large international issues being sold in more than one market simultaneously (euroequity issues) were in syndication at the time, and the deteriorating prices of existing secondary issues were immediately felt on the underwriters' books. Since the syndicates were international, many investment bankers felt the brunt of the U.S. market drop and reacted quickly to cut losses. Their reaction spilled into other markets.

In the period immediately preceding the October market break, foreign portfolio investments had increased across the board. Nonresident transactions in U.S. equities (gross purchases and sales) rose from $159 billion in 1985 to $277 billion in 1986. In the nine months preceding the break, volume had reached $360 billion. Similar increases were seen in the Canadian, German, and Japanese markets.[25] Rapid selling certainly followed, but whether it was enough to produce a genuine market crash of international proportions is doubtful. The question is: Were the transmission mechanisms large or adequate enough to cause a widespread price rout, or did they simply contribute to the process in a meaningful but not material way?

Regardless of the mechanisms involved, the reaction of foreign investors to U.S. equities was clear. In the fourth quarter of 1987, gross activity in equities continued at the record pace set in the first nine months but foreigners became sellers on a net basis. Gross activity amounted to $122 billion but net sales totaled $7.25 billion. The largest sellers were the British, accounting for some $5 billion alone. The Swiss followed with $2 billion. Canadians remained net buyers with $533 million. The Japanese equally were net buyers, accounting for $1.85 billion in purchases. But not all of the sales meant that the funds left the United States. During the fourth quarter, the British were net buyers of U.S. Treasury bonds. Of the $3.9 billion they purchased in 1987, $3.7 billion were in the fourth quarter alone. The Japanese were net sellers of Treasury bonds during the same three-month period along with the Swiss.[26]

After the market break, the traditional flight to quality began, spilling over into the first quarter of the following year. Between January and the end of March 1988, net purchases of U.S. Treasury bonds exceeded those in all of the preceding year. Gross activity in equities declined and foreigners were net sellers for the quarter. The second quarter produced much the same results. Gross activity in equities was almost identical to the first quarter

($96 billion) and net purchases managed a mild gain of $588 million. A trend that had begun immediately after the market break continued and was becoming more obvious by early 1989. Japanese interest in U.S. equities rose substantially, almost matching and, in some cases, exceeding European gross activity for the first time.[27] This occurred at the same time that Japanese investment in Treasury bonds was also increasing, along with direct investment.

Much of the Japanese interest in U.S. equities can be attributed to the relative values on the Tokyo stock market at the time. The Japanese market indices were trading at historic high levels and the average price-earnings ratio of Japanese stocks was several times that of U.S. shares. As a result, many U.S. stocks appeared inexpensive to Japanese investors. British investors, on the other hand, were more sensitive to the severe price drops in the U.S. markets. Not having a large trade balance with the United States, and therefore more sensitive to market movements, they instead liquidated in favor of either Treasury bonds or repatriation of their funds.

While portfolio investments did eventually increase after the market break, the original market recovery did so without the help of the usual foreign investors. Although the New York Stock Exchange had taken precautionary measures against a repeat of October 1987 by initiating a "circuit breaker" on equities trading, foreign interest was slow to return. The circuit breaker provided for a halt in trading if the market fell by more than 250 points in a trading day, and provided further stoppages if a market decline should continue. Nevertheless, overseas equity market returns, on a cumulative basis, were greater than U.S. returns between October 1987 and the middle of 1989. It was not until mid–1989 that foreign investors began to return, investing $4.5 billion in the second quarter of the year.[28]

The decline of the dollar continued after the Plaza agreement reached by the Group of Seven (G7) in the autumn of 1985, and continued through the Louvre accords reached in Paris in the winter of 1987. The Plaza agreements called for concerted efforts by the Group of Seven members to bring about a depreciation of the dollar. This would be accomplished mainly by member central banks selling dollars in favor of their own or other currencies. In that respect, they were successful. Between 1985 and 1986, the effective exchange rate of the dollar, as measured against currencies of fifteen other industrial countries, fell by 16.5 percent. By the end of 1987, it had fallen another 11 percent, and by the end of 1989 the total depreciation measured almost 29 percent. The currency that gained the most during the same time was the yen, about 48 percent.[29]

Once the dollar had fallen from its previous heights, the intent of the G7 was to agree on a set of economic indicators that all its members could monitor to achieve some standardization in their intervention efforts. Once an agreed level of currency exchange rates could be found, the members would adopt economic policy changes in order to support it. But the general policy did not work particularly well. The yen found additional support in the market after the Louvre conference and increased in value against the dollar despite the desires of the Federal Reserve and the Bank of Japan. Some of the yen's strongest gains against the dollar came in the months immediately following Louvre. As a result, the dollar decline continued and the major currencies were still floating in an exchange-rate environment characterized by volatility and the lack of coherent or coordinated policies by the central banks most integrally involved.

The currency market in October 1987 was anything but stable, and fears of a vacillating dollar, plus the interest-rate fears accompanying them, helped create the conditions that caused the market break. Some of those fears were based on interest-rate volatility: would the Federal Reserve or other central banks have to raise interest rates with currency considerations in mind? If it did, what would be the implications for the credit markets as a whole? Those questions were never sufficiently answered, and the stock market began its October decline. In those terms, the market break was the most notable example of financial "internationalization," or integration, since the demise of the Bretton Woods system fifteen years before.

The 1980s ended on a more traditional note than had been seen in several years. In 1989, net purchases of U.S. equities rose to $10.1 billion. Of that amount, $4.5 billion came from the United Kingdom and $3.3 billion from Japan. The usual European investors—the Germans and Swiss—were net sellers along with the Canadians. Both the Japanese and the British feared domestic interest-rate rises and increasing domestic economic problems, and they continued to diversify as a result. However, the Japanese amount invested was overshadowed by the amounts that Japanese investors were committing to European markets in anticipation of European economic integration in 1992. In 1987, 48 percent of Japanese net purchases of foreign securities were made in the European Community; by mid–1989 the amount had risen to over 67 percent.[30]

The deregulation of the financial system that began with the Monetary Control Act in 1980 received further impetus from the Garn–St. Germain Depository Institutions Act of 1982. Deposit rates at financial institutions were now effectively deregulated, and depository institutions were given more latitude in booking assets. The new financial environment had international repercussions as well. U.S. financial markets had a profound effect on foreign financial markets. The British deregulation of financial markets in 1986 resulted in a new stock exchange structure and procedures that owed much to the American system. Negotiated commissions on stock transactions were introduced; an automated over-the-counter style system replaced the floor procedures of the London Stock Exchange; and a dual-capacity trading system, fashioned after the U.S. specialist system, replaced the older single-capacity system. Better investor-protection rules were also introduced in Britain and the regulatory system was enhanced to correct trading abuses.

On the domestic side, the international effect on U.S. financial institutions was more subtle but still quite important. The number of foreign banks practicing in the United States continued to increase, and many of those banks brought with them financial innovations from their home countries or the euromarket. The floating, or adjustable, interest rate product and the swap concept were but two examples. These new practices and products gave U.S. domestic banks more flexibility. But more important, the idea of universal banking played a major role in fashioning the thinking of U.S. commercial bankers and policymakers. A universal bank is one that performs commercial and investment banking under the same roof without the constraints of regulatory legislations such as the Glass-Steagall Act. The best examples of financial systems practicing universal banking were West Germany and Switzerland. Banks in those countries had the opportunity to both make short-term loans and operate in the long-term market by underwriting securities for customers. In addition to exerting financial power through both capacities, these banks had the advantage of an additional profit center, something U.S. banks did not enjoy.[31]

Domestic commercial banks had long been advocates of universal banking, since they saw it as a natural function of commercial banks. Investment banks naturally took the opposite view, regarding commercial bank intrusions into their government-granted monopoly as unwarranted. While commercial banks had made some progress in returning to the investment banking practices that the 1933 banking legislation had caused them to relinquish, the banking and thrift crisis of the late 1980s and early 1990s led to legislation that would again integrate the two banking industries. Arguing that a restructuring of the banking system was in the best interests of the economy, the Bush administration announced proposals in the spring of 1991 aimed at effectively abolishing the Glass-Steagall Act and the McFadden Act. The proposals made by Treasury Secretary Nicholas Brady called for an end to geographic restrictions on commercial banks, the reintroduction of commercial banks to the securities underwriting business, and the ability of nonbank companies to buy commercial banks if desired. Clearly, the proposals aimed to create a U.S. financial system more akin to the European.

The entrepôt idea had received a boost in 1990 and again in 1991, when the Securities and Exchange Commission changed its rules concerning the amount of information that must be disclosed by a foreign company when it sells new securities in the United States. The relaxation of disclosure rules affected both bonds and stocks. In the former case, the new SEC rule (144A) made it easier for foreign companies to issue private placements in the United States. Traditionally, private placements were securities not registered with the SEC, usually sold to a handful of private institutional investors. The move was intended to draw back some of capital-raising business that had been lost to the euromarket in the past fifteen years.

In the case of stocks, the SEC relaxed its disclosure requirements for foreign companies if the stock of which was traded on U.S. stock exchanges through American Depository Receipts, or ADRs. These receipts allowed U.S. investors to hold a foreign stock without directly incurring a foreign exchange risk. Investors paid for the stock in dollars. The dollars actually purchased an ADR, a receipt that gave the holder the right to the specified number of foreign shares. The receipts traded on the exchanges alongside U.S. stocks and were subject to normal disclosure rules. If a foreign company subsequently wanted to raise more equity capital, it had to provide financial disclosure, as any other listed company. As the number of U.S. investors buying foreign shares grew in the 1980s, some new foreign issues, particularly those involving takeovers, were raised abroad and could not be subscribed to by domestic investors because the foreign firms found the listing process in the United States too difficult and time-consuming. The SEC estimated that, in 1990, Americans holding foreign stocks were excluded from more than eighty-five offerings in which they might otherwise have participated.[32]

The most significant fact to emerge from the SEC decisions was the change in disclosure rules to suit foreigners, citing the U.S. investor as the beneficiary. While the benefits and shortcomings of the rulings may not be evident for some time, it is apparent that the SEC change of heart was aimed at bringing more foreign securities business back to the United States by requiring no more information than those companies would provide to their own securities authorities. The move proved successful within a short time. In 1983, 585 stocks were represented by ADRs on the U.S. stock markets; by 1990 the number had risen to 836. More important, many of the foreign companies having ADRs outstanding planned to raise more capital via the receipts and use the funds to make acquisitions in the United States.[33] When this was combined with the eased withholding tax on foreign investors for new issues of Treasury bonds six years before, it was clear that various U.S. regulatory bodies were lessening the stringent requirements that had proved a disincentive for foreign investment.

As the 1980s came to a close, increasing direct foreign investment began to account for a larger percentage holding of U.S. assets. The political pressures brought on by these noticeable changes resulted in a change by the Commerce Department regarding the methods by which it valued foreign holdings in the United States, as well as U.S. holdings overseas. Nevertheless, the results using different valuations could vary materially. Foreign direct investment in the United States, measured by historical costs, was $403.7 billion in 1990 while U.S. direct investment abroad was valued at $421.6 billion using the same method. This continued the trend seen earlier whereby the two figures began to vacillate marginally from year to year. However, the massive overseas investment advantage once enjoyed by the United States had disappeared.

If foreign direct investments in the United States were measured by current methods, the numbers would be larger. On a current-cost basis, they were valued at almost $466 billion; on a stock-market value basis they were $530.4 billion.[34] The newer methods can not be applied to U.S. holdings overseas because some countries lack adequate pricing mechanisms. However, it could be assumed that the value of U.S. direct investment abroad was substantially more in 1990 than direct investments in the United States because of the longstanding nature of some of those investments, as mentioned in the Introduction. Statistically, this change in valuation methods could, therefore, produce substantially different results and could lead to a reevaluation of the assumption that the United States had become the world's greatest debtor nation for the second time in the century.

Of equal, but less noticed, importance is the amount of portfolio investment by foreigners, especially in U.S. Treasury securities. In the 1980s, an increasing amount of Treasury debt was purchased by foreigners, especially at new-issue auctions. The continuing presence was acknowledged by the Federal Reserve when it admitted several foreign securities houses to its list of recognized primary dealers. By the end of 1990, foreign holdings of Treasury securities were about $135 billion, representing about 10 percent of the total amount outstanding. At the same time, foreign holdings of stocks totaled about $261 billion, while holdings of corporate and agency bonds amounted to $229 billion.[35] The stock figures showed an increase of about 60 percent over the previous five years, while the corporate and agency bond numbers rose about four times over their 1986 levels. Treasury holdings also gained about four times over the 1986 figures, indicating the continuing preference for fixed-income investments.

British, Dutch, and Canadian investors held 54 percent of all foreign direct investments, although the Japanese portion rose rapidly to 16 percent of the total, from 4 percent in 1980. Total (nonbank) employment provided by foreign direct investment amounted to approximately 4.1 percent of the workforce, representing about 14.7 percent of total business assets. Firms owned or controlled by foreign companies generated $853 billion in sales, with manufacturing accounting for $258 billion of the total and wholesale trade $271 billion. The net income of the foreign-owned affiliates was $12 billion. The British were the largest employers and the Japanese were second. The states that benefited the most were New York, New Jersey, and Pennsylvania on the East Coast and California on the West Coast.[36]

Many states actively courted foreign investment by establishing duty-free, or enterprise, zones designed to entice foreign manufacturing and trade with tax-free incentives. Most of the states with the highest number of foreign companies had zones established by the mid–1980s, and as a result, were able to maintain relatively low unemployment numbers until the recession of 1990. The establishment of those areas, plus the active recruitment of foreign investment, indicates that purchase of U.S. assets by foreign companies was as much a matter of recruitment as it was a foreign exchange and/or marketing decision by the investing companies. Throughout the history of foreign direct and portfolio investments, Americans have courted foreign capital as much as foreigners have looked favorably to the United States for stability when their home markets could or did not produce a decent return.

NOTES

1. See Charles R. Geisst, *Visionary Capitalism: Financial Markets and the American Dream in the Twentieth Century* (New York: Praeger, 1990), Chap. 3, for more detailed background on the deregulatory legislation of the early 1980s.

2. Ibid., pp. 72–73.

3. Securities Industry Association, *The International Market: Growth in Primary and Secondary Activity* (New York: Securities Industry Association, 1987), p. 12.

4. Ibid., p. 14.

5. Brendan Brown and Charles R. Geisst, *Financial Futures Markets* (New York: St. Martin's Press, 1983), p. 104.

6. Securities Industry Association, *The International Market*, pp. 12–13.

7. Ibid., p. 14.

8. Ibid., p. 20.

9. Standard & Poor's Corporation, *Standard & Poor's Analyst's Handbook* (New York: Standard & Poor's Corporation, 1988).

10. Roger G. Ibbotson and Rex Sinquefield, *Stocks, Bonds, Bills, and Inflation: Historical Returns (1926–1987)* (Homewood, IL: Dow Jones Irwin, 1989), p. 58.

11. Securities Industry Association, *The International Market*, p. 21.

12. Comparisons based on Euromoney Publications, *Euromoney International Finance Yearbook* (London: Euromoney Publications, 1989), p. 214 ff.

13. The relatively low level of diversification of U.S. investors, as compared to European and Japanese counterparts, holds for bonds as well as stocks. For instance, in 1983, foreign bonds as a percentage of resident bond holdings was 2.7 percent for the United States as opposed to 6 percent for Japan, 6.7 percent for Germany, and almost 17 percent for the United Kingdom. By 1989, the numbers had changed for all but the United States; the Japanese increased to 19 percent, the Germans to 18 percent, and the British to almost 44 percent. In stocks, the same was true. Foreign equities as a percentage of resident equity holdings was 1.3 percent in 1983 and 2.5 percent in 1989. The Japanese were a negligible 0.3 percent rising to 1 percent, the Germans a constant 12 percent, and the British 21 percent rising to 25 percent. See Morgan Guaranty Trust, "Japanese Investment in U.S. Securities," April 19, 1991.

14. U.S. Department of Commerce, *Survey of Current Business*, various issues. In 1990, the Commerce Department announced that it was changing the method of valuing U.S. investments abroad. The Bureau of Economic Analysis (BEA), the office that prepares the foreign investment surveys for the Commerce Department, planned to switch to a method that valued these investments abroad on a current basis rather than a historical one. By using book values as the basis for direct investments abroad, there is an assumption that the value of U.S. investment is being seriously misstated—that is, underestimated. "Consequently, because U.S. direct investment

abroad is more 'mature,' on average, than foreign direct investment in the United States, it is subject to larger understatement." See Russell B. Scholl, "International Investment Position: Component Detail for 1989." *Survey of Current Business*, June 1990, p. 54.

15. Vincent Reinhart, "Macroeconomic Influences on the U.S.–Japan Trade Imbalance," Federal Reserve Bank of New York *Quarterly Review*, Spring 1986, p. 8.

16. Susan Hickok, Linda Bell, and Janet Ceglowski, "The Competitiveness of U.S. Manufactured Goods: Recent Changes and Prospects," Federal Reserve Bank of New York *Quarterly Review*, Spring 1988, p. 8.

17. Ibid.

18. Ibid.

19. David Garvin, *Managing Quality: The Strategic and Competitive Edge* (New York: The Free Press, 1988), p. 1. It was not perceptions alone that motivated consumers to buy foreign-made consumer durables. As Garvin notes (Chap. 11), in a controlled study of quality in 1981–82 of Japanese and U.S.-made air-conditioners, the U.S. products were less attractive than Japanese in terms of more defective parts and materials, more assembly-line defect rates, and more service calls per unit under warranty coverage.

20. See Geisst, *Visionary Capitalism*, Chap. 4, for a more detailed account of the agricultural crisis of 1985–87.

21. R. David Belli, "Foreign Direct Investment in the United States: Highlights from the 1980 Benchmark Survey," *Survey of Current Business*, October 1983.

22. See Morgan Guaranty Trust, "Japanese Investments," p. 4.

23. Federal Reserve *Bulletin*, December 1987.

24. Paul Bennett and Jeanette Kelleher, "The International Transmission of Stock Price Disruption in October 1987," Federal Reserve Bank of New York *Quarterly Bulletin*, p. 17.

25. Robert Aderhold, Christine Cumming, and Alison Harwood, "International Linkages among Equities Markets and the October 1987 Market Break," Federal Reserve Bank of New York *Quarterly Bulletin*, Summer 1988, pp. 36–45.

26. Securities Industry Association, "Foreign Activity," October 21, 1988, p. 10.

27. Ibid., January 25, 1989.

28. Ibid., October 4, 1989.

29. Based upon Morgan Guaranty Trust's effective exchange rates. See J. P. Morgan & Co., *World Financial Markets*, February 1990.

30. Ibid., May 4, 1990, p. 3.

31. See Geisst, *Visionary Capitalism*, Chap. 3, for the background on this topic.

32. *New York Times*, June 5, 1991.

33. "American Depository Receipts," *The Economist*, June 15, 1991, p. 73.

34. U.S. Department of Commerce, *Survey of Current Business*, June 1990 and June 1991.

35. Ibid.

36. U.S. Department of Commerce, *Survey of Current Business*, July 1990. The number of people employed by foreign companies was determined for both multinational and small companies with partial foreign ownership. For example, in New Jersey, over 170,000 people were employed by over 1,000 firms with foreign controlling interests. The New Jersey Chamber of Commerce attributed the employment to 268 Japanese firms, 176 German, 135 British, 50 Canadian, 69 Dutch, and 83 Korean companies. The actual amount of foreign interest in each was not divulged.

Conclusion

Foreign investment in the United States since 1920 has undergone some radical changes while at the same time remaining relatively consistent. For most of the period, a stable core of British, Canadian, and northern European direct investment helped finance manufacturing and trading enterprises and remained relatively constant, despite wars and radical changes in the international monetary system. A great deal of this investment produced products that many U.S. consumers would identify as domestic, not realizing that they were produced by foreign-controlled companies. A great deal of this anonymity has to do with common language and culture; British, Canadian, and Dutch firms have been in the country for so long that their origins have long since receded into the background.

On the portfolio side, U.S. securities have long been a favorite of foreign investors, especially as the dollar became the international currency of choice for trading and investing. Foreign investing in the markets has usually followed the trend set by domestic investors, although it certainly has been ruled by foreign exchange considerations. In the 1920s, when short-term profit was a paramount importance to investors, foreign investors speculated. In the 1980s, when fixed-income investing became popular, foreigners bought increasing numbers of dollars-denominated bonds. Their appetite for fixed-income instruments in the 1960s and 1970s helped the eurobond market develop as a major capital market. After the late 1970s, it could no longer be considered an overseas appendage of the domestic dollar market.

But central to these fast-moving developments that saw the international monetary system abandon the gold exchange standard and the fixed parity system in favor of floating exchange rates was the relatively regulation-free environment that characterized U.S. attitudes toward investment in the country itself. Although the United States has maintained a tariff structure since the days of the Hawley-Smoot Act, few if any meaningful restrictions have been placed on the import or export of capital. In the 1920s, a decidedly entrepôt atmosphere was encouraged as foreign governments and companies were able to use the U.S. capital markets to raise money. Over the years, the markets have remained receptive to foreigners through the Yankee bond market and the use of ADRs. Even the most American of all capital market regulations, those surrounding disclosure, have been relaxed of late so that foreigners can continue to use the domestic capital markets to raise funds.

The one event crucial to the development of the entrepôt market outside the United States was the emergence of the eurobond market in the mid–1960s. The same spirit that had established the Yankee bond market was seized upon by British authorities eager to reestablish London as the financial capital of the world, without having to use sterling in the process. The success of the eurobond market in the ensuing years kept the entrepôt spirit alive but obviously changed its locale. Rather than use New York as its center, entrepôt capitalism became firmly entrenched in London. The one consolation was that its currency of choice was still the U.S. dollar. The function could still be provided, although the structure of the marketplace had changed. But even the entrepôt concept, which had served the U.S. trade balance with varying degrees of success over the years, became somewhat idiosyncratic as new, innovative types of financings were developed in the capital markets. New products and developments spanned more than one market in a race toward global integration of the stock and credit markets.

Despite the remarkably stable nature of European and Canadian investment in the twentieth century, structural changes began to occur after the demise of the Bretton Woods fixed parity system in 1972. Investment flow into the United States increased as the dollar weakened on the foreign exchange markets, although the inflow was now geared toward direct rather than portfolio investment. European and Japanese companies began opening manufacturing subsidiaries in the United States in an attempt to gain closer access to the large domestic market while at the same time circumventing import duties. The increased investment by foreign companies continued through the 1980s, and by 1989 had changed the balance that the United States had enjoyed for most of the postwar period: direct foreign investment in the United States exceeded U.S. direct investment abroad for the first time.

A slight reversal of this trend occurred after the United States–Canada free trade pact was passed in 1988. The agreement provided for eventual abolition of trade barriers between the two countries, in both direct and portfolio investments. It also provided methods of settling trade and investment disputes and allowed for easy repatriation of earnings by expatriate companies located across the border. Shortly after the legislation was passed, some Canadian companies began to move operations to the United States despite the relaxed atmosphere, citing better unit labor costs and less restrictive domestic practices.

Following the emergence of floating foreign exchange rates, the increasing foreign influence in U.S. manufacturing, trading, and banking became more noticeable. Through a combination of imports and domestically produced goods with foreign brand names, foreign manufacturers especially had a profound effect upon the U.S. marketplace. Domestic companies lost market share to foreigners in increasing numbers. But consumers benefited through higher quality domestically produced goods. At the same time, employment at the foreign-owned companies rose along with the level of wages paid and the amount of assets controlled by foreigners.

Complaints about foreign ownership of U.S. assets have been heard since the mid–1970s. Prior to that time, the tables were turned; the U.S. economic reach into the internal affairs of others, as well as the export of American popular culture, were the main complaints of foreigners in the late 1950s and 1960s. But the foreign purchases of U.S. assets are a sign of the continued success of the dollar in the international marketplace. As long as the dollar remains the major reserve and trading currency, foreigners will be compelled to hold it. And as long as the United States continues to run trade deficits, there will be an additional incentive for foreign holders to invest those dollars in U.S. assets. In this respect, the United States is a victim of its own success.

U.S. economic policy has always favored foreign investment. Put another way, policy has never dissuaded investment, especially portfolio investment, despite the layer of protective tariffs erected occasionally since the 1930s. In those cases where foreign control of certain vital industries has been proscribed (outright control of 51 percent of voting stock, not the 10 percent used to define controlling interest), pragmitism usually has reigned. When certain industries otherwise protected from outright foreign control fell upon hard times, the rules were usually liberalized to keep them on their feet. The commercial airline industry is but one example.

The one major concern that foreign investment underscores is exchange-rate volatility. Foreign investment in any country usually receives its major impetus from favorable exchange rates, whether the market dictates—as in the case of most hard currencies—or the governments accommodate investors—as in the case of the soft currencies. Ever since the Depression and the Hawley-Smoot Act the direct relation between exchange rates and investment flow has been established. Recent concern with increasing direct foreign investment has occurred simultaneously with growing attractiveness of the U.S. marketplace. This poses a dilemma for those opposed to increased foreign investment. In an environment that encourages foreign direct investment, it is unrealistic to criticize its effects. The United States can ill afford to complain about foreign influence on one hand and court it on the other.

Despite concerns over foreign direct investments and the purchase of U.S. real estate by foreigners, the amount of foreign investment in securities has, for the most part, been overlooked. The market break of 1987 linked the world's major stock markets, although the precise nature of the connections is disputed. The U.S. market break was linked to the falling indices in other markets because international investors were able to react quickly to a new international environment of deregulation that made cross-border investment much easier than it had been in the past. In this atmosphere, hot money takes on added velocity since it can now be moved from market to market efficiently, with fewer transaction costs. Potentially, large foreign investment in U.S. securities is more dangerous to the domestic economy than is foreign direct investment, which is an integral part of the economy. A foreign investor intent on selling large amounts in Treasury bonds will have a more profound impact on domestic interest rates than will increased direct investment hoping for a low rate of financing. It is apparent that concerns about foreign investment are not well placed; portfolio investment is intrinsically more risky to the domestic economy than is direct investment.

Yet neither type of foreign investment can be controlled—not as long as the dollar remains the major trading and reserve currency. Dissuading foreigners from investing either directly or indirectly is tantamount to encourage exchange-rate volatility; those holding dollars would not have sufficient motivation to invest them in the United States, thereby putting selling pressure on the currency in the foreign exchange markets. Although the entrepôt market was never a deliberate or planned strategy, it has worked tolerably well in the relatively relaxed atmosphere surrounding investment in the United States over the last century. The underlying reason why that atmosphere is so tolerant is the state of affairs in the foreign exchange market.

As history has shown, serious attention has been paid to foreign direct investment in the United States only since the mid- to late 1970s, when the dollar was weak in relation to other major hard currencies. Since 1972, the major central banks have tried various methods to achieve desirable exchange rates, with varying degrees of success. The Federal Reserve, for example, avoided intervention on behalf of the dollar for the first part of the Reagan administration in the 1980s, until the Plaza meeting in late 1985. After that time, it acted in concert with the other G7 members to achieve a depreciation of the dollar, causing a 30 percent fall and eventually helping reduce the U.S. merchandise trade deficit. But in the entire post–Bretton Woods period, no specific exchange-rate policy designed to achieve stability was introduced to replace floating exchange rates, with the aim of achieving some stability in the markets. As a result, periods of general dollar weakness, in 1972–80 and again in 1986–90, led to increasing amounts of foreign capital invested in U.S. assets. Even the period of extraordinary dollar strength in 1981–85 showed an increase in foreign investment, indicating that the trend was difficult to change.

Against that background, U.S. industry and consumers nevertheless benefited from increased investment on two counts. First, opening foreign manufacturing and banking facilities helped expose the marketplace to different production methods and new financial techniques. The quality of U.S.-manufactured goods increased as a result, and the financial markets benefited from the flexibility that many of the new instruments introduced. Drivers of U.S.-made automobiles and borrowers of adjustable-rate mortgages are two examples of consumers benefiting from the import of foreign capital and financial concepts.

Second, foreign portfolio investment has had a noticeable effect on the term structure of interest rates since the second half of the 1980s. As the budget deficit grew and the household savings rate remained low, foreign investment in Treasury bonds especially has help keep domestic interest rates at lower levels than they might otherwise have been. Many of these effects are difficult to quantify or qualify, since foreign portfolio investment could change rapidly, especially in the deregulated financial environment of the 1980s. But without that portfolio investment, the financial markets would have had a more difficult time funding the budget deficit.

Foreign investment has been an integral part of financing the American Dream since the nineteenth century. Likewise, foreign money has found the demographics and politics of the United States provide a large market and a safe haven for money. Trends since 1972 have underscored the central role that foreign capital has played in U.S. economic development. As with immigration trends, the structure and origin of foreign investment has changed over the years. The U.S. attitudes and receptiveness to capital inflow may vary, but should not fail to recognize that the United States has been a home for immigrant capital throughout its history.

Bibliography

Aderhold, Robert, Christine Cumming, and Alison Harwood. "International Linkages among Equity Markets and the October 1987 Market Break." Federal Reserve Bank of New York *Quarterly Review*, Summer 1988, pp. 34–46.

Anderson, Clay. *A Half-Century of Federal Reserve Policymaking, 1914–1964*. Philadelphia: Federal Reserve Bank of Philadelphia, 1965.

Anderson, Gordon B. "The Effect of the War on New Security Issues in the United States." American Academy of Political and Social Science, *The Annals*, November 1916, pp. 115–27.

Aufricht, Hans. *The International Monetary Fund: Legal Bases, Structure, Functions*. New York: Praeger, 1964.

Baker, James C., and Gerald Bradford. *American Banks Abroad: Edge Act Companies and Multinational Banking*. New York: Praeger, 1974.

Bell, Linda A. "Wage Rigidity in West Germany: A Comparison with U.S. Experience." Federal Reserve Bank of New York *Quarterly Review*, Autumn 1988, pp. 11–21.

Belli, R. David. "Foreign Direct Investment in the United States: Highlights from the 1980 Benchmark Survey." *Survey of Current Business*, October 1983.

Bennett, Paul, and Jeanette Kelleher. "The International Transmission of Stock Price Disruption in October 1987." Federal Reserve Bank of New York *Quarterly Review*, Summer 1988, pp. 17–33.

Brandes, Joseph. *Herbert Hoover and Economic Diplomacy*. Pittsburgh: University of Pittsburgh Press, 1962.

Brady, Nicholas F., et al. *Report of the Presidential Task Force on Market Mechanisms*. Washington, DC: U.S. Government Printing Office, 1988.

Brown, Brendan, and Charles R. Geisst. *Financial Futures Markets*. New York: St. Martin's Press, 1983.

Cairncross, Alec. *Control of Long-term Capital Movements*. Washington, DC: The Brookings Institution, 1973.

Chown, John F., and Robert Valentine. *The International Bond Market in the 1960s: Its Development and Operation*. New York: Praeger, 1968.

Clarke, Stephen V. O. *Central Bank Cooperation 1924–31*. New York: Federal Reserve Bank of New York, 1967.

———. *Exchange-Rate Stabilization in the Mid 1930s: Negotiating the Tripartite Agreement*. Princeton: Department of Economics, Princeton University, 1977.

Comptroller General of the United States. *Controlling Foreign Investment in National Interest Sectors of the U.S. Economy*. Washington, DC; General Accounting Office, 1977.

Conference Board. *Foreign Investment in the United States: Policy, Problems and Obstacles*. New York: The Conference Board, 1974.

Dale, Richard. *The Regulation of International Banking*. Englewood Cliffs, NJ: Prentice Hall, 1984.

Daniels, John D. *Recent Foreign Direct Manufacturing Investment in the United States: An Interview Study of the Decision Process*. New York: Praeger, 1971.

Dickens, Paul D. *Foreign Long-Term Investment in the United States, 1937–39*. Washington, DC: U.S. Department of Commerce, 1940.

Dunning, John H. *Studies in International Investment*. London: George Allen & Unwin, 1970.

The Economist. Various issues.

Einzig, Paul. *The History of Foreign Exchange*, 2nd ed. London: Macmillan, 1970.

———. *A Textbook on Foreign Exchange*. London: Macmillan, 1969.

Euromoney Publications, *International Finance Yearbook*. London: Euromoney Publications, 1989.

Falk, Richard. *Legal Order in a Violent World*. Princeton: Princeton University Press, 1968.

Federal Reserve Bank of New York. *Quarterly Review*. Various issues.

Federal Reserve System. *Annual Report*. Various issues.

———. *Bulletin*. Various issues.

Fisher, Irving. "The Rate of Interest After the War." American Academy of Political and Social Science, *The Annals* 68 (November, 1916), pp. 245–56.

Friedman, Milton, and Anna Schwartz. *A Monetary History of the United States, 1867–1960*. Princeton: Princeton University Press, 1963.

Garvin, David. *Managing Quality: The Strategic and Competitive Edge*. New York: The Free Press, 1988.

Geisst, Charles R. *Raising International Capital: International Bond Markets and the European Institutions*. London: Saxon House, 1980.

———. *Visionary Capitalism: Financial Markets and the American Dream in the Twentieth Century*. New York: Praeger, 1990.

Gold, Joseph. *Legal and Institutional Aspects of the International Monetary System: Selected Essays*. Washington, DC: International Monetary Fund, 1979.

Graham, Edward M., and Paul Krugman. *Foreign Direct Investment in the United States*. Washington, DC: Institute for International Economics, 1989.

Greider, William. *Secrets of the Temple: How the Federal Reserve Runs the Country*. New York: Simon & Schuster, 1987.

Griffiths, Brian. *Invisible Barriers to Invisible Trade*. London: Macmillan, 1975.

Hakkio, Craig, and Richard Roberts. "Has the Dollar Fallen Enough?" Federal Reserve Bank of Kansas City *Economic Review*, July-August 1987, pp. 24–41.

Hardouvelis, Gikas. "Evidence on Stock Market Speculative Bubbles: Japan, the United States, and Great Britain." Federal Reserve Bank of New York *Quarterly Review*, Summer 1988, pp. 4–16.

Hayes, Samuel, and Philip Hubbard. *Investment Banking: A Tale of Three Cities*. Cambridge, MA: Harvard Business School Press, 1990.

Heilbroner, Robert L. *The Worldly Philosophers*. New York: Simon & Schuster, 1961.

Hickok, Susan, Linda Bell, and Janet Ceglowski. "The Competitiveness of U.S. Manufactured Goods: Recent Changes and Prospects," Federal Reserve Bank of New York *Quarterly Review*, Spring 1988, pp. 7–22.

Hobson, J. A. *Imperialism*. Ann Arbor: University of Michigan Press, 1965.

Ibbotson, Roger, and Rex Sinquefield. *Stocks, Bonds, Bills, and Inflation: Historical Returns (1926–1987)*. Homewood, IL: Dow Jones Irwin, 1989.

International Monetary Fund. *Annual Report*. Various issues.

————. *International Financial Statistics Yearbook*. Various issues.

Katseli-Papaefstratiou, Louka. *The Reemergence of the Purchasing Power Parity Doctrine in the 1970s*. Princeton: Princeton University, 1979.

Kindelberger, Charles. *International Short-Term Capital Movements*. New York: Augustus M. Kelley, 1965.

Kojima, Kiyoshi. *Direct Foreign Investment*. New York: Praeger, 1978.

Krooss, Herman, ed. *Documentary History of Banking and Currency in the United States*. vol. 4. New York: Chelsea House, 1969.

Lees, Francis A. *Foreign Banking and Investment in the United States: Issues and Alternatives*. New York: John Wiley & Sons, 1976.

———— and Maximo Eng. *International Financial Markets*. New York: Praeger, 1975.

Leftwich, Robert P. "Foreign Direct Investments in the United States, 1962–71." *Survey of Current Business*, February 1973.

————. "Foreign Direct Investment in the United States in 1973." *Survey of Current Business*, August 1974.

Lenin, V. I. *Selected Works*. Moscow: Progress Publishers, 1970.

Levy, Marc M. *Foreign Investment in the United States*. New York: John Wiley & Sons, 1989.

Lewis, Cleona. *The United States and Foreign Investment Problems*. Washington, DC: The Brookings Institution, 1948.

"London and New York as Financial Centers." American Academy of Political and Social Sciences, *The Annals* 68 (November 1916).

J. P. Morgan & Co. *World Financial Markets*. Various issues.

Morgan Guaranty Trust. "Japanese Investment in U.S. Securities," April 19, 1991.

Nolle, Daniel, and Charles Pigott. "The Changing Commodity Composition of U.S. Imports from Japan." Federal Reserve Bank of New York *Quarterly Review*, Spring 1986, pp. 12–18.

Northedge, F. S., and M. J. Grieve. *A Hundred Years of International Relations*. New York: Praeger, 1971.

Organization for Economic Cooperation and Development. "Controls and Impediments Affecting Inward Direct Investment in OECD Member Countries." Paris, September 1987.

———. "Controls on International Capital Movements: Experience with Controls on International Portfolio Operations in Shares and Bonds." Paris, January 1981.

———. *Financial Market Trends*. Various Issues.

Orion Bank, Ltd. *International Capital Markets: An Investors' Guide*. London: Euromoney Publications, 1979.

Owens, Jeffrey P. *Growth of the Euro-Dollar Market*. Bangor: University of Wales Press, 1974.

Patterson, E. M., ed. *America's Changing Investment Market*. Philadelphia: American Academy of Political and Social Science, 1916.

Phillips, David M. *Legal Restraints on Foreign Direct Investment in the United States*, vol. 7, Appendix K. In U.S. Department of Commerce, *Foreign Direct Investment in the United States*. Washington, DC: U.S. Department of Commerce, 1976.

Pizer, Samuel, and Zalie V. Warner. "Foreign Business Investments in the United States." *Survey of Current Business*. Washington, DC: U.S. Department of Commerce, 1960.

Preston, Allyson, ed. *Euromoney International Finance Yearbook*. London: Euromoney Publications, 1989.

Price Waterhouse. *Foreign Investment in U.S. Real Property*. Price Waterhouse Company, 1988.

Reid, Margaret. *The Secondary Banking Crisis, 1973–75*. London: Macmillan, 1982.

Reinhart, Vincent. "Macroeconomic Influences on the U.S.–Japan Trade Imbalance." Federal Reserve Bank of New York *Quarterly Review*, Spring 1986, pp. 6–11.

Salomon Brothers. *Prospects for the Credit Markets in 1978*. New York: Salomon Brothers, 1978.

Scholl, Russell B. "International Investment Position: Component Detail for 1989." *Survey of Current Business*, June 1990, pp. 54–65.

Securities Industry Association. "Foreign Activity." Various issues.

———. *The International Market: Growth in Primary and Secondary Activity*. New York: Securities Industry Association, 1987.

Servan-Schreiber, J.-J. *The American Challenge*, trans. Ronald Steel. New York: Atheneum, 1968.

Solomon, Robert. *The International Monetary System, 1945–1976*. New York: Harper & Row, 1977.

Staley, Eugene. *War and the Private Investor*. Chicago: University of Chicago Press, 1935.

Standard & Poor's Corporation. *Standard & Poor's Analyst's Handbook*. New York: Standard & Poor's Corporation, 1988.

Studenski, Paul, and Herman Krooss. *Financial History of the United States*. New York: McGraw-Hill, 1952.

The Study Group on FDI. *Foreign Direct Investment 1973–87*. New York: Group of Thirty, 1984.

U.S. Department of Commerce. "The Balance of International Payments of the

United States in 1927." Bulletin Number 552. Washington, DC: U.S. Department of Commerce, May 1928.

————. "The Balance of International Payments of the United States in 1929." Bulletin Number 698. Washington, DC: U.S. Department of Commerce, 1929.

————. *Foreign Direct Investment in the United States*, Vol. 3. Washington, DC: U.S. Department of Commerce, April 1976.

————. *Foreign Direct Investment in the United States, 1976, Completed Transactions*. Washington, DC: U.S. Department of Commerce, December 1977.

————. *Foreign Direct Investment in the United States. Completed Transactions, 1974–1983*, Vol. I. Washington, DC: U.S. Department of Commerce, June 1985.

————. *Foreign Direct Investment in the United States, 1980*. Washington, DC: U.S. Department of Commerce, 1983.

————. *Foreign Direct Investment in the United States, 1987 Transactions*. Washington, DC: U.S. Department of Commerce, 1988.

————. *Foreign Investments in the United States*. Washington, DC: U.S. Government Printing Office, 1937.

————. *Foreign Long-Term Investment in the United States*. Washington, DC: U.S. Government Printing Office, 1940.

————. *Historical Statistics of the United States: Colonial Times to 1970*. Vol. 2. Washington, DC: U.S. Bureau of the Census, 1975.

————. *Selected Data on U.S. Direct Investment Abroad, 1950–76*. Washington, DC: U.S. Department of Commerce, 1982.

————. *Survey of Current Business*. Various issues.

————. *U.S. Direct Investment Abroad: Balance of Payments and Direct Investment Position Estimates, 1977–81*. Washington, DC: U.S. Department of Commerce, 1986.

U.S. House of Representatives. "Report to the Special Commissioner of the Revenue upon the Industry, Trade, Commerce &c. of the United States for the Year 1869." Executive Document No. 27. 41st Cong., 2nd Sess. 1869.

U.S. Senate. "Report of the Secretary of the Treasury in Answer to a Resolution of the Senate Calling for the Amount of American Securities Held in Europe & Other Foreign Countries, on the 30th June 1853." Executive Document No. 42. 33rd Cong. 1st Sess., 1854.

U.S. Treasury Department. *Census of Foreign-Owned Assets in the United States*. Washington, DC: U.S. Government Printing Office, 1945.

Veblen, Thorstein, *The Theory of the Leisure Class*. New York: Modern Library, 1934.

Webley, Simon. *Foreign Direct Investment in the United States: Opportunities and Impediments*. London: British-North American Committee, 1974.

Wilkins, Mira. *The History of Foreign Investment in the United States to 1914*. Cambridge, MA: Harvard University Press, 1989.

Williamson, John. *The Exchange Rate System*. Washington, DC: Institute for International Economics, 1985.

Yaseen, Leonard, ed. *Direct Investment in the United States*. New York: European-American Banking Corporation, 1974.

Yoshida, Momoru. *Japanese Direct Manufacturing Investment in the United States*. New York: Praeger, 1987.

Index

WIDENER UNIVERSITY
WOLFGRAM
LIBRARY
CHESTER, PA.

ABOUT THE AUTHOR

CHARLES R. GEISST has worked as an investment banker in London and has taught both political science and finance. He is the author of several other books, including *A Guide to the Financial Markets*, *A Guide to Financial Institutions*, *Financial Futures Markets*, and *Visionary Capitalism: Financial Markets and the American Dream in the Twentieth Century* (Praeger, 1990).